BEETHOVEN'S
SYMPHONIES

Sinfonia grande

Louis van Beethoven

BEETHOVEN'S SYMPHONIES

AN ARTISTIC VISION

LEWIS LOCKWOOD

W. W. NORTON & COMPANY

Independent Publishers Since 1923

New York · London

For information about permission to reproduce selections from this book,
write to Permissions, W. W. Norton & Company, Inc.,
500 Fifth Avenue, New York, NY 10110

For information about special discounts for bulk purchases, please contact
W. W. Norton Special Sales at specialsales@wwnorton.com or 800-233-4830

Manufacturing by Quad Graphics Fairfield
Book design by JAMdesign
Production manager: Julia Druskin

Library of Congress Cataloging-in-Publication Data

Lockwood, Lewis.
Beethoven's symphonies : an artistic vision / Lewis Lockwood. — First
edition.
    pages cm
Includes bibliographical references and index.
ISBN 978-0-393-07644-8 (hardcover)
1. Beethoven, Ludwig van, 1770–1827. Symphonies. 2. Symphony—19th
century. I. Title.
ML410.B42L62 2015
784.2'184092—dc23
                         2015022306

W. W. Norton & Company, Inc.
500 Fifth Avenue, New York, N.Y. 10110
www.wwnorton.com

W. W. Norton & Company Ltd.
Castle House, 75/76 Wells Street, London W1T 3QT

1 2 3 4 5 6 7 8 9 0

Poets are sieves

Brimming rose leaves;

Yielding when prod,

Attar of God.

—M.W.L.

CONTENTS

ILLUSTRATIONS

EXAMPLES

All the music examples included or mentioned in this
book may be found at musicexamples.com

PREFACE

A new book on the Beethoven Symphonies calls for justification. Readers may wonder what can possibly be added to current levels of familiarity with these famous works, which remain the core of the classical concert repertoire. Living as we do in an age of lightning-quick access to oceans of information, it is natural to assume that pretty much anything important about Beethoven is probably available at the touch of a finger.

And yet it is not true. Not true for many aspects of his life and career, and certainly not for the deeper understanding of his works and his artistic evolution. This book aims to provide an introduction to the Beethoven symphonies as individual works of art, with a focus on their historical, biographical, and creative origins. More than any other great composer of the past, Beethoven left to posterity a vast body of material that documents the early stages of almost every work he ever wrote. This patrimony is contained in the desk sketchbooks that he used at home and in the smaller pocket sketchbooks that he carried with him out of doors, especially in his later years. They have the potential to show us Beethoven as a working composer, deeply engaged in what he accepted as a lifetime commitment to bring forth "all that I felt was within me," as he wrote in his Heiligenstadt Testament of 1802. That he managed to keep this ever-growing mass of sketch material largely intact suggests that he was protecting his inner creative world from the difficulties of his daily life across the years.

The Beethoven sketchbooks were first studied in the nineteenth century by the pioneering scholar Gustav Nottebohm, a friend of Brahms, whose essays and monographs are still fundamental. Yet for many reasons, only a handful have been published in fully reliable editions. This is partly because Beethoven's musical notation is often hard to read and partly because Beethoven scholarship and the larger field of historical musicology in the twentieth century moved in other directions. Even now only about twenty percent of this vast material is available in transcription, and it was as late as 1985 that the first comprehensive catalogue of the sketchbooks was published, by Douglas Johnson, Alan Tyson, and Robert Winter.[1]

This book reflects my years of Beethoven study and teaching, and is directly influenced by my recent work on the *Eroica* Sketchbook, the product of seven years of close collaboration with my colleague Alan Gosman. Our work resulted in the publication of its first complete critical edition in 2013.[2] This sketchbook contains, among other things, the great mass of Beethoven's known sketches for the *Eroica* Symphony and other works of its time, including the "Waldstein" Sonata. This project strengthened my belief that engagement with the primary sources of artistic masterworks remains a vital source of insight. Such engagement has the capacity to create links between history, biography, and analysis, and it opens up an unparalleled view of the inner musical world in which a great composer's works originated.

A further consequence of these efforts will be found in the appendix to this book, which offers a synoptic overview of what we know of the incipient ideas for symphonies that Beethoven entered into his sketchbooks over the years. Many of these concept sketches for symphonies, though not all, have recently been discussed in a pathbreaking study by Erica Buurman.[3] Her study, which is devoted entirely to sketches for multi-movement works, not those for single movements, also includes many concept sketches for works in other genres, such as the string quartets and piano sonatas.

My appendix is limited to Beethoven's entries for symphonies, but does include those entries in which Beethoven wrote down ideas for single movements. A very few of the concept sketches listed in the appendix are for works that Beethoven went on to complete, including most conspicuously, the *Eroica* Symphony. It also includes his preliminary ideas for two movements of the Fifth Symphony, which he wrote down in this same *Eroica* Sketchbook, years before he came back to complete the Fifth in its final form. These entries are discussed in my chapters on the *Eroica* and the Fifth Symphonies.

Especially illuminating are a whole series of brief concept sketches, each marked "Sinfonia" or "Sinfonie," which Beethoven wrote down as he was thinking about possible symphonies that never got beyond this incipient stage. In 1809, for example, we find brief ideas for symphonies in G minor, G major, and even a passing verbal reference to a symphony in A minor. Three years later, while writing the Seventh and Eighth Symphonies, he sketched ideas for possible symphonies in D minor, in B-flat major, in E minor, and in E-flat major, all of which remained gleams in his imagination. All of these and other entries combine to justify the view that for Beethoven the symphony was a lifetime preoccupation to which he returned at various times for both inner and outer reasons. These laconic entries reveal some of the rich creative soil from which the nine completed major works grew. Awareness of such a background enlarges our understanding of the finished works, and it should contribute to a larger and more wide-ranging portrait of Beethoven as a symphonic thinker than we have had before.

In short, this book can be read as a series of historically informed critical essays on each of the symphonies. In some chapters the historical and biographical background is prominent. In others, where the documentation permits, I offer a broad picture of aspects of the compositional background. The music examples in the book have been kept to a minimum but all the examples will be found at the Web site (musicexamples.com).

This project has been in gestation for many years, and I am glad to acknowledge the help and advice of many friends and colleagues, including Alan Gosman, Theodore Albrecht, Matthew Cron, Lucy Turner, and Elizabeth Williamson. My colleague Jeremy Yudkin kindly read and offered valuable comments on my entire manuscript. I owe special thanks to Michael Ochs, whose friendship, editorial skill, and suggestions for this book, as for my earlier Beethoven publications, have been invaluable. Equal recognition goes to Maribeth Payne, music editor at W. W. Norton, for her close reading and help at every stage, and also to Michael Fauver. As always, my deep thanks to my wife, Ava Bry Penman, for her encouragement and patience during the writing of this book. And finally, I dedicate this book to the memory of my mother, Madeline Wartell Lockwood, a poet and writer, who put Romain Rolland's *Jean Christophe* into my hands when I was sixteen and kindled my love of music and literature. The poem on my dedication page is by her.

LEWIS LOCKWOOD
Brookline, Massachusetts

BEETHOVEN'S
SYMPHONIES

Beethoven's birthplace in Bonn, now the seat of the Beethoven-Haus
and Beethoven Museum (Beethoven-Haus, Bonn / Bridgeman Images)

"THE TRIUMPH OF THIS ART"

INDIVIDUALITY AND THE IDEA
OF THE SYMPHONY

In January 1826, little more than a year before his death, Beethoven was visited by the young violinist Karl Holz, a trusted member of his circle in Vienna. Holz's part of their exchange is recorded in one of the conversation books with which the aging and deaf composer communicated with others during the last years of his life. As usual, Holz wrote down what he had to say and Beethoven spoke his answers.

HOLZ: That is what I always miss in Mozart's instrumental music.

BEETHOVEN:————.

HOLZ: Especially the instrumental music.—A specific character in an instrumental work. That is, one does not find in his [Mozart's] works a representation [*Darstellung*] analogous to a state of the soul, as one does in yours.

BEETHOVEN:————.

HOLZ: I always ask myself, when I listen to something, what does it represent?

BEETHOVEN:————.

HOLZ: Your works have, throughout, a really exceptional character.

BEETHOVEN:————.

HOLZ: I would explain the difference between Mozart's and your instrumental works in this way. For one of your works a poet could only write one poem, while to a Mozart work he could write three or four analogous ones.[1]

Whatever Beethoven's responses may have been, the force of Holz's remarks remains as clear today as it was then, as the highly profiled individuality of each of Beethoven's symphonies continues to stamp them in the memory of everyone who knows them. This is true of musicians at all levels, including the historically minded, who tend to see them within the contexts that surrounded and informed the music of the period. It is true of modern cultural critics who see them as bearers of poetic, programmatic or social meanings. And it is true of the vast majority of listeners and concert-goers who enjoy these works in performance or recordings no matter how many times they hear them. Generations of listeners have come to Beethoven's symphonies not only for their artistic wholeness and integrity, but to gain access to experience that only artworks on this level can convey.

To the world at large, then, to all who know these works on the many levels of perception that are shared by professionals and laymen, their most salient features are their power of emotional expression, their cogency, and their individuality. Critics voiced these judgments in Beethoven's time, and they remain valid in the vastly transformed musical world of the present, as we near the 250th anniversary of his birth. Taken as a group, his symphonies, like his string quartets and piano sonatas, exhibit the family resemblances we should expect from nine works in the same genre by one composer, but their singularity outweighs their common features. I will argue that these works were not merely conceived as individual projects but were the products of an artistic vision that persisted throughout Beethoven's lifetime; a vision that grew from his early formative years to a larger ambition to revolutionize the genre and reconstruct it on a new level of significance.

Once Beethoven had arrived in Vienna from Bonn late in 1792, he set about establishing his career as pianist and composer, writing and publishing his first piano sonatas, variations, and keyboard chamber music. By the late 1790s, with a string quintet and his Opus 9 string trios in hand, it was time to expand his role as the apparent successor to Mozart and the still living Haydn by turning to the string quartet and the symphony. And so by 1800 he was busily at work on his first string quartets, those of Opus 18—and was also ready to present his First Symphony, a strong but not radical first essay into the highly competitive world of the most public of genres. He proceeded over the next few years to transform his idea of the symphony, to expand its range of expression, and to make the symphony his largest vehicle of communication to audiences of his own time and to posterity.

We can imagine Beethoven in 1800 thinking back over the great body of the Haydn and Mozart symphonies, at least some of which he had played in Bonn as a young violist in the Bonn court orchestra. The Bonn repertoire included works from across Europe, from France to Hungary, offering exposure to a broad continental spectrum of symphonies by many composers now obscure but who generated an enormous literature of music that is still only partially known even to specialists. To cite a recent major study of eighteenth-century symphonies by a group of scholars, we know of the existence in the early classical period of thousands of works by hundreds of composers.[2]

Though Beethoven could obviously have known only a tiny fraction of such a gigantic mass of music, we should imagine that he shared with his fellow Bonn musicians a latent awareness of this panoramic background. He would have had a sense that his first attempts as a composer would fit into a vast and well-formed body of tradition, whose formulas he would first assimilate and then transform in the light of his idiosyncratic striving for originality, which emerged early and then developed into a lifelong sense of purpose.

When he started work on his first symphony in the mid-1790s, Beethoven was well aware of Haydn's recent masterpieces, his twelve "London" symphonies (Nos. 93–104) written between 1791 and 1795, more than a few of which were performed in Vienna as early as 1793.[3] Mozart's later symphonies were at least as important models, especially the six great works of Mozart's last ten years, from the "Haffner" symphony of 1782 through the "Linz" and "Prague" of 1783 and 1784. But significant above all for Beethoven's idea of the symphony were Mozart's final trilogy—the symphonies in E-flat (K. 543), the G-minor (K. 550), and the "Jupiter" in C major (K. 551). When Mozart had written all three in a mere six weeks in the summer of 1788, the seventeen-year-old Beethoven was still in Bonn but was anxious to get back to Vienna, to which he had traveled in 1787 in hopes of becoming Mozart's pupil. Recent research has shown that this journey of 1787 was not a matter of little more than two weeks, as had formerly been believed, but lasted for ten weeks. It is possible that the young Beethoven might have met Mozart at that time.[4]

His ambition to capture the "spirit of Mozart" but also to find his own voice is writ large in early works, including the three piano quartets of 1785, based directly on Mozart models.[5] Beethoven's awareness of his Mozartian inheritance is clearly evident in his works but most pointedly in a C-minor passage that Beethoven wrote down on a sketch leaf in 1790. After jotting down the musical passage, he wrote this ironic note between the staves: "This entire passage is stolen from Mozart's Symphony in c where the Andante in 6/8. . . ." Beethoven then rewrites the passage on the same page and proudly labels it "Beethoven *ipse*," i.e., "Beethoven himself."[6]

Other evidence of Beethoven's indebtedness, his mind filled with Mozartian themes, is found in later sketches. In 1803, when he was laboring over the first movement of the *Eroica* symphony, Beethoven found himself writing down a theme from a Mozart piano concerto. Mozart's theme, which opens his last concerto, K. 595, had been in 6/8 meter and in B-flat major, but Beethoven writes it in 3/4 meter and in E-flat major, that is, in the meter and key of the *Eroica* first movement that he was sketching.[7] Similar evidence of his indebtedness to Mozart and Haydn in the early works is not hard to find. And yet from early on we are equally struck by his impatient urge to be independent, to become a great artist, to be "Beethoven *ipse*" in his music and in every aspect of his life. In a letter from late October or early November 1792 to his former teacher in Bonn, Christian Gottlob Neefe, Beethoven writes:

> I thank you for your advice, which you have so often shared with me in my pursuit of my divine art. If I become a great man, you will share in the credit. And that will delight you all the more since you may be convinced . . . [breaks off][8]

* * *

Beethoven's lifetime restriction of his completed symphonies to nine—less than a tenth as many as Haydn, less than a fourth as many as Mozart—was due in part to his living in changing times. In earlier decades the writing of symphonies had often been a matter of steady output by composers who were typically supported by a private patron in a local court establishment with regular concerts put on for the enjoyment and pleasure of the patron and his friends. At least this had been the pattern at Esterházy, where Haydn had produced his symphonies for most of his career until his late London period. For Beethoven, this situation had prevailed at Bonn, but after 1800 the entire patronage situation was changing, as many patrons could maintain their musical forces only with difficulty. But there was more than this behind his ambitions in this genre. More important by far was his sense of larger purpose, his feeling that each work, especially after the Third, the *Eroica*, should be a singular achievement worthy of his highest aspirations. As a free-lance artist, he waged a long struggle to maintain himself by every means available—by fees from publishers for first editions of his music, in an age without copyright; by personal dedications of his works to wealthy patrons; by subscription concerts; and most essentially, by the direct financial support he received from a few devoted aristocratic patrons, first from Prince Karl Lichnowsky and later from a few others, above all the Archduke Rudolph.

With the rise of bourgeois audiences seeking entertainment in opera houses and, occasionally, in orchestral concerts but with regular public concert seasons only beginning to emerge, occasions for the performance of new symphonies had to be manufactured. In the absence of concert halls designed for the purpose, conditions in Vienna were not encouraging for the composition and performance of symphonies, despite its active musical life. In fact, the genre was in a state of decline during these years. As one scholar puts it, "Whereas most composers avoided the genre, Beethoven wrote symphonies despite the prevailing circumstances, an act of defiance that was integral to the composer's artistic outlook."[9]

The further progress of the genre in Vienna only became possible after 1815 with the defeat of Napoleon, the return of peace to Austria after decades of war, and the rise of public concert life spearheaded by the recently founded Gesellschaft der Musikfreunde, an important society of amateurs. But Beethoven's persistent refusal to let his legacy be shaped by contingency is shown by the fact that eight of his nine symphonies were completed by 1812, with only the Ninth remaining a distant future project. Of course, by 1812 he had also completed many works in genres for salons and domestic music-making—piano sonatas, keyboard chamber music, string quartets, and vocal works.

Nonetheless, Beethoven's restless determination to achieve originality and yet remain within the framework of the highest musical traditions of the past brought him back again and again to the symphony, as we see not only from the completed works but from the many brief concept sketches for symphonies that crop up in his sketchbooks, most of them remaining embryonic ideas that never developed but all of them enriching our knowledge of the imaginative background behind the famous nine symphonies.

We may well disagree with Holz's remark that Mozart, at least in the towering compositions of his last years, had not created artworks as fully individual as any of Beethoven's. But what Holz felt, and many have felt ever since, was that Beethoven's symphonies and other mature instrumental works, along with *Fidelio* and the *Missa Solemnis*, not to mention the late quartets, emerge from the well-springs of a restless and searching creative self, get deeper into the souls of listeners, and arouse emotional responses more powerful than even the most finely wrought works of his immediate predecessors. Perhaps this is why Holz said that for each work a listener might be moved to write only one poem, not three or four analogous ones.

Throughout his career, Beethoven's ambition drove him to a constant search for varied modes of expression. That he aimed to reach his listeners in new ways and as directly as possible is spelled out in his inscription on the Kyrie of the *Missa Solemnis*—"from the heart, may it go to the heart." These words were nominally meant for the dedicatee, Archduke Rudolph, but implicitly they are addressed to mankind, like Schiller declaring in the "Ode to Joy," "Be embraced, O ye millions." A parallel urgency is evident in a letter of 1819—"in the world of art, as in the whole of creation, freedom and progress are the main objectives."[10] The pianist-composer Busoni described Mozart's music as "god-like," but said of Beethoven that he "brought the human dimension [*das Menschliche*] into music for the first time."[11]

Other artists have felt the expanded emotional scope of Beethoven's music. Writers from Balzac and Dostoevsky to Thomas Mann and others, and visual artists such as Antoine Bourdelle, who made the composer a lifelong subject, have all expressed the influence of

Beethoven on their own lives. Among modern writers, perhaps surprisingly, we find Samuel Beckett, whose works record his recognition of an implacable world in which the individual can do nothing but try to endure. But Beckett below the surface was a true Beethoven admirer, as we know from his letters and some of his works. Struck by the groups of silent measures that occur in the first movement of the Seventh Symphony, Beckett wrote in a letter of 1937 that

> language is like a veil which one has to tear apart in order to get to those things (or the nothingness) lying behind it . . . Is there any reason why that terrifyingly arbitrary materiality of the word surface should not be dissolved, as for example the sound surface of Beethoven's Seventh Symphony is devoured by huge black pauses, so that for pages on end we cannot perceive it as other than a dizzying patch of sounds connecting unfathomable chasms of silence?[12]

* * *

As early as the Second Symphony and then far more with the *Eroica* and the later symphonies, Beethoven reshaped the symphonic canon. After the *Eroica* each symphony continued this expansion in a new way. We see that in his orchestral music Beethoven drew upon the gains he was making in other sectors—the piano sonatas and variations, the keyboard chamber music, and the string quartets—and honed his skills as well in his overtures, his incidental music for the stage, and his large-scale vocal works with orchestra, including his masses and oratorios and such adventurous works as the Choral Fantasia. After 1805 he also drew on all he learned while composing and revising his opera, *Leonore* (later renamed *Fidelio*). By the time he wrote the first movement of the Ninth in the early 1820s, he could bring to his orchestral writing some of the subtleties and complexities that he had achieved in his late middle-period string quartets.

"THE TRIUMPH OF THIS ART"

In the early nineteenth century, the symphony was coming to be seen as "the highest genre of instrumental music."[13] As early as 1803, when the *Eroica* had not yet been finished, let alone heard, an anonymous critic wrote that

> Symphonies are the triumph of this art [of music]. Freely and without limits an artist can conjure up within them a whole world of feelings, dancing merriment and triumphant joy, the sweet yearning of love and the deepest pain, gentle peace and mischievous caprice, playful jest and fearful gravity pour forth and touch the sympathetic strings of the heart, the feelings, and the imagination. The whole mass of instruments is at his command.[14]

Praising Mozart and Haydn for having created symphonic works "that deserve great admiration," he then hailed Beethoven, "a newcomer in art who, however, approaching the great masters, in particular has made this great field of instrumental music his own." Since this critic knew only Beethoven's First and Second, he echoed the feeling that the European musical world was ready for a composer who could fulfill the expectations of a new age. As the nineteenth century began, many felt that Beethoven might be that composer.

Moreover, the mysticism with which the German Romantics clothed their view of the world helped to give music primacy among the arts—instrumental music above all—as a seemingly autonomous world of expression. As adumbrated by Novalis, this belief in the high mystical qualities of musical expression was readily endorsed by a generation of German Romantics, including Tieck, Wackenroder, and E. T. A. Hoffmann.[15] Though Beethoven's relationship to Romanticism was more oblique than direct, he found ways to enter into this new domain of experience, living in a time in which such views were rapidly gaining currency. His quest for personal expression, though still imbued with Enlightenment ideals, stood well within the high Romantic landscape that was then emerging in literature, art, and drama.

By the time Hoffmann wrote his celebrated review of the Fifth Symphony in 1810, Beethoven had completed his first six symphonies. As a writer of fantastic novels and stories but also a highly knowledgeable musician and composer, Hoffmann defended Beethoven's "powerful genius" from the conservative critics who found his musical language hard to understand and his music emotionally "unbridled." He wrote of the Fifth Symphony that "it leads the listener imperiously forward into the spirit world of the infinite!" and that Beethoven's instrumental music "opens up to us . . . the realm of the monstrous and the immeasurable."[16]

Such views were not held only by musicians and writers on music. Schopenhauer's influential tract *The World as Will and Representation*, of which the first part was published in 1819, before the Ninth Symphony, is a prime example. By the time the second part appeared in 1844, Mendelssohn and Schumann were in their prime, the young Wagner had come on the scene, and German musical Romanticism had reached its first peak. Beethoven was Schopenhauer's favorite composer, and Beethoven's symphonies shaped Schopenhauer's view of music more than any other works. In the second part of his treatise, Schopenhauer presents music as the art-form most nearly capable of revealing "the innermost nature of the world [. . . it] expresses the profoundest wisdom in a language that his [the composer's] reasoning faculty does not understand." He continues:

> a symphony by Beethoven presents us with the greatest confusion which yet has the most perfect order as its foundation; with the most vehement conflict which is transformed the next moment into the most beautiful harmony. It is *rerum concordia discors*, a true and complete picture of the nature of the world . . . All the human passions and emotions speak from this symphony: joy, grief, love,

hatred, terror, hope, and so on in innumerable shades, yet all, as it were, only in the abstract and without any particularization . . . We certainly have an inclination to realize it while we listen, to clothe it in the imagination with flesh and bone, and to see in it all the different scenes of life and nature. On the whole, however, this does not promote an understanding or enjoyment of it, but rather gives it a strange and arbitrary addition. It is therefore better to interpret it purely and in its immediacy.[17]

MODELS AND MOVEMENT-PLANS

By "models," I am not referring to the conventional four-movement patterns that Beethoven inherited from his forebears, nor to the symphonic works by earlier composers that influenced his ways of shaping his own, however real that influence. I use the term to refer to Beethoven's own capsule summations of his basic ideas for symphonies and symphonic movements as we find them, mainly, in his sketchbooks. These concept sketches and movement-plans, sometimes only in musical notation but sometimes also using words, show his initial ideas for a movement or a work, including how it should begin and sometimes some of its other features. These brief notations are rich in implications, and at times they convey the character and contrasts he was seeking. By writing down the essentials of a movement or work in abbreviated form, he could establish what its primary lineaments might be, and even if the movement-sequence changed later, at least one basic movement-idea often remained intact, one that could serve as the invariant against which he could set the other movements. We do not have such notations for every work, but enough of them survive to give us a good idea of how he went about planning and thinking about his larger works. Such movement-plans survive for piano sonatas, orchestral works, and quartets; not in very large numbers, so far as we can now tell, but not in negligible ones either.

Just recently, after I had completed this book, Erica Buurman made a valuable contribution to our knowledge of these concept sketches and movement-plans in an as yet unpublished dissertation completed in 2013.[18] Her wide-ranging study encompasses not only concept sketches for symphonies but reaches out more broadly to the other genres of Beethoven's instrumental works. She also includes reference to a number of concise plans for unfinished works, some of which were previously known to the Beethoven literature and some that were not. I offer a provisional listing of the known concept-sketches for symphonies in the appendix to this book, and I make reference to her findings in the instances in which her discussion of such movement-plans overlaps with mine. The eventual publication of all of these models and movement-plans would be enlightening.

For the purposes of this book, the central point is that such brief ideas for symphonies appear in Beethoven's sketches and sketchbooks from before the First Symphony to very late in his life. They show that his desire to write symphonies was not just an intermittent matter, which came alive only when opportunities for performances came his way, but that the idea of writing symphonies persisted through his mature lifetime. They show us that for Beethoven the symphony was a lifetime preoccupation.

In the symphony and the string quartet, from the eighteenth to the early twentieth century—as long as these traditional genres remained intact or influential—the familiar four-movement scheme rules. Its basic form is that of a fast sonata-form first movement that sets the pattern for the whole; a slow movement in a contrasting key and meter; a third movement in the home tonic, derived from Baroque antecedents as the classic "Menuetto," converted by Beethoven into the dynamic "Scherzo;" and a rapid finale in the home tonic key, either a sonata-form movement, a rondo, or at times a hybrid, the sonata-rondo. Traditionally the finale rivals the first movement in content and can surpass it in energy, but is lighter in tone, and simpler and more direct in expression.

This tradition holds for Beethoven despite some deviations, as in the return of the third movement within the finale in the Fifth, the five-movement form of the Sixth, or even the introduction of voices in the finale of the Ninth. An important variable is the slow introduction to the first movement, inherited from Haydn and some works by Mozart. Beethoven employed it to good effect in his first two symphonies and originally planned a slow introduction for the *Eroica* in its embryonic stage in 1802 but then abandoned it when the work grew large. Once beyond the *Eroica* he returned to the slow introduction for the Fourth and Seventh Symphonies, including highly developed opening sections that establish aspects of sonority and structure for the Allegro first movements that grow out of them. They provide each work with a richly developed prologue.

The "characteristic" or programmatic symphony had been cultivated in the eighteenth century and was mentioned prominently by critics in Beethoven's lifetime.[19] Two of his symphonies—the *Eroica* and the "Pastoral"—bear titles that immediately mark them as members of this subgenre, and both were published with subtitles that further modify and characterize their intended mode of reception. Both subtitles resulted from complex changes of mind. The phrase "composed to celebrate the memory of a great man" was first used for the *Eroica*, so far as we know, only when it was published in 1806, two full years after its composition and the revocation of its dedication to Napoleon. And Beethoven arrived at the subtitle for the "Pastoral"—"more the expression of feelings than tone painting"—only after trying out various verbal formulations while looking for the right way to deal with the paradox of both asserting and denying that the work belonged to the category of illustrative music. I will come back to these points later.

CHRONOLOGY

Although the chronology of the symphonies is clear enough in broad outline, the picture becomes more complex when we look more closely at the evidence for Beethoven's initial ideas for each work, its elaboration and completion, its first performance, and its publication.

The First Symphony was published in 1801 by Hoffmeister in Leipzig, eighteen months after its premiere in April 1800. Thereafter Beethoven seems to have begun fully intensive work on each symphony just as the preceding one was nearing publication or had recently been printed. He first conceived the idea of the Third as a symphony in 1802 but did not complete it until the second half of 1803, all the while awaiting the publication of the Second, which came out in March 1804. A two-year span separates the completion of the Third in 1804 from its publication in October 1806, which is about the time at which he finished the autograph manuscript of the Fourth. As I will discuss, he apparently hatched his first ideas for what became the Fifth, and at least two movements of the Sixth, early in 1804, well before his main work on the Fourth two years later. Accordingly, it looks as if Beethoven had a primary conception of the Fifth and Sixth Symphonies in mind before he began work on the Fourth. The Fifth and Sixth then lay waiting to be fleshed out in full form in 1807 and 1808. At that time publication seems to have been quicker, as both of these appeared in 1809. In 1811 and 1812 Beethoven composed the Seventh and Eighth, in close succession, but for various reasons they did not come out in print until 1816 and 1817. The trajectory of the Ninth was longer and more complicated. He thought about a D-minor symphony as early as 1812 (actually the seed of such a work already existed in 1804) but did not put down definite ideas for it before 1815, by which time the Seventh and Eighth were close to publication.

Beethoven's symphonies fall into five phases. In the first phase, up to and including the First Symphony, he is establishing his credentials, having delayed the writing of a symphony until he had an opportunity for a public concert, something not easy to mount at that time. The second phase runs from 1801 to 1806, embracing the Second, the Third, his first ideas for the Fifth and to some extent the Sixth. Then came the all-consuming project of his opera *Leonore* (1804–6) and its two great overtures (*Leonore* Nos. 2 and 3), then the Fourth. As to the finished works, it is plausible to argue that the Second, Third, and Fourth Symphonies all participate in the major breakthrough that is often ascribed exclusively to the *Eroica*, of course in different ways.

Beginning in 1807 and 1808 there follow the third and fourth phases. The third encompasses the Fifth and Sixth symphonies, which were completed in 1808 and were originally so closely intertwined that their opus numbers, 67 and 68, were initially assigned in the reverse order. The fourth phase brings the Seventh and Eighth Symphonies, published with the successive opus numbers 92 and 93. Between 1813 and 1819 he had fleeting ideas for symphonies, as his entire outlook deepened and changed, but nothing came of them. His full-scale work on the Ninth took place from 1822 to 1824.

The main work on the Ninth is the fifth and final phase of his symphonic production. Although he made sketches for a possible Tenth, leaving a trail that has attracted at least one attempted reconstruction, the evidence makes clear that between 1824, when he finished the Ninth, and March 1827, when he died, Beethoven gave serious thought to such a possibility but did not complete any work for orchestra, let alone a new symphony. During these years, he was entirely enveloped in the world of the late quartets, and, except for a few piano pieces and canons, they absorbed all the creative energy of his last few years.[20]

Beethoven ca. 1801, engraving by Johann Joseph Neidl
after a drawing by Gandolph Ernst Stainhauser von
Treuberg (The Cobbe Collection Trust, UK / Bridgeman Images)

1

THE FIRST SYMPHONY

SYMPHONY, OPERA, AND DRAMA AT BONN

The Electoral court at Bonn in the 1780s boasted a highly skilled orchestra and an ambitious opera theater, both supported vigorously by the Elector Max Franz after his accession in 1784. Max Franz was an enthusiastic music-lover, a dedicated Mozart admirer, and a true patron who was anxious to keep musical performance at Bonn on a very high level. One result of Max Franz's recruitment of good players was the young Beethoven's contact with performers of exceptional caliber for a provincial court. The orchestra's leader and principal violinist was Franz Anton Ries (1755–1846), from whom Beethoven took some violin lessons.[1] From 1785 on Beethoven would also have known the gifted Bohemian cellist and composer Joseph Reicha (1752–1795), who came to Bonn from service at the South German court of Oettingen-Wallerstein, and brought with him his nephew Anton Reicha, later an important theorist and pedagogue in France.[2] Other first-class string players in Beethoven's later years in Bonn were the brilliant cellist Bernhard Romberg and his violinist cousin Andreas Romberg, both of whom went on to impressive European careers. And among the horn players was Nikolaus Simrock, later an important music publisher at Bonn.[3] It was a lively civic environment in which local musical enthusiasts could hear recent and new music by a range of composers from across the continent, with orchestral works by Haydn and Mozart liberally represented.

In this setting, the teenage Beethoven, son and grandson of Bonn musicians, was coming of age as a brilliant musical talent. In addition to his intense studies as pianist and budding composer, he played viola in the orchestra for opera and symphonic works.[4] This early experience of high-level music-making surely remained in his memory later in Vienna when he had to rely on groups maintained by his patrons or else assemble them himself for his own occasional benefit concerts.[5]

Though orchestras were not nearly as large as they later became, the symphony stood in contrast to domestic music, and the potential analogies between symphony and opera as public art-forms, along with spoken drama, were certainly apparent. In the early 1780s, when Beethoven was making his first attempts at composition, drama in Bonn and in all the major centers across the German-speaking lands was in a state of transformation. "National" theaters had sprung into being since the earlier 1770s, both in imperial Vienna and in smaller princely courts, including Bonn.

In these years, the new German literary masters, from Lessing onward, were reaching their first heights in plays that abandoned traditional plots in favor of conflicts that pitted individuals against one another and sometimes against the established norms of society. Their works replaced roles that called for high-flown speech in favor of everyday characters who talked like the citizens in the audience. In Bonn, those favoring this new trend included Christian Gott-lob Neefe, who had come to Bonn in 1779, became court organist in 1782, and was Beethoven's most important early music teacher. Neefe also belonged to the Bavarian Illuminati, a group on the left margin of Freemasonry that was strongly promoting new and pro-gressive ideas in politics and literature.[6]

In the 1780s, the citizens of Bonn could feel the seismic political and social changes that were breaking out across the Rhine in Paris and would soon explode in 1789 in the French Revolution. In the German states and cities, despite fear of bloody revolution, artists and writers were stirred by the French upheaval and the new political ideas behind it, which for them were intermingled with enthusiasm for the new idealistic philosophy of Kant. In drama, the prime mover was Friedrich Schiller, whose first plays astonished the public with their power of expression and messages of social unrest. Consider this description of Schiller's early play *The Robbers*, at its premiere in Mannheim in January 1782:

> The theater was like a madhouse—rolling eyes, clenched fists, hoarse cries in the auditorium. Strangers fell sobbing into one anothers' arms, women on the point of fainting staggered towards the exit. There was a universal commotion as in chaos, out of which a new creation bursts forth.[7]

This same play was given at Bonn later that year by the Grossman company, whose leader was the main figure in theatrical productions of opera and spoken drama in Bonn and who was on good personal terms with Beethoven's family.[8] The music director for Grossman's theater group was none other than Neefe. Schiller's powerful dramas fired the ambitions of the younger generation of German artists and intellectuals, and Beethoven's lifelong admiration for Schiller took root during this time and in this context.[9]

There can be no doubt that the young Beethoven's basic musical models were Haydn and Mozart, especially Mozart; and Bach above all in the later years. But the immediacy of Schiller's impact on his audiences—his dramas with their well-made plots, credible characters, and heroic themes—could well have provided for Beethoven a larger image of what he might achieve in his orchestral music of the future: the ability to stir large audiences to emotional depths they

had not experienced before. Notwithstanding his admiration for
Goethe as the largest figure in German literary culture, he became
uncomfortable with Goethe's role as court poet to the aristocracy.
But his reverence for Schiller remained strong, and it intensified
after Schiller's death in 1805.

Beethoven knew many passages from Schiller's plays by heart
and quoted them in letters and conversation. When Beethoven left
Bonn for Vienna in 1792, three entries in his departure album prepared by friends quoted Schiller's *Don Carlos*, and in his first months
in Vienna in 1793 Beethoven himself wrote down a passage from
this same play that might well have resonated with his sense of his
own state of mind, newly arrived as he was in Viennese society:

> Hot blood is my fault—my crime is that I am young. I am not
> wicked, truly wicked. Even though wildly surging emotions may
> betray my heart, yet my heart is good.[10]

In a much later letter to the Archduke Rudolph, his patron and
pupil, Beethoven compared himself to "Sir Davison," a character in
Schiller's *Mary Stuart*, and it is noteworthy that he did not have to
explain the allusion.[11] From early on, Beethoven was inspired by the
same faith in the potential betterment of mankind and in political
freedom that he found in Schiller. As early as the 1790s he planned
to make a setting of Schiller's *Ode to Joy*, finally realized in the finale
of the Ninth Symphony. Witnesses to Beethoven's later years, among
them Franz Grillparzer and Karl Holz, tell us that Beethoven "held
Schiller in very high regard" and that "Beethoven had underlined
everything in Schiller's poems that constituted his [own] confession
of faith."[12]

THE FIRST SYMPHONY: AN OVERVIEW

Movement	Meter	Key
1. Adagio molto	4/4	C major
Allegro con brio	2/2	C major
2. Andante cantabile con moto	3/8	F major
3. Menuetto: Allegro molto e vivace	3/4	C major
4. Adagio	2/4	C major
Allegro molto e vivace	2/4	C major

If some of Beethoven's early chamber works from his first Vienna years seemed to reveal a degree of "hot blood" and "wildly surging emotions," the First Symphony is not one of them. Rather, the work gives the impression of being a supremely competent but carefully modulated entry into the public world of the symphony, a work in which the young Beethoven seems to be largely emulating Haydn and Mozart rather than challenging the great tradition that they represented and in which he was now making his formal debut. Only in the remarkable Menuetto movement does the young composer break the mold.

The Adagio Introduction follows the great models of Haydn's recent London symphonies in that it offers novel harmonic twists, prepares the arrival of the main Allegro, and lays the foundation for its most striking passages. The Allegro itself is lively and vivacious, its opening figures affirming the tonic C major with strongly accented figures that contrast nicely with the eventual second group themes, in which the winds come to the fore in playful alternation with one another. Below the surface there are patterns of procedure that have been found to be derived from earlier works, especially the development section, which has been shown to be structurally modeled on the comparable section in Mozart's "Jupiter" Symphony, also in C major.[13]

Beethoven's choice of key for the slow movement, F major, the subdominant, is conservative, although it reflects the stress on this same subordinate tonality that had been heard at the very opening measure of the Introduction. Since in major-mode symphonies the slow movement was the only full movement that could provide large-scale tonal contrast, Beethoven's choice is cautious when compared to his early trios or sonatas.[14] In his thirty-one published works that precede this symphony, only seven use the subdominant key for a slow movement within a major-key context.

The Menuetto is the truly new element in this symphony. It is really a full-blooded scherzo despite the name, the most striking movement in the symphony, an outburst of energy and imagination—it is Beethoven's decisive break with the symphonic Minuet of the eighteenth century. We feel that with this movement of his First Symphony Beethoven is in process of discovering his "Scherzo" personality, his way of harnessing incessant rhythmic repetitions of short figures within a context of relentless forward motion. This type of movement is to become a hallmark of his later symphonic style. In short, this "Menuetto" is really his first symphonic Scherzo.

Haydn's robust symphonic third movements in the London symphonies are the most relevant for comparison, more so than Mozart's orchestral Minuets with their genial smoothness of contour, as in the "Jupiter" Symphony. A comparison with Haydn's Symphony 103 (the "Drumroll")—even with regard to the lengths of sections—shows the ambition that animates Beethoven's third movement. Haydn writes a "Menuetto" of 48 bars in two sections, each repeated as is customary; then a slightly shorter Trio of 41 bars, with the same binary form and two repeats; then the whole Menuetto "da capo" (repeated in full with or without the inner repeats).

On paper, Beethoven's format looks the same, but the entire character of the movement is new. His "Menuetto" is divided into two utterly unequal parts, with a mere 8 bars for the first section and an enormous 71 bars for the second part. As usual, both are repeated, but with immense vigor and a quasi-development of motives in the second section. The Trio is shorter and more lyrical, as is usual in the classical third movement, and the return to the repeat of the entire Menuetto brings back the swiftness and power that is the trademark of this movement.

While Haydn's Menuetto implies a moderate tempo, in Beethoven's the character of the thematic material demands a rapid tempo; this is also confirmed by the inscription "Allegro molto e vivace."[15] The upward-sweeping scalar theme, with its decisively marked-off subphrases, generates short motives that he uses to great effect in the expanded second section of the Menuetto, which contains remarkable chromatic modulatory passages in *pianissimo* that suddenly erupt in the *fortissimo* return of the first theme.

The finale, emulating many a Haydn 2/4 Allegro or Presto finale, is replete with spirit, verve, and charm. It opens with a touch of humor, something like a miniature sketch-process that builds up the first theme one fragment at a time, adding a new note with each repetition and culminating at last in the clever theme. This opening theme itself is a little masterpiece of comedy, somewhat akin to the finale theme of the First Piano Concerto, and it is followed by many lively moments. Near the end of the movement, new ideas appear, among them the march-like segment in the Coda and the crescendo that runs from the march to the sustained *fortissimo* climax at the end. It matches the peroration that brought the first movement to a powerful close.

THE CREATIVE BACKGROUND

I begin with some of the concept sketches for symphonies that were not completed but that led eventually to the First Symphony, and include some that bear directly on that work as it was finished and performed in 1800. Beethoven marked each one "Sinfonia."

Example 1. Draft for an unfinished "Sinfonia" in C Minor, ca. 1788, mm. 1–6

Source: Kafka Papers, fols. 70r–v; Beethoven, Autograph Miscellany, pp. 175f. and comments, 291 (Hess 298).

Probably from 1788, the draft in Example 1 (see also Web Example A) opens with a striking theme that Beethoven had used in one of his piano quartets of 1785, written when he was fourteen. The whole draft is a substantial two-stave sketch of more than one hundred measures for the first movement exposition of a Symphony in C Minor marked "Presto" 3/4. The theme begins exactly as in the piano quartet but thereafter the "Sinfonia" draft develops more consistently.[16] The sweeping, upward contour of the first two measures moves swiftly into a syncopated continuation without a break, moving forward in a manner that anticipates the dark "C-minor mood" of several works from Beethoven's first Vienna period.[17]

This sketch anticipates the spirit and the contour of the opening of the Scherzo of his Fifth Symphony, and, as Beethoven himself noted on a later sketch page, it has a thematic affinity with the opening theme of the finale of Mozart's G Minor Symphony. If this C-minor torso was drafted in 1788 or 1789, it is quite possible that Beethoven could already have known the G-minor Symphony, which Mozart had written in the summer of 1788. This Mozart masterpiece could easily have made its way to Bonn as soon as it could be copied, since there was no greater Mozart enthusiast than the Elector Max Franz in all Europe.

Example 2. Concept Sketch for an unfinished "Sinfonia" in C major, 1790, mm. 1–6

Source: Kafka Papers, fol. 88v; Beethoven, Autograph Miscellany, vol. 2, 228.

Example 2 shows a curious and humdrum "Sinfonia" sketch in C Major from about October 1790 that seems to have been conceived as the opening of a first movement. After the opening figures, with their simple repetitions of neighbor-note figures around the tonic pitch of C, the remainder works with equally square-cut repetitive patterns of repeated chords, three to a measure, a pattern that suggests the Menuetto of the First Symphony, still ten years in the future. It is odd that this passage appears on the verso of the same page in which Beethoven wrote that phrase in C Minor, referred to earlier, which he had labeled as "stolen from Mozart."[18]

I take a sketch in E major (Web Example B) out of chronological order (it comes from about 1797) so as to keep discussion of the C-major First Symphony sketches together. This smooth, flowing melody in 2/4, probably Andante and marked "Sinfonia," is clearly for a slow movement, and had it been developed could have ranked with Beethoven's best early 2/4 Andantes.[19] Although the key signature clearly designates E major, Beethoven writes "in F" at the top of the second page, showing that he thought of transposing it.[20] The E-major slow movement suggests a symphony in A major, though for that plan we have no corroboration. But his further idea, of putting the movement into F major, suggests that this Andante could have found a home within a symphony in C major, which was indeed a project that he had very much in mind in 1797.

An extended set of ideas for a C-major symphony[21] (Web Example C) occupied Beethoven in 1795 and again in 1796, perhaps written in connection with his visit to the court of Friedrich Wilhelm II in Berlin from May to July 1796. He may have started the symphony in Vienna in 1795 in hopes of getting it performed at an orchestral concert in Berlin (which did not materialize), and continued to work on it after returning to Vienna.[22]

These sketches for an early unfinished symphony are the most extensive for any early Beethoven work now known, and some of these materials found a home in the First Symphony a few years later. Here Beethoven is looking back at early sketches as he gets fully into a new major work, something that he did in later years as well and over much longer stretches of time. As Douglas Johnson has shown, the 1795–96 material includes nine or ten drafts for a slow introduction, even including a score fragment, plus drafts for the Allegro exposition of the first movement, with revisions. Beethoven also attempted to lay out the coda of the first movement. Intermingled with these sketches are brief ideas for the three other movements of the symphony, none of which got further at this time.[23]

What remains memorable from these sketches is his later decision to use the main theme of this early Allegro first movement as the principal theme of the finale of the First Symphony. This transfer of a main theme from a first movement to a finale is rare in Beethoven's compositional procedures, so far as we know. It must have taken place around 1799, when he was getting the whole work into final form for its first performance early in 1800, the event that marked his debut as a symphonic composer before the Viennese public.

PREMIERE AND SIGNIFICANCE

On April 2, 1800, the Burgtheater in Vienna witnessed a benefit concert of new compositions by Beethoven, mingled with works by Haydn and Mozart. This concert, which he had hoped to mount earlier, was a major step in Beethoven's campaign for public recognition. The program, though not all of the details, is extant in a Viennese newspaper advertisement and a review in the *Allgemeine Musikalische Zeitung,* which called it "the most interesting public concert for a long time."[24]

1. A grand symphony by Mozart[25]
2. An aria from Haydn's *Creation,* sung by Mlle. Saal
3. A grand concerto for piano and orchestra, played by Beethoven
4. Beethoven's Septet, Op. 20, "most humbly and obediently dedicated to her Majesty the Empress"
5. A duet from the *Creation* sung by Herr and Mademoiselle Saal
6. Beethoven's improvising at the piano
7. Beethoven's new grand symphony [his First Symphony, Opus 21]

Some implications are apparent. Following convention, Beethoven opened and closed with a symphony, placing his own at the end. But his choice of the opening work sets his own first symphony in direct competition to one by Mozart rather than Haydn, the greatest living old master, who was still active. Perhaps to do honor to Haydn's recent works and to signal his respect, Beethoven included two numbers from *The Creation,* still fresh after its premiere in this same Burgtheater only a year earlier. As pianist in this concert, Beethoven was bidding for acclaim as both soloist and improvisor, though the theme or themes on which he improvised are unknown. Nor are we sure which concerto he played, though it was probably the First, since the Third was not yet ready. In an act of careful planning, he paired these two large-scale orchestral compositions with his divertimento-like Septet, a work he knew would bring him popular success and that might smooth the way for better reception of his more difficult new compositions.[26]

The *AMZ* critic had harsh words for the orchestra players. He claimed there were quarrels over who should direct the performance, as "Beethoven thought he could not entrust the direction to Mr. Conti [the main director of this Italian opera orchestra] and could entrust it to no one better than Mr. Wranitsky."[27] The orchestra did not want to play under him, and the critic reports that they played badly: "in the second part of the symphony they became so lax that in spite of all efforts, no fire could any longer be brought forth in their playing, especially not in the wind instruments."[28]

During the half-decade from 1795 to 1800 Beethoven had become the new man of the hour in Vienna both as a pianist and as a composer. He had begun to publish with his Opus 1 Piano Trios of 1795, the first piano trios to have four movements, and followed them the next year with his equally novel and stylistically wide-ranging Opus 2 Piano Sonatas. He was stepping forward as Haydn's legitimate heir and, on the eve of a new century and an uncertain future for music in the wake of Mozart's death, he was working to secure his future greatness. Aware of his own need for tighter control of his technique, he had apprenticed himself to Haydn as counterpoint student; then, disappointed with Haydn's laxity as teacher, he had gone to the master of traditional counterpoint, Johann Georg Albrechtsberger.[29] Summing up his sense of purpose and his urgency to feel fully free as an artist, he had noted on a sketch leaf in 1794 that "another half-year of counterpoint and he will be able to do as he wishes."[30]

To the contemporary critics who could have no inkling of the future, the First Symphony demonstrated Beethoven's skill and command despite the orchestra's poor showing. To some of them, the First Symphony seemed less bizarre and unusual than his "most recent fortepiano works."[31] But to many later nineteenth-century commentators, who could look back with full knowledge of the enlarged world of the later Beethoven symphonies, the First Symphony seemed to be a timid and attenuated beginning. Witness Berlioz, who complained that "it is music admirably framed: clear, vivacious . . . cold, and sometime even mean—as in the final rondo—truly musical childishness; in a word, Beethoven is not here."[32]

Though Berlioz was acutely sensitive to Beethoven's works and styles, his dismissal now seems overstated. A closer examination of the symphony as a whole, and especially its dynamic Scherzo, shows that it is indeed a "farewell to the eighteenth century," as Donald Francis Tovey called it. Despite some retrospective and comfortably accessible features, it is sprinkled with passages and procedures that point ahead to the later Beethoven.[33]

The house in which Beethoven wrote his Heiligenstadt Testament in 1802
(Museum Karlsplatz, Vienna / Bridgeman Images)

2

THE SECOND SYMPHONY

OVERVIEW

If the First Symphony is a genteel farewell to the preceding century, the Second is in turn a vivid contrast to the First. In its richness of content and high individuality, this symphony signals the end of Beethoven's first maturity in his orchestral music, just at the same time that his allegiance to his classical models is giving way to the increasingly dynamic and expressive style of his middle period. In the Second Symphony, the dissimilarities both within and between movements are much stronger than in the First, and although the instrumentation is the same, the interplay of orchestral colors is far more dramatic and more intricate, the disruptions and surprises far more abrupt. Though no written-out movement plan for the Second Symphony survives, we can infer one from the finished work. The basic model is broadly the same as that of the First Symphony: the familiar four-movement scheme with a slow introduction to begin, but the introduction is almost three times the length of that of the First.

	Movement	Key	Meter	Measures
1.	Adagio	D major	3/4	33
	Allegro con brio		4/4	327
2.	Larghetto	A major	3/8	276
3.	Scherzo: Allegro	D major	3/4	84
	Trio		3/4	46
4.	Allegro molto	D major	Alla breve	442

The opening Adagio is a large musical statement, whose contrasts of dynamics, of orchestral choirs, and of winds and strings presage the dramatic features of the Allegro. It has been proposed that this introduction is modeled on that of Mozart's "Prague" Symphony, in the same key, and forms another example of Beethoven's strong indebtedness to Mozart throughout his early years.[1] But if the "Prague" lurks in the background, it does so at a distance. Beethoven's assertiveness in the rapid movements is now beyond the range of Mozart or Haydn. This Adagio is rife with subtleties of sound and harmony that show him moving forward in new directions.

The first movement Allegro opens with a taut, brisk theme marked in its first measure by the strong rhythmic contrast of a long-held first note and then a figure of four rapid sixteenth-notes that serves as an intensified upbeat to the next bar, which has the same pattern; then come four equal quarter-beats to complete the phrase, and these too form a motivic unit. The intensified upbeat will have a life of its own later in the movement, when the four-sixteenths figure comes into its own near the end of the exposition in a passage of high mystery that moves from *pianissimo* to *fortissimo* in a mere six bars.[2] The whole movement is filled with dramatic contrasts, both in the large and in the small. Thus, the second subject has the flavor of a military march that is announced in the clarinets, bassoons and horns, with an answering salvo from the full orchestra; then the same pair of phrases comes again, this time in a higher register with an expanded range of sound.[3] And a brilliant stroke of integration is heard at the end of the development section: as its harmonic motions pass through subordinate keys to reach the expected dominant harmony and prepare the arrival of the recapitulation. Beethoven uses the same downward-sweeping scale in the first violins that had originally formed the transition from the slow introduction to the opening of the Allegro itself. Most striking of all is the tremendous passage in the coda in which the lower strings move upward through successive chromatic steps under shifting harmonies above, all in fortissimo and leading to the triumphant ending.

The Larghetto is a gem of the first water. This is Beethoven's first truly mature orchestral slow movement, matching the most beautiful major-mode slow movements of his earlier sonatas or chamber music.[4] It is dramatically different from the intense first movement, while the finale regains and extends the tension of the first movement right to the end, culminating in a closing passage that bewildered contemporary observers.[5] Against these "strange" products of Beethoven's imagination, the slow movement left "nothing to be desired" in clarity and melodic beauty, as a critic put it in 1812.[6] Beethoven gains the unforgettable richness of sonority of the opening measures by restricting the melody and its flowing accompaniment to the orchestral strings in middle register—that is, low register for the violins, high for the cellos, and with the basses silent until the closing cadence. And from beginning to end there is a high degree of melodic inventiveness, rhythmic variety, and smoothness of surface that presages many a later Beethoven slow movement in triple meter (e.g., that of the "Harp" Quartet, Op. 74) or the best of Schubert.

The Scherzo, so-named for the first time in his symphonies, resumes the first movement's energetic drive but with simpler means. In its first section a close dialogue of strings and winds alternates three-note scalar figures in *forte* and *piano*, then closes each phrase *fortissimo*, echoing the powerful contrasts of the first Allegro and, in its tender way, the Larghetto. And in the second section of the Scherzo, the three-note rising figure from the opening theme of the movement is tossed back and forth between the two violin sections under a new theme in the winds, the whole effect being one of veiled intensity that then grows into the dynamic ending of the Scherzo proper. The Trio extends its material into new tonal areas, opening with winds alone in a gentler manner than the preceding Scherzo, then continuing with gruff replies from the strings alone. Then the two ensembles of the orchestra, the winds and strings, present the opening material once more before joining in the final measures—this time softly, to contrast with the ending of the Scherzo.

The finale opens with one of Beethoven's most astonishing and dynamic short figures (Example 3).[7]

Example 3. Second Symphony, opening theme of the Finale

It begins with a two-note upward-moving fragment, then a brief continuation that stops with two hammer-blows. This striking first motif gives way to a quiet, running theme that suddenly ends with two more hammer-blows, now in a sudden *forte*. If we imagine that Beethoven might have begun this theme with its *pianissimo* running figures instead of its wild opening gesture in *forte*, the radical novelty of his way of formulating striking local contrasts immediately stands out in comparison to the thematic manner of most of his predecessors. These opening volatile elements and richly developed later themes are all Beethoven needs to generate a long finale in sonata-rondo form, in which a return of the first large section appears at the beginning of the middle section of the movement.[8]

The coda, by far the longest part of the movement, is almost a transformed second recapitulation. After the first part has run its course, the hurtling motion comes to a fermata, ushering in the most dramatic completion in all of early Beethoven, after which another fermata halts the tumult again and several final statements of the original opening motif bring the tempestuous finale and the whole symphony to its end.[9]

VIEWPOINTS

The Second Symphony is often seen as a way-station between Beethoven's formative years and his defiant stride into a new domain with the *Eroica* in 1803–4. Now, not even the keenest tracers of Haydn's and Mozart's influence doubt that the *Eroica* creates a new framework for the genre. But the *Eroica*'s prominence has masked the evidence that the Second Symphony was heard in its own time (and can still be heard in ours) as a decisive departure from tradition. In intensity, energy, and individuality, it leaps beyond those modestly progressive tendencies that we have found in the First. It seems fair to say that if Beethoven had never written any but the first two symphonies, the Second would have signaled a new stage of expression that strongly influenced the younger composers who were coming of age around 1820, led by Schubert and extending beyond him.[10]

Its innovations run parallel to those of the piano sonatas that Beethoven wrote between 1799 and 1802, from his masterly B-flat major sonata, Opus 22, to the trilogy of Opus 31, which dramatically deepened his sonata style.[11] In fact, the Second Symphony has been shown to have close structural affinities with his piano sonata Opus 28, also in D major, written in 1801 and published in 1802.[12] Both belong to the early stages of Beethoven's search for what he was then calling his "new way," while the *Eroica* lifts that search and his entire symphonic vision to a higher plane and lays a foundation for the freedom and complexity of many of his later works. Yet without the innovations of the Second Symphony the *Eroica* might not have been possible.

Another critical commonplace is that the brightness and energy of the Second's fast movements and the calm beauty of its slow movement surprise us in giving no hint of Beethoven's growing torment over his deafness, although he wrote it during the time when the seriousness of his hearing loss was coming upon him. This condition, which emerged early and lasted a lifetime, had apparently begun around 1796, when he was twenty-five, and became progressively worse over the next five to six years. By the summer of 1801, he was reporting his deafness in letters to two trusted friends, Franz Wegeler and Karl Amenda, and in October 1802 he wrote the poignant private document that became known as the Heiligenstadt Testament

Like all significant historical documents, the Testament can be read and pondered many times over without diminishing its meaning and importance. It is a personal declaration in the form of a will, addressed to his brothers and to posterity, which Beethoven kept hidden all his life and which was discovered after his death.[13] To Wegeler he reports his alarming symptoms of the past two years: increasing deafness, pain, social isolation, and fear of loss of his professional standing. We have the testimony of one of his close friends, Stephen von Breuning, that marked psychological difficulties emerged along with his growing fear of what deafness would mean for his professional career and personal relationships.

In one of his letters to Wegeler, Beethoven writes:

> Heaven knows what is to become of me. Vering [his physician] tells me that my hearing will certain improve, though not completely. Already I have often cursed my Creator and my existence. Plutarch has shown me the path of resignation. If it is all possible, I will defy my fate, though I feel that as long as I live there will be moments when I will be God's unhappiest creature.[14]

And earlier in the same letter:

> For almost two years I have ceased to attend any social functions, just because I find it impossible to say to people—I am deaf. If I had any other profession I might be able to cope with my infirmity; but in my profession it is a terrible handicap. And if my enemies, of whom I have a fair number, were to hear about it, what would they say?

And in the Heiligenstadt Testament:

> Such incidents [as when he was unable to hear what others were hearing] drove me almost to despair; a little more of that and I would have ended my life—it was only my art that held me back. Ah, it seemed to me impossible to leave the world until I had brought forth all that I felt was within me. So I endured this wretched existence—truly wretched for so susceptible a body, which can be thrown by a sudden change from the best condition to the very worst.[15]

The reality of his suffering and anxiety is beyond question. Yet there is no easy way to link this crisis directly, let alone causally, with his current work as a composer beyond the truism that a traumatic condition of this kind inevitably magnified his awareness of frailty and mortality. If anything, it fortified his resolution to hold fast, to keep up his intense productivity as a way of overcoming pain and loss. Taking the measure of his inner strength, he adds, in a second letter to Wegeler, the visionary remarks, "Oh, if only I could be rid of it [my deafness] I would embrace the world" [and] "Every day brings me nearer to the goal which I feel but cannot describe."[16]

It is natural to believe that the emotional character of a work of art should directly reflect what we take to be the artist's prevailing emotional and psychological state at the time of its creation. But one can argue with equal cogency that with a deeply centered personality like Beethoven's, his will to create and his strength of purpose could just as readily lead, consciously or unconsciously, to a disjunction that enables very different results. We sense the complexities of this issue as soon as we ask what we really mean by "psychological state"—as if we could imagine a well-functioning individual governed by one supposedly well-defined and steady-state condition rather than being perpetually swept from day to day by contending and contradictory psychic forces and impulses. The issue goes deep into all that we mean by biography, and it goes without saying that much of what we want to know is hidden from view. The literary biographer Richard Ellman once remarked on what he found to be, in his subjects, "the secret or at least tacit life [that] underlies the one we are thought to live . . . writers generally allow some access to their unspoken histories . . . but visiting hours are short; parts of the ground are cordoned off."[17]

When earlier Beethoven biographers adopted the view that his best works, the ones into which he put his heart and soul, must reflect his dominant psychological condition, they were adhering to a literal-minded belief in the aesthetic unity of life and work. On this assumption, Beethoven could be portrayed as a prototype of the suffering Romantic artist whose struggle with disability found immediate expression in his most important works.[18] His deafness could be taken as the central and even the immediate cause of his creation of a "heroic" body of music, and his great works represent aesthetic embodiments of his triumph over personal afflictions, the hero overcoming adversity. This was the thesis made famous by J. W. N. Sullivan in his book on Beethoven's "spiritual development."[19] It proposes a direct connection between the "deafness crisis" and the "heroic style" that is embodied most completely in the *Eroica,* which literally carried the title "Heroic Symphony." This viewpoint inevitably caused the Second Symphony to recede in importance, since an artist of Beethoven's stature is not supposed to be able to write viva-

cious and energetic works like this one at a time of torment, and so
the work was seen to be in some way below the level of an assumed
biographical and artistic standard. Thus Sullivan had little or nothing to say about the Second Symphony. About the Fourth, Sixth,
and Eighth he offers this judgment:

> Beethoven himself did not always plumb the depths. He was not
> always busy with major problems and the most significant spiritual
> experiences. Such works as the fourth, sixth, and eighth sympho-
> nies depict states of mind that require no such intensity of real-
> ization . . . They are not in the main line of Beethoven's spiritual
> development.[20]

A hard look at the Second Symphony, however, tells a different
story. The Second is characterized by a strongly mercurial emotional
climate both within and between movements. It breathes a new
spirit of the age; it uses starkly contrasting elements in surprising
ways; and it shows new uses of orchestral colors singly and in combination. It heralds the higher level of cyclic unity and expression that
became a normal resource in many of Beethoven's later works. One
contemporary critic found it to be "of a depth, power, and artistic
knowledge like very few," while another saw it as "a work full of new,
original ideas . . . which however would benefit from the shortening
of some passages and by the sacrifice of many modulations that are
far too strange."[21]

THE IMMEDIATE BACKGROUND, 1800–1802

For Beethoven, who turned thirty at the end of 1800, this was a
time of continued progress and experimentation. In addition to the
keyboard sonatas, he was moving forward on other fronts. The new
violin sonatas Opus 23 and 24 (1800–1801) fleshed out the growing body of his accompanied sonatas; his String Quintet Opus 29

(1801), with its unusual harmonic design, stood alongside the Opus 9 trios and the Opus 18 quartets. And the two sets of Piano Variations, Opus 34 and 35, "both written in a really new manner, and quite different from each other," as he described them, deepened the genre of keyboard variations, a familiar form since his childhood.[22]

His ballet *The Creatures of Prometheus* was relevant in another way. It was first staged in March of 1801 at the royal palace theater in Vienna. The ballet's overture famously resembles the First Symphony not only in the harmonically unstable opening of its slow introduction but also in aspects of its Allegro. And the finale of *Prometheus*, with its "festive dancing," uses the same material as his "Contredanse" (No. 7 of his 1800–1801 set of ballroom dances) and also connects directly to the Piano Variations Opus 35 and to the finale of the *Eroica*. All four are based on the same theme and bass. Other movements in the ballet link to the Second Symphony, above all the March, No. 8. Its vigorous D-major Allegro con brio presages the first movement of the symphony, and the opening solo timpani figure expands into a unison orchestral continuation and foreshadows the coda that ends the first movement. It is interesting to note that in his main sketchbook of late 1800 and early 1801, the main source for his sketches for the Second Symphony, while Beethoven was working on *Prometheus*, he also had a brief flickering idea for a possible "Sinfonia" in C major, which, although it came to nothing, is one more indication that the range of possible symphonies that crowded his mind was very broad.[23]

The ballet's orchestration also paved the way for the symphony. Beethoven was freer to experiment in theater music than in the symphony—witness the use of solo cello and of harp, the light and shadow of coloristic effects in the introduction "La tempesta," and in the "Pastorale." Beethoven probably had certain players of the royal theater orchestra in mind as he wrote these passages. From the first notes of the Second Symphony's Adagio Introduction, we are in a different sound-world from that of the First, and the experiments of *Prometheus* enabled Beethoven to control a new array of orchestral colors. Although some have relegated *Prometheus* to the category of a light-weight *pièce d'occasion,* it forms a bridge between the First and Second Symphonies, even if it inevitably lacks their concentration of ideas. It was deliberately tailored to the conventions of theater music, which had no need of the developmental types of discourse that were expected in the symphony, at least not until the operatic revolution wrought much later by Wagner.

Another factor in the new style of the Second appears to be the growing importance of French music by post-revolutionary composers, primarily Méhul, Cherubini, Gossec, and Rodolphe Kreutzer. Connections between Beethoven's newly emerging orchestral style and French composers began to be noticed in Beethoven's lifetime, in reviews by Hoffmann and others.[24] How and to what extent did French orchestral music directly influence Beethoven's emerging new style? We can confidently detect French influence on Beethoven in his opera and in his interest in the French schools of string playing, especially the French violin tradition led by Rodolphe Kreutzer, Pierre Baillot, and Pierre Rode, all of whom he met at various times between 1798 and 1812.[25] We know that Beethoven admired the operas of Cherubini and Méhul, as he confessed to Ries and later to Cipriani Potter. Further, the first version of *Leonore* (1804–5) clearly owes considerably to Cherubini, and of course its plot and its entire ethos stems from French post-Revolutionary events. Many French operas of these years inevitably reflected the political upheavals of 1789 and embraced the themes of personal freedom and the universal rights of man. Even though the Reign of Terror, the struggles of the 1790s, and the rise of Napoleon had shaken the faith of outsiders in the ideals of the Revolution, Beethoven by 1800 had become strongly engaged on a personal level with ideas of heroism in several different forms.

The Piano Sonata Op. 26, with its "Funeral March on the death of a Hero" (anticipating the slow movement of the *Eroica*), the *Prometheus* ballet, the monumental Piano Variations and Fugue in E-flat major for piano, Op. 35; and above all the *Eroica* itself, which Beethoven originally intended to name "Bonaparte" until he changed his mind, all illustrate this engagement.

As to thematic connections between the Second Symphony and instrumental works by Méhul, Gossec, and their contemporaries, all such claims remain unproven. Furthermore, a review of concert programs in Vienna between 1789 and 1804 shows that little or no French orchestral music was performed there.[26] On the other hand, there does appear to be a broad and general relationship between French revolutionary musical styles and the newly emerging Beethovenian symphonic style—including the use of massive orchestral forces, a quality of grandeur and potency, and even some occasional references to military rhythms and instruments.[27] Einstein even defined a "military style" for certain French works of this period, including the violin concertos by Viotti.[28] For Beethoven, the march, especially the military march, was prominent all through his first twenty years in Vienna, a period of almost perpetual war and invasion, as Austria found itself in conflict first with the post-Revolutionary French regime and then with Napoleon. Vienna housed important military garrisons, while its poorer citizens suffered for years under the burdens of war, inflation, economic deprivation, and social unrest.[29]

The march as a genre fit well with Beethoven's unflagging interest in composing varied types of independent pieces for public occasions, and he cultivated it at all levels—from popular examples to march-like movements of the highest seriousness—and often at the same time.[30] But general style, atmosphere, and aesthetic purpose are not the same as thematic dependence. The Second Symphony belongs to that phase of his growth at which these influences could find a point of entry into the fabric of his work and the broad shaping of a multi-movement composition. But the surviving sketches give us no reason to look for "reminiscences" in the conventional musicological sense.

THE COMPOSITIONAL BACKGROUND: STAGES OF COMPOSITION

For the First Symphony, we possess sketches for Beethoven's earlier concept of a C-major symphony, but not for the final stage as he developed it in 1799. For the Second, on the other hand, there is abundant extant evidence for its earlier pre-compositional stages. Beethoven began sketching the first movement sometime in 1800 and he continued to develop it through 1801 and into 1802.[31] It looks as though he settled on the first movement and finale before coming to the two inner movements, but we have a concept sketch for a slow movement in G major in the so-called Kessler Sketchbook that is enlightening, written about 1801–2 (Example 4; see also Web Example D).

Example 4. "Andante sinfonia," concept sketch for a slow movement in G major for a "Sinfonia," 1801–2

Source: Kessler Sketchbook, f. 8v.

This short thematic idea is rich in implications. It consists of an eight-measure first period in G major, 3/8, marked "Corni soli," followed by an answering second eight-measure period marked "tutti." It appears among sketches for the Second Symphony finale, and its partial resemblance to the beautiful opening theme of the A-major Larghetto of that work clearly suggests that it was intended for that movement.[32] The sound of two horns in the opening phrase is unmistakably Romantic, especially as followed by the implied orchestral tutti in the concluding phrase. But although the melodic contour is partially suggestive of the Larghetto's beginning, it also foreshadows another well-known Beethoven theme, namely the principal second theme of the slow movement of the Fifth Symphony. As we will see, Beethoven wrote down significant ideas for the first and third movements of the Fifth sometime in early 1804 but he did not turn to the full composition of the symphony before 1807. So it appears that this delicate organism, apparently jotted down early in 1802, may have been a progenitor of two different slow movements.

As early as March 1802, when the Second Symphony was not yet finished, Beethoven's brother Carl offered the new symphony to Breitkopf and Härtel. But the offer was withdrawn almost at once, as Beethoven hoped to have it performed at a benefit concert in April of 1802. The concert did not take place, but if it had he would have premiered this new symphony along with a Concertante in D Major for Piano, Violin, Cello and orchestra, a Rondo in A Major for Piano and orchestra, and possibly an Andante in G Major for Flute, Bassoon, and string orchestra—all of which remained unfinished along with a few other ideas for concerto-like works.[33] Setting the other projects aside, he continued work on the symphony.

Between November 1802 and March of 1803, Beethoven negotiated new terms for it with the publishing house André, then withdrew it when Härtel offered a still higher price. It was finally premiered on 5 April 1803 in a concert in the Theater-an-der Wien, but almost another year elapsed before it was published (in parts, as was customary) by the Bureau d'Arts et d'Industrie in Vienna. Despite the loss of the autograph score and any early corrected copies, it appears that Beethoven revised the work after its first performance and that he finished the score in final form as late as the winter of 1803–4, prior to its publication in March 1804. In other words, the final

touching-up of the Second Symphony took place while Beethoven
was in the midst of composing the "Eroica."

The surviving sketches for the first movement enable us to reconstruct its formation in broad terms. First, the idea of a slow introduction was essential from the start, but it was originally to be in 4/4,
not triple meter; and its early state included a slow-tempo version of
what later became the principal second-group theme of the Allegro.
The first-movement continuity drafts are a textbook demonstration
of the way in which Beethoven developed a slow introduction and its
subsequent Allegro exposition in close connection with one another,
shifting and changing his basic ideas for both sections as part of one
larger process.

The first theme of the Allegro sketch begins with an arpeggiated
tonic triad extended as a theme, but there is more here than meets
the eye.[34] In this form it is far too static in content and rhythmic form to be of real use for Beethoven's purposes, but from it
he gradually generates the final version of the first theme, which
maintains the basic frame but cuts the material into well-defined
motivic units that can function both together and apart, a technique that he used frequently. The first theme contrasts vividly with
the main second-group theme, with its presentation in the winds,
its march-derived rhythms, its extension of rhythmic content to
include some similarities to the tail of the first theme, and much
that is completely new. Within four successive attempts at a continuity draft for the exposition, Beethoven finds his way to what
is nearly the final form of the exposition of the first movement in
its basic outline. The economy of motion and the sureness of the
transformation serve even at this stage to realize the implications of
the motivic units of the two main themes. The supposedly dogged
labor of sketching may well have taken very little real time once he
settled on the basic material and caught the spirit of the movement
as he wanted it to be.

The further sketches do not seem to have been made directly in the final order of the movements, as would later be a normal practice for Beethoven. Here the apparent order entailed extensive work first on movements 1, 3 and 4; the second movement was at first nowhere in sight. The basic phases of gestation look like this:

Phase 1, winter 1800–1801 to spring 1802: work on movements 1, 3, and 4;
Phase 2, later in 1801 to spring 1802: work on movement 2 and conclusion of sketching of 4.

The autograph is lost, but Ries provides an indication that Beethoven was still making revisions in the slow movement after the work had reached its supposedly final stage. Ries writes:

> There was something most striking in the Larghetto quasi Andante of the Symphony in D just mentioned; which Beethoven had presented to me as a score in his own hand and which was unfortunately stolen from me by a friend, out of pure friendship. This Larghetto is so beautiful, so purely and happily conceived, the voice-leading so natural, that one can hardly imagine anything in it was ever changed. The design was indeed from the beginning as it is now. However, in the second violins, almost in the very first staves, a very significant part of the accompaniment was changed in some places and at some points also in the violas. But everything is so carefully crossed out that I could never discover the original idea despite great effort. I also questioned Beethoven about it, who retorted drily, "It is better that way."[35]

Contemporary critics found the slow movement beautiful, but wrote that the finale was "bizarre, wild, and shrill."[36] Its emotional exuberance, its relentless sense of directed motion in the small and in the large, was beyond their comprehension. And yet, although the Second broke new ground, indeed must rank as a major turning point in his career, the further growth of Beethoven's symphonic thinking was on such a scale as to relegate it to the role of being more a predecessor of the later symphonies than the landmark that it really was in its own time.

Title page of the *Eroica* Symphony, a manuscript copy of the autograph, showing Beethoven's annotations and his erasure of the original dedication to Napoleon Bonaparte (Gesellschaft der Musikfreunde, Vienna / Art Resource)

3

THE *EROICA* SYMPHONY

Movement	Key	Meter	Measures
1. Allegro con brio	E♭ major	3/4	691
2. Marcia funebre:			
Adagio assai	C minor	2/4	247
3. Scherzo:			
Allegro vivace	E♭ major	3/4	442
4. Finale:			
Allegro molto	E♭ major	2/4	473

"In his own opinion it is the greatest work that he has yet written. Beethoven played it for me recently, and I believe that heaven and earth will tremble when it is performed." Thus Beethoven's pupil Ferdinand Ries wrote to his friend Nikolaus Simrock, the Bonn music publisher, on October 22, 1803, adding that the composer wants to sell the symphony to Simrock for 100 gulden (a fair-sized sum).[1] Ries further tells Simrock that Beethoven would like to dedicate the work to Bonaparte, but that his Austrian patron, Prince Joseph Lobkowitz, has offered to pay 400 gulden to own the work for half a year, and if that plan works out then Beethoven would name the work "Bonaparte" in homage to Napoleon, rather than dedicate it to him. Finally, Ries says that the firm of Breitkopf and Härtel has already offered 180 gulden for the symphony, together with the "Kreutzer" sonata for violin and piano, but Beethoven does not want to sell them the works "because his brother [Carl] is conspiring with them."

Ries's letter is eloquent, not least for his description of Beethoven playing his new symphony on the piano. We have one other report of Beethoven's playing a portion of the *Eroica* at about this time, namely that in the late summer of 1803 he played the finale of the symphony for the painter Willibrord Joseph Mähler—and then "at its close but without a pause, he continued in free fantasia for two hours."[2] Ries's prediction that future orchestral performances would "shake heaven and earth" largely came true. For with this new work, Beethoven not only created his most powerful large-scale composition to date, but also lifted the genre of the symphony onto a new level of expression and grandeur.

As this new symphony began to be known through its first performances, its length and immensity were apparent to Beethoven's contemporaries, and some found it bewildering. And as it became more widely known (after its premiere in 1805 and its first publication in 1806), its special significance became a watchword. In instrumental music this work launched Beethoven's "heroic style," a concept that became embedded in later criticism and biography and for many Beethovenians served to intertwine these two dimensions, his life and work. Its special status remains essential in modern discussions of his artistic career, despite inevitable reappraisals.

Almost two hundred years after Ries's letter, Scott Burnham wrote that the *Eroica* came to be seen as the "one work [by which] Beethoven is said to liberate music from the stays of eighteenth-century convention, singlehandedly bringing music into a new age by giving it a transcendent voice equal to Western man's most cherished values." He argued that Beethoven's enlargement of the symphonic model encompasses all four movements, though most comments on the mythic power of the work focus on the first movement, which "singlehandedly altered the fate of sonata form, the defining form of the classical style, not to mention that of the symphony."[3]

The story of Beethoven's original plan to dedicate the symphony to Napoleon, or name it for him, and his angry decision to tear up this tribute on hearing of Napoleon's coronation as Emperor, is not a myth. It was documented by Ries in a later account published in 1838, and is also reported by Anton Schindler in his biography of 1840. It is graphically illustrated by the title page of the best-known surviving manuscript copy of the score (see illustration at the head of this chapter), no doubt the same one that Ries describes in a famous passage:

> In this symphony Beethoven had *Buonaparte* in mind, but as he was when he was First Consul. Beethoven admired him very much at the time, and compared him to the greatest Roman Consuls. I and several of his other close friends saw this symphony, already copied out in score, lying on his table with the word *"Buonaparte"* at the extreme top of the title page and at the extreme bottom "Luigi van Beethoven" but no other words. Whether and with what the space between was to be filled out I do not know. I was the first to bring him the news that Buonaparte had proclaimed himself emperor, whereupon he flew into a rage and cried out, "Is he then, too, nothing more than an ordinary man! Now he will trample on all the rights of man and only indulge his ambition. He will exalt himself above all others and become a tyrant!" Beethoven went to the table, grasped the title page at the top, tore it in two, and threw it on the floor. The first page was newly written and only then did the symphony receive the title *Sinfonia Eroica.*[4]

Although this tale has become a staple in Beethoven biography, in some ways it remains ambiguous, for we can follow Beethoven's changes of mind over the dedication and title only up to a point. There is no doubt that during the 1790s, when Napoleon, as general of the French armies, was winning victories in Italy and electrifying all of Europe, Beethoven saw him as the rising hero of post-revolutionary France. His admiration continued as Napoleon accumulated increasing political power as First Consul (1799–1804), though we do see Beethoven expressing some personal doubt in 1802, when Napoleon signed his Concordat with the Pope in order to suppress royalist counter-revolutionary movements in France.[5]

Beethoven's disenchantment must have grown dramatically in May of 1804, when the French senate granted Napoleon the hereditary title of Emperor, thus sealing off any lingering hope that his regime might keep alive any vestige of the old French revolutionary ideals. And yet, on August 26th of that year Beethoven was telling his publisher that "the title of the symphony is really 'Bonaparte.'"[6] It is true that on the famous copy of the score with its mutilated title page, the words "intitolata Bonaparte" were so strongly effaced that holes were cut through the page. But it is also true that at the bottom of this same title page Beethoven wrote, in pencil, "geschrieben auf Bonaparte" (written about Bonaparte), as if he was still considering the possibility of leaving the name on the work after all. After August 1804, we have no further evidence, and can only assume that Napoleon's formal coronation as Emperor on December 2 must have terminated any thought of dedicating the work to him, let alone naming it for him.

The symphony was published in Vienna in October 1806, more than two years after Beethoven's letter of August 1804 and eighteen months after its first performance in 1805. On the title page, after "Sinfonia eroica" appear the words, "composed to celebrate the remembrance of a great man" (*composta per festeggiare il souvenire di un grand Uomo*). Inevitably the question has remained as to whether this subtitle could refer between the lines to Napoleon, as he was before his coronation, or could perhaps refer to another "great man" who might have seized Beethoven's imagination (among the suggested candidates is Prince Louis Ferdinand of Prussia, who was killed in battle in 1806). Another—and to my mind more convincing—view is that in 1806, with the work about to appear in print before the world, Beethoven intended its title and subtitle to refer more broadly not to any single individual but to an ideal, mythic figure, whose heroism is represented by the power and weight of this symphony and whose death is commemorated by its Funeral March as second movement.

THE EMPIRE OF THE MIND

We do well to consider this dedication in the context of Beethoven's idea of greatness and human fallibility. Beethoven's belief in his own artistic potential had awakened early and remained unshaken, fortified not only by his rise to European fame but by his Utopian faith in the power of art to move the world, a belief that artists could still harbor in his time. It only strengthened as he grew older, but it was already there in his first maturity, when he was writing for the immediate public, and it remained strong in his middle years, when he was writing for an ideal public, only a few of them his contemporaries. In his last years it became an obsessive conviction, despite the fact that his most recondite works, the late quartets, were scarcely understood in his lifetime and seemed likely to be accepted only in the distant future, as indeed proved to be the case.

Throughout his life Beethoven found it next to impossible to deal effectively with practical necessities, beset as he was by his perpetual need for money, his incessant problems with publishers and fees, his lack of a fixed position, his surly dependence on aristocratic patrons, and most of all by the growing social isolation brought on by his deafness and compounded by his difficult personality. But through the years of his personal struggles he kept alive an idealistic pride in who he was and what he could create, displaying not only the heroism of achievement, but the heroism of endurance as he saw it personified in the imprisoned Florestan, the suffering hero of his only opera.[7]

In 1801, he dreamed of a Utopian "market for art" [a *Magasin der Kunst*] to which an artist "would only have to bring his works and take as much money as he needed . . . but, as it is, an artist has to be to a certain extent a business man as well, and how can he manage to do that."[8]

In later years he returns to the comparison of artists and aristocrats, including monarchs. In 1814, as the crowned heads and diplomats of Europe were gathering at the Congress of Vienna to plan the future of Europe after the overthrow of Napoleon, Beethoven wrote to a Viennese lawyer and musician, Johann Nepomuk Kanka,

> You yourself know that a man's spirit, the active creative spirit, must not be tied down to the wretched necessities of life. And this business robs me of many other things conducive to a happy existence. I have been compelled . . . to set bounds to my inclination to work by means of my art for human beings in distress—I shall not say anything to you about our monarchs, and so forth, or about our monarchies . . . I much prefer the empire of the mind, and I regard it as the highest of all spiritual and worldly monarchies.[9]

And in his letters to the Archduke Rudolph, Beethoven again and again reminds the royal prince who is master and who is pupil. Rudolph, the youngest brother of the reigning Emperor of Austria, was a talented composer and pianist who accepted his role as musical apprentice and recognized Beethoven's mastery, while at the same time furnishing him with financial support.[10]

This same theme, the opposition of artistic ideals and hard realities, dominates Beethoven's feelings in his last years. Witness this letter to Prince Nikolai Galitzin, who had commissioned the first three of his late quartets:

Believe me when I say that my supreme aim is that my art should
be welcomed by the noblest and most cultured people. Unfortu-
nately we are dragged down from the celestial element in art only
too rudely into the earthly and human sides of life.[11]

Coming of age in the time when Kantian ideals were in the air,
Beethoven kept the faith that a work of the stature of the *Eroica*
would carry significance long after the achievements of any patron
or dedicatee—even Napoleon—had faded into history.

THE EMERGENCE OF THE *EROICA*

The origins of the *Eroica* are unlike those of any other work by
Beethoven. By "origins" I mean essentially two things. Broadly it
refers to the relationship of a work to his own earlier achievements
and to the relevant context in which he brought it to completion. In
the narrow sense it refers to what we can learn from the abundant
evidence that lets us glimpse the emergence of the symphony from
its earliest stages of conception, as documented by his sketches. The
surviving sketches for this symphony have been partially known for
more than a century and have been widely quoted in the scholarly
and popular literature. But the entire known sketch material for the
Eroica has only very recently been fully transcribed and published,
and so we can trace the early phases of its evolution far more clearly
than ever before.[12]

We begin with the broader background. By 1802, Beethoven was
riding a wave of growing popularity as the coming figure in musical life, not only in Vienna but across Europe. As Beethoven wrote
in the same letter of 1801 to Franz Wegeler in which he revealed
his deafness, he could now work on three or four compositions at a
time. Publishers were clamoring for his music and his future success,
which had grown steadily since his arrival from the Rhineland ten
years earlier, was now assured.[13]

In the course of 1802, along with the Second Symphony, the oratorio *Christus am Ölberge* (*Christ on the Mount of Olives*), the three violin sonatas of Opus 30, and some other works, Beethoven wrote two sets of piano variations that capped his contributions to this genre. One was his Opus 34, Six Variations in F major on an original theme; the other was his Opus 35, Fifteen Variations and Fugue in E-flat Major. Both were innovative in different ways. The Opus 34 set brings each variation in a different key and meter. Opus 35 is large in size and scope, ending with a fugal finale, and it commands special attention by virtue of its direct connection to the *Eroica* Symphony.

The Opus 35 Variations

As is well known, the thematic material and organizational plan of the Opus 35 Variations directly foreshadow the finale of the *Eroica*, which emerges as a freely structured set of variations on the same "Basso del Tema" (the bass of the theme) and the upper-line "Tema" (theme) that had served for the piano variations. Beethoven had also used this same thematic material twice before—as a contredanse for the Viennese ballroom repertoire and in the finale to his ballet *Prometheus*, both composed in the winter of 1800–1801. It is the only theme that Beethoven ever used for so many separate works over his lifetime. It is always in the same key, E-flat major, and his use of it in the finale of his new symphony shows that it harbored special meaning for him, perhaps connected to the myth of Prometheus as the hero who brings civilization to mankind, one of the dramatic themes of the ballet. Beethoven was proud of these variations, and even intended to have a prefatory statement included with the publication explaining that they were not only "distinctly different from my earlier ones" but that he meant by assigning them opus numbers that "I have included them in the proper numerical series of my greater musical works, all the more since the themes are by me."[14]

THE "UR-*EROICA*" OF 1802

Sometime in the later part of 1802, either before leaving Heiligenstadt in mid-October to return to Vienna or shortly after his return,
Beethoven completed his sketches for the Opus 35 variations, entering them into his principal sketchbook for that year, later known as
the "Wielhorsky Sketchbook."[15] What counts for our discussion is
a two-page movement plan in E-flat major that directly follows the
sketches for the Opus 35 Variations. This preliminary draft for a
multi-movement work is the earliest known set of musical ideas for
what became the *Eroica* Symphony, and it speaks eloquently about
Beethoven's earliest vision of this work (see Web Example E). The
"Ur-*Eroica*" movement-plan shows four essential features:

1. A brief outline of a slow introduction in 4/4 time, with a triadic beginning and a rising chromatic ending—two features
   that retain their identity all the way to the *Eroica*'s opening
   theme in the final version, for which a slow introduction was
   jettisoned in favor of the powerful opening hammer-blows in
   the full orchestra;
2. A draft of the first movement exposition, in E-flat major and
   in 3/4 meter. For the opening Allegro theme Beethoven writes
   down only six measures, all in the tonic key as we should expect,
   but opening with the same intervals as the Bass of the Theme
   from Opus 35. Later on the same page he tries out another
   version of the opening theme, still embryonic by comparison
   with the final version but more substantial in content. On the
   next page he writes out another draft of the exposition—still
   fairly simple but containing brief thematic ideas that he could
   later employ as the first movement took shape.
3. This early plan continues with a slow movement in C major
   and in 6/8 meter. Beethoven writes an opening theme and its
   extensions, then a passage in D-flat major with the significant

mark "fag[otto]" (bassoon) below the staff, thus confirming that he is thinking of a work for orchestra. We realize with some astonishment that the first phrase of this 6/8 Adagio theme would resurface years later in a vastly different context, as the opening melodic gesture of the slow movement of Beethoven's last string quartet, Opus 135.

4. Directly after the slow movement sketch, he enters two very brief ideas for a "Menuetto serioso," the third movement, and its contrasting Trio. At this stage Beethoven is still using the term "Menuetto" instead of "Scherzo," but the adjective "serioso," the opposite of "scherzando," is one he used very sparingly.[16]

This "Ur-*Eroica*" movement plan gives no explicit indication of what the finale is to be, but there cannot be any doubt that Beethoven intended from the start to use the same theme and bass of the theme that he had just worked out in full detail in the Opus 35 variations, which indeed proved to be the case. Nowhere is there any indication of his having an idea for a different finale, either in this sketchbook or in the one that followed, which contains far more developed sketches for the symphony. This is in contrast to the movement-plan for the Fifth Symphony in the *Eroica* Sketchbook and other sketch leaves, where Beethoven tries out different ideas for a finale that bear no resemblance to the finale of the finished work.

What do we learn from the "Ur-*Eroica*" movement plan? Essentially, these points:

1. Beethoven's initial conception of his Third Symphony emerged directly from the Opus 35 Variations, which was to form the basis for the symphony's finale. His task was to use the same basic material, but in the more continuous sectional design needed for a symphonic finale, and he would flesh out

the finale only after working out the basic continuities of the three earlier movements.

2. He would suppress the slow introduction to the first movement, thus differentiating the opening of the Third from his first two symphonies.

3. Beethoven began with the idea of an Adagio 6/8 slow movement in C major, which he then proceeded to replace with the Funeral March in C minor.

The last point is the most telling. It shows that in the "Ur-*Eroica*" stage, Beethoven was planning an expressive Adagio slow movement and that, apart from the *Prometheus* ballet connection, there is no visible sign of the "heroic" or any other programmatic idea for this movement or the symphony as a whole. But by the time he began to work on the symphony in the opening pages of the *Eroica* Sketchbook, perhaps not very long after the "Ur-*Eroica*" plan, the Funeral March had replaced the 6/8 Adagio and had utterly transformed the character of the new symphony. It now directly evoked the public mourning of a departed hero. A few years earlier, he had written a simpler but effective funeral march "for the death of a hero" in his Piano Sonata in A-flat major, Opus 26, but this new and extended slow movement is on a much grander scale.

This change of plan for the slow movement is momentous. With this Funeral March, Beethoven introduces death and commemoration into the genre of the symphony for the first time. The low-pitched upbeat flourishes in the basses that open the movement seem to allude to the ruffle of covered military drums in a funeral procession, as if an imagined phalanx of soldiers in a slow-step march rhythm accompany a fallen hero to his grave. Not that Beethoven's aim was to depict a scene in its details, since his idea is certainly to create a movement that is "more the expression of feelings than tone-painting"—his own phrase for the subtitle of the "Pastoral" Symphony.[17] In his sketches for the "Pastoral," as I will demonstrate, Beethoven tried out other wordings to express his reservations about tone-painting. But this Adagio in C minor infuses the whole symphony with a new range of emotional meanings as it ennobles and uplifts the symphonic experience. It points directly to what Beethoven may have felt when he decided two years later that the final title should refer not simply to an implied hero, but to a fallen one—"Heroic Symphony composed to celebrate the memory of a great man" (*Sinfonia Eroica composta per festeggiare il sovvenire di un grand Uomo*).

We can pause for a moment over the word *sovvenire*. Beethoven's written Italian was serviceable enough and he was learning to set the language to music, as we see from several current vocal works and from his recent studies in Italian text-setting with Salieri, especially in 1801.[18] *Sovvenire* means not only "to remember" or "to recall," as in the French and Anglicized French "souvenir," but in Italian has the secondary meaning, "to assist." So the flavor of his 1806 subtitle "*festeggiare il sovvenire di un grand Uomo*" seems to carry the meaning "to celebrate the recalling to memory of a great man." This phrase distances the Funeral March and the whole work from being seen as a descriptive enactment of funeral rites; rather it lends it the character of a measured yet powerful and all-embracing remembrance of heroic greatness. The slow movement evokes the memory of the death of the heroic figure that is the generic subject of the work, while its middle section in C major expresses hope and resolution. The other movements in their own ways offer different perspectives on the issue of heroism and of greatness. Once Beethoven had torn up his original title page, he could envisage the whole work as embodying an unprecedented and visionary musical tribute, not to any individual but to the timeless ideals of the heroic. As one scholar said about the culminating ending of the great first movement, "its *telos* is the future."[19]

A few more words on the Funeral March are in order. It was a familiar genre both in revolutionary French music and in contem-

porary operas such as Fernando Paer's *Achille*. According to Ferdinand Ries, Paer's march was the inspiration for the *Eroica*'s slow
movement. Quite likely Beethoven knew this opera by Paer, as he
certainly knew his *Leonore*, based on the same plot as Beethoven's
own, but there is no further evidence to back up Ries's assertion,
made many years after the fact. Still, Beethoven had met Paer a
few years earlier, and it would be surprising if he had not at least
glanced at *Achille* when writing his own celebration of the heroic.[20]
Beethoven, like many of his contemporaries, read Homer and Plu-
tarch, and in this era the heroes of classical Greece and Rome were
important symbolic figures in art, literature, music, and political
life. They could be summoned up to glorify the warriors of modern
times, as in the paintings of Jacques-Louis David, the major painter
of Revolutionary France and then of the Napoleonic era.

The hero of the "Heroic Symphony" remains a mythic figure,
and just as the work embodies Beethoven's idealism and belief in the
power of greatness, it can be understood as being about heroism at a
level beyond the reach of any single human being.

THE EARLY RECEPTION OF THE *EROICA*

When the new symphony was first performed in public on April 7,
1805 in the Theater an der Wien, with Beethoven conducting, most
listeners and certainly the critics were overwhelmed by its length
and power, and they reacted accordingly. One reviewer divided the
concert-goers into three groups. The first were "Beethoven's special
friends," who, he said, thought it a masterpiece, though admittedly
beyond the understanding of the general public; but they were sure
it would eventually be accepted. He compared them to a second
group which "utterly denies this work any artistic value [saying
that] it manifests a completely unbounded striving for distinction
and oddity [with its] strange modulations and violent transitions."
Between them he imagined a third small group, who

admit that the symphony contains many beautiful qualities but . . . that the endless duration of this longest and perhaps most difficult of all symphonies exhausts even connoisseurs, becomes unbearable to the mere amateur. They wish that Mr. v. B. would use his well-known great talent to give us works that resemble his first two symphonies . . . his graceful Septet in E♭, the spirited Quintet in D Major [*sic*], and others of his earlier compositions, which will place B. forever in the ranks of the foremost instrumental composers . . .[21]

As we read these early critics and many others who wrote music criticism that is often surprisingly detailed and insightful alongside much that is of less distinction, we are struck by the sense of immediacy and importance they attached to such new music by the composers of their time, not only Beethoven, but also his contemporaries. Far from simply accepting or rejecting what was new and difficult in Beethoven's music, they heard his music, as a modern scholar has shown, "in a rather complicated way." That is, as he puts it, "to the same extent that they recognized a transcendent dimension in it, they heard seemingly old-fashioned representations of concrete, objective meanings as well, which they saw as raised to new heights of realism by Beethoven's musical language."[22]

This is not the place to expand on the ample early critical literature on Beethoven, except to mention E. T. A. Hoffmann and Adolf Bernhard Marx, two important critics who helped shape the prevailing image of his music for decades to come. Hoffmann's famous review of the Fifth Symphony, written in 1810, struck deeply into the minds of many writers who followed him, whether or not they agreed with his highly charged language and his claim that the Fifth symphony "opens up the kingdom of the gigantic and the immeasurable."[23] Marx, among the most influential critics of his time and an important figure in early nineteenth-century formal analysis, saw the *Eroica* as "not merely a great work, like others; rather it is . . .

decisive for the entire sphere of our art . . . a work that brought music to a new and higher plane of consciousness."[24]

But just as Hoffmann and Marx defined the parameters of Beethoven criticism for the first half of the nineteenth century, Wagner did so for the second half—and his influence reached much further. For him, in an essay of 1841, the heroic aspects of this symphony could not reflect Napoleon but rather had to be ascribed to Beethoven himself, who "saw before him the territory within which he could accomplish the same thing that Bonaparte had achieved in the fields of Italy."[25] There was, however, another side to Wagner's lifelong devotion to Beethoven and above all to Beethoven's orchestral music, which he portrayed to his own advantage as having exhausted the expressive possibilities of instrumental music, thus creating the rich soil from which he, Wagner, could develop the music drama. We see this other side of Wagner's appreciation of the *Eroica* in a revealing anecdote told by a young composer, Felix Draeseke, who visited him in Lucerne in August 1859.

In a memoir, Draeseke recalled how on a very hot August afternoon, Wagner began to sing the first movement of the Eroica. He fell into a very violent passion, sang on and on, became very overheated, quite beside himself, and didn't stop until he had come to the very end of the Exposition. "What is that?" he cried out to me. To which I naturally replied, "the Eroica." "Now then, isn't melody enough? Must you always have your crazy harmonies along with it?"—At first I didn't understand what he meant by that. When he later calmed down he explained to me that the melodic flow in the Beethoven symphonies streams forth inexhaustibly, and that by means of these melodies one can clearly recall to memory the whole symphony.[26]

It should be noted that Wagner had then just completed *Tristan*, his most pathbreaking work to date and one whose innovations in harmony have long overshadowed its own melodic content.

The anecdote suggests that one of the greatest musical minds in Western history could hear the *Eroica* as primarily a stream of melodies, a long continuous flow of ideas that listeners could sing from beginning to end. This is not the way in which most commentators tend to hear mature Beethoven, whether his symphonies or other works, and it forms a healthy antidote to the view that Beethoven was weaker in melodic invention than in the developmental processes by which he could work out the complex consequences of short melodic motives, certainly an important aspect of many of his works. About the developmental aspect in his later music dramas, Wagner would later write, as if he were describing a Beethoven symphony, "the whole artwork is a thorough web of basic themes, which, as in a symphonic movement, relate to one another through contrast, mutual complementation, formation of new shapes, articulation, and connection."[27] And also, "If there had not been a Beethoven, I could not have composed as I have."

For the other side of nineteenth-century music, that of the concert hall rather than the opera house, the *Eroica* became a fundamental monument for the major composers who continued the symphonic tradition after Beethoven, certainly including Mendelssohn, Schumann, Brahms, and others—but it also remained a primary experience for Berlioz and later Romantic composers who were seeking to infuse their works with programmatic narratives. Beethoven towered over the music of the nineteenth century like a figure on a high plateau, one that many later nineteenth-century composers aspired to reach, each in his own way, each with a sense of the need to integrate their experience of Beethoven with the current stylistic conditions of their own generation and to find their individual voices within that generation.[28]

LENGTH AND DENSITY

For many decades after its composition, the *Eroica* was recognized not only for its vastness of conception, but also its length, as the single work that greatly extended the traditional time-scale for symphonic compositions. That Beethoven was well aware of this is clear from a note in Italian that was printed on the first violin part in the first edition:

> Since this symphony has deliberately been written at greater length than is usual, it should . . . be performed closer to the beginning than to the end of an Academy [a concert], shortly after an Overture, an Aria, and a Concerto; for if it is heard too late, it will lose its own, proper effect for listeners who will be tired out by the preceding compositions.[29]

"Deliberately written at greater length than is usual." It is unlikely that anyone but Beethoven could have written these words. Assuming likely tempi for its four movements, written ten years before the appearance of the metronome, its weight of content and commensurate scope put severe demands on contemporary listeners, as we have seen.

What this work required was not simply that listeners extend their attention spans to unheard-of lengths, but that they try to perceive musical content of greater density than they generally expected from symphonic works intended for large audiences in public settings, not for connoisseurs in private salons. For in the *Eroica* Beethoven created a musical fabric far more dense and interwoven than in earlier orchestral works, even the brilliant Second Symphony, or in any but his most highly developed piano sonatas, keyboard chamber music, or early string quartets.

This level of complexity is apparent from the very beginning of the first movement and then all the way through it, as the opening theme, with its triadic beginning and chromatic continuation, influences many of the subordinate themes and motives that spread out across the landscape of the exposition. The first theme thus takes on two fundamental roles. On the one hand it is a carefully fashioned and memorable opening theme, though not a symmetrical one; on the other, its characteristic motives are elements Beethoven can use later, in various ways, to fashion his web of secondary themes and passages. The connections are sometimes more literal, sometimes less, but they are ever-present, and along with the other essential aspects of musical structure they create a sense in the listener's ear that the long journey through each movement is not simply a process of extension, but entails a greatly enlarged chain of thematic units linked by surface contrast but also by underlying connections.[30] This is primarily true for the first movement but it is somewhat true for the two middle movements and is manifest in the connected variations that form the finale.

Contemporaries report Beethoven saying that in his greater works he composed with what he called an "image" in mind. Although some commentators have readily believed that it was a literary or pictorial image, it seems more likely that it was essentially a basic musical idea, a primary shape or gestalt—what Roger Sessions called, straightforwardly, "a musical idea" that gives rise to a train of thought. This viewpoint fits well what we see in most of Beethoven's sketches, that he often began a work with a "concept sketch"—a basic thematic shape that has a definite form in pitch content and rhythm. Such a primary idea could remain an anchor, an invariant, against which he could build successive elaborations and contrasts as he worked out the larger shape of a movement or a piece.[31] When laying out his ideas more broadly for a large cyclic work he would begin by planning one of the movements in detail, not necessarily the first movement, and then hold this movement steady while he decided what other movements to place against it.[32]

For the *Eroica* first movement sketches, the invariants are certainly these:

1. The key, E-flat major, which may well have had Masonic associations for him, as it was the key of Mozart's great Masonic opera *The Magic Flute*, a Beethoven favorite; and also we find

what appear to be Masonic symbols in the margins of at least two pages of the *Eroica* Sketchbook.[33]

2. The meter and tempo (3/4 Allegro), and a 3/4 that often moves in two-measure modules that can imply 6/4, with off-beat accents and syncopation as types of rhythmic contrast.

3. The opening theme with its triadic beginning on scale-steps 1, 3, and 5, with chromatic continuation, as well as its initial location in bass register and successive restatements in higher register and with increasing orchestral forces.

The first theme is a triadic "turning-theme," that is, a theme in which the melodic line begins on an anchoring pitch, moves away from that starting point, moves again in the opposite direction, then returns to its starting point. This portion of the theme unequivocally expresses the tonic, the home key, which it is the purpose of the opening bars of the movement to establish as its musical center. Then follows what has been called a chromatic "cloud," in which the tonic pitch moves down by half-steps, then upward through the same half-steps back to the tonic. This chromatic figure, sometimes falling, sometimes rising, appears conspicuously at various points in the movement, sometimes as the tail end of an important secondary theme, as well as in the coda.[34]

But it is the triadic motion of the first two measures and its structure as a turning theme that most strongly influences the later thematic content, and it does so not only literally, as at the end of the exposition, but even in a seeming transition passage between statements of the first theme in the opening section of the movement.[35] Listeners may not hear this connection readily or immediately, but it is there, and when they do hear it, the infusion of significance into what might otherwise be a routine transition becomes apparent. This sample can stand for many within the movement.

SOME ASPECTS OF THE LATER MOVEMENTS

Marcia funebre

Hector Berlioz, a Beethoven devotee to the core, called this Funeral March "a drama in itself." For him the symphony's subtitle in the first edition clearly meant that not only the Funeral March but the whole work could best be understood as a commemoration of a fallen hero. He added, "I know no other example in music of a style wherein grief is so able to sustain itself consistently in forms of such purity and nobility of expression."[36]

The movement extends the March as a movement-type, not the quick-step military march but the slow-step funeral march, to a large and amply developed ternary form in which the principal theme has the functions of a refrain, as in a rondo form.[37] The enlargement provides Beethoven with room for contrasting themes within the C-minor first section but also for the C-major ("Maggiore" section) in which the preceding tragedy gives way to a utopian vision of hope. Later, when the funereal main theme returns, there is room for a further expansion by way of a fugal episode and then another return of the main theme in G minor. Finally, after a shocking *fortissimo* plunge, the way is clear for a final statement, a full reprise of the main theme in C minor, now in the oboe, Beethoven's preferred instrument for moments of high pathos. At the end of the movement the main theme crumbles into short phrases interspersed with silences. Again Berlioz:

> When these shreds of the lugubrious melody are bare, alone, broken, and have passed one by one to the tonic, the wind instruments cry out as if it was the last farewell of the warriors to their companions in arms.[38]

In 1821, when word came to Beethoven that Napoleon had died on Saint Helena, he is reported to have said, "I have already composed the music for that catastrophe."

Scherzo: Allegro vivace

More than twice the length of either of the third movements he had composed for his First and Second Symphonies, this movement launches the genre of the large symphonic Scherzo that would live on through the later nineteenth century. To those commentators who yearned to find a single narrative throughout the whole symphony, it seemed curious that, after the profound funeral rites for the hero that they found in the slow movement, he should come back to life in the Scherzo. But what they missed is that Beethoven was not writing a sequential biography of a single hero, but composing a transcendent symphony on the subject of the heroic that would offer different perspectives on this ideal. His larger aim was to extend and ennoble the symphony in a work in which the four-movement plan, with its traditional sequence of basic tempi and keys, would survive and flourish in its enlarged dimensions.

The quiet animation of the opening, with its *pianissimo* and staccato figures in the strings, leading to a descending theme on the dominant, is a typical gambit that enables Beethoven to build the intensity as the whole orchestra eventually takes command and restates the descending theme in *fortissimo*, then hurtles forward with enormous energy to its powerful final cadence. The Trio contrasts as sharply as possible, with its three French horns (three horns appear here for the first time in the symphonic tradition) vigorously declaiming what to many early listeners sounded like stylized calls to battle, but with an expressivity that no military music could possess. In a remark that rings as true today as it did in the late nineteenth century, George Grove said of these passages that, "surely, if ever horns talked like flesh and blood, and in their own human accents, they do it here."[39]

To the traditional three-part Menuetto or Scherzo Beethoven adds a coda, even marking the term in the score (unusual for him). This closing section in its short span encapsulates the pattern of rapid growth from a mysterious *pianissimo* to a rousing *fortissimo* ending that, in the large, was the plan for the Scherzo as a whole.

And in doing so he offers a thematic reference back to the chromatic "cloud" of the first movement—the same rising chromatic motion through three notes, landing on the tonic, that he had used in the coda of the first movement. That he planned this special effect at the end of the Scherzo from the beginning is clear from an incomplete verbal remark he inserted over his very first sketches for this movement: *"am Ende Coda eine Fremde* [—]" (at the end of the Coda a strange [figure? voice?]).[40] Here the rising chromatic figure is assigned mainly to the winds while the tympani quietly repeat the tonic and dominant notes of the home key, E-flat major, in the same two-note pairing that had begun the Scherzo, and just as mysteriously.

Finale: Allegro molto

Whether the direct connection of the finale to *Prometheus* implies more than merely their shared thematic basis remains controversial. One view is that the dramatic plot of the ballet influences the symphony, though this seems questionable.[41] The ballet plot is certainly an Enlightenment narrative with the Titan Prometheus as protagonist, here presented not as fire-bringer or suffering victim of Zeus's wrath, but as a benign maker of civilization who instills life into clay figures who become human and gain access to the arts and sciences. But the differences in musical weight between the two works are much greater than the similarities, for Beethoven's ballet music for *Prometheus* belongs to another world, that of theatrical dance music. In that world, to which he managed to accommodate himself this once, everything was conditioned by the solo dance numbers allotted to the principal characters, who include the god Apollo, the mythological Pan, Bacchus, and Orpheus (whose lyre is represented by pizzicato chords), and the muses Melpomene and Thalia. Ballet was not a comfortable venue for Beethoven, but he wrote effectively for it this one time, using orchestral colors and special effects that would not find a place in his symphonies, concertos, or overtures—for example an elaborate cello cadenza.

When he came to the idea of using the same E-flat major theme and bass as material for his largest piano variations to date in Opus 35, he was clearly aiming to show what riches could be reaped from these simple musical elements. And when he then decided to construct an entire symphony that would in various degrees be based on these same elements, and to use them in literal form in the finale, it meant a further raising of the aesthetic level, in that now in the last movement the strict sectional structure of the classical variation— each variation being a fully closed short piece—would give way to a far freer, more imaginative movement in which the sections are connected to one another without pause.

In effect, this was the meaning of Beethoven's idea of the "fantasia," inherited from Mozart and Haydn but now very much his own. "Fantasia" as a term and concept remained vitally important for Beethoven all his life; it meant a freely developed genre that emerged from his lifetime love of improvisation. But in composed works it also meant that the segments of a multi-sectional or multi-movement piece would follow one another without a pause, as in the keyboard fantasias of Mozart and Haydn, among others. His main completed example is the 1809 "Fantasia" for piano solo, Op. 77, a work of strong originality that begins in G minor and ends in B major. It has all the earmarks of a written-out improvisatory composition, with strongly contrasting sections that flow from one to the other without a break, fitting the genre. In his two sonatas of Op. 27, both entitled "*Sonata quasi una fantasia*" (the second being the "Moonlight" sonata), the movements are complete and separate, but at the end of the opening and interior movements he writes the word "*attacca*," to tell the performer not to pause but to plunge right into the next movement.[42] The same principle, connecting highly contrasting segments within one large movement, governs the *Eroica* finale, in which he transforms the basic material of the Opus 35 Variations into a symphonic finale and rewrites substantial material accordingly. And looking ahead, we see him adopting the same principle for his Choral Fantasia, Op. 80, and ultimately for the finale of the Ninth Symphony.

Even so, in his first movement-plan for the finale, Beethoven used the term "Variations" as a heading and even thought of using a clarinet solo and a horn solo along the way, along with a "Fuga" and an Adagio segment. Of these only the last two survived into his early drafts, of which he made three distinct versions.[43] Later drafts of the movement do not survive, but we can tell from the final version that he was able to blend the outline of a connected variation movement with a large three-part form, of which the Andante would form the reprise and would lead to the final culmination. A telling stroke was the decision to extend the Andante through an intensely expressive passage in A-flat major, which links to the comparable closing section in the Funeral March.

For all its originality, the finale has had a mixed reception, since for some later listeners it did not wholly satisfy the desire to have a last movement that fully encompasses and resolves the cumulative experience of the first three movements, as is surely the case with the Fifth Symphony and its triumphant finale. As Burnham notes, this view is conditioned by the "depth of our attachment to the end-orientation model," in which a finale should be the culmination of all that has gone before.[44] Such a view may stem from the simplicity of the Theme and Bass themselves; to some extent from the introductory section of the finale, in which after his opening G-minor outburst Beethoven gradually builds up the structure by first stating the Bass itself, in a dialogue of strings and winds; then he repeats the process while moving the Bass up an octave with new contrapuntal elements; then he states it a third time, now with the "Bass" in the top voice, in the violins; and then at last he ushers in the upper-line Theme itself, in the winds. The whole introduction is like a demonstration of the composition process within the final work, and it mirrors exactly what he had done in Op. 35. Patient listeners are amply rewarded by the richness of the material that follows; but one must admit that it is only in the last phases of the finale that many feel the epic qualities that had been embodied in the earlier movements.

The Eroica's fourth movement can be seen as a primary example of what might be called Beethoven's finale problem. In a lifetime of making decisions about the character and content of three- and four-movement cyclic works, when it came to first movements, or the first two or three movements, Beethoven's certainty as to what his material should be never seemed to flag, despite the arduous work he then devoted to perfecting them. But sometimes he remained less certain when it came to the finale of a large work, as we see in several famous cases in which he changed his mind about the finale. The most famous example is the B-flat Major Quartet Opus 130, of which the original finale was the vast fugue which he later agreed to separate from the main body of the work and publish separately as the "Grosse Fuge," Op. 133, after which he wrote the "little" finale that became established as the final movement. Another substitution, less well known, was the finale of the "Kreutzer" Sonata, Op. 47, which he had originally intended for the A-major Violin Sonata, Op. 30, No. 1. And even in the case of the Ninth Symphony finale, with its setting of Schiller's Ode to Joy and its combination of variation form and fantasia, the sketches show that Beethoven gave at least some consideration to an instrumental finale in D minor.[45] His main theme for that projected movement did not disappear but resurfaced as the opening theme of the finale of the A-minor Quartet Op. 132.

No such indecision seems to have attended the *Eroica*'s finale. On the contrary, the evidence strongly supports the idea that the finale, derived directly from Op. 35, was the anchor against which he composed the rest of the symphony. But if Beethoven did not nurture doubts, even favorable critics in his time questioned the effect of the opening building-up of the Bass of the Theme and then the Theme, coming after the colossal experience of the preceding movements. And although no one has ever failed to see the skill and imagination with which Beethoven develops these elements in all that follows, above all in the Poco Andante, we can identify a long chain of commentators for whom this finale did not seem to fully match the glories of what had come before.[46]

Thayer reported the following conversation between Beethoven and Christoph Kuffner in 1817. By this time, all but the Ninth had been composed and were widely known.[47] Early that summer, Beethoven was once again staying in Heiligenstadt, where he was visited by Kuffner, a Viennese writer and civil servant. Kuffner was also something of a musician and was on good enough terms with Beethoven to be his dinner companion that summer at a Gasthaus in nearby Nussdorf. Kuffner later reported this exchange, according to his younger acquaintance Franz Krenn, who told it to Thayer in 1859:

KUFFNER: Tell me frankly, which is your favorite among your symphonies?
BEETHOVEN (in great good humor): Eh! Eh! The "Eroica."
KUFFNER: I should have guessed the "C Minor."
BEETHOVEN: No, the "Eroica."

Perhaps it was not a coincidence that such a conversation should have taken place in Heiligenstadt, of all the country villages in which Beethoven had stayed during his summer residences over the years. This was the place, after all, in which, fifteen years earlier, Beethoven had passed through the greatest personal crisis of his life.

Consider the postscript to the Heiligenstadt Testament, dated October 10, 1802:

As the leaves of autumn fall and are withered,—so likewise has my hope been blighted—I leave here—almost as I came—even the high courage—which often inspired me in the beautiful days of summer—has disappeared. Oh Providence—grant me at last but one day of pure *joy*—it is so long since real joy echoed in my heart—Oh when—Oh when, Oh Divine One—shall I feel it

again in the temple of nature and of mankind—Never? No, Oh
That would be too hard.

Studying Beethoven's working papers enables us to relate the
confessional testament to his compositional life, for him the basic
raison d'être of his existence. In 1802, Heiligenstadt had been a place
of suffering and of the failure of his hopes for recovery, but it had
also been the place in which he had come to terms with his deafness
and had regained his determination to live and to fulfill his ambitions. He had already prepared himself for both, as we see from the
letter to Wegeler a year earlier, where he had written: "if it is at all
possible I will defy my Fate, though there will be moments when I
will be the unhappiest of God's creatures."[48] Returning to Heiligenstadt years later, Beethoven was revisiting the place in which he had
completed the piano variations that had seized his imagination and
spurred him to create this symphony.

Beethoven in 1806, painting by Isidor Neugass

(Private collection / Bridgeman Images)

4

THE FOURTH SYMPHONY

Robert Schumann once called it "the Greek-like slender one in B-flat major," and elsewhere, "a slender Greek maiden between two Norse giants."[1] His metaphor, endlessly quoted in program notes, depicts the Fourth Symphony as a delicate creature poised between the muscular *Eroica* and Fifth rather than as a robust and independent masterwork that can stand up to its companions on either side. His image fits well with the gendered categories by which Romantic music theory often characterized the contrasting themes of sonata-form movements (the first theme as assertively masculine, the second lyrical and shyly feminine). But more telling is that he thinks of his maiden as "Greek," by which he meant the artistic classics of antiquity, including its famous sculptured human figures. His language evokes memories of the procession of young women in the Parthenon frieze who carry vessels for the sacrifices that must be made to the gods. Above all else, Schumann sees this symphony as classic in its proportions, well-made, beautifully wrought, worthy to be ranked with the ideal of noble simplicity in classical art that the Romantic period inherited from the Enlightenment.

Schumann's affection for this smaller, "lighter" symphony remained influential, as it gave voice to the feeling shared by listeners of being awestruck and overwhelmed by the Third and Fifth, the sense that these works so amply redefined the symphonic experience that the Fourth was felt to be a deviation, to some even a regression.[2] To the musical world of the mid- and late nineteenth century, it seemed clear that Beethoven had returned to the idea of a symphony of smaller dimensions, on the scale of Haydn, though one in which the three fast movements displayed highly charged rhythmic energy and accessible and memorable thematic ideas, plus an Adagio of great melodic beauty that evokes a world of Romantic feeling. It was this world that Beethoven entered in this slow movement and in a few other works, among them the song cycle *An die ferne Geliebte*, written nine years later.

Two aspects of the Fourth proclaim its independence of conception from the *Eroica:* its instrumentation and its movement-lengths. The orchestra now includes only one flute, which means not simply a smaller wind section but a less sonorous use of upper registers in the woodwinds (although woodwind solo passages are frequent and important). With its paired horns and trumpets, the orchestra for this work is the one usually associated with contemporary concertos rather than symphonies. The four movements of the Fourth are strikingly compact when compared to the outsized lengths of those of the *Eroica*, and its modes of continuity in the rapid movements are primarily engaged with motion and action, not with density of musical ideas and textures. The four movements are laid out as follows:

Movement	Key	Meter	Measures
1. Adagio	B♭ major	Alla breve	38
Allegro vivace	B♭ major	Alla breve	460 (cf. *Eroica*, 691)
2. Adagio	E♭ major	3/4	104 (cf. *Eroica*, 247)
Rondo (no repeats)			
3. Allegro vivace (5-part	B♭ major	3/4	397 (cf. *Eroica*, 442,
scherzo & trio)			3-part scherzo)
4. Allegro ma non troppo	B♭ major	2/4	355 (cf. *Eroica*, 473,
(sonata form,			Allegro molto)
exposition repeated)			

GENESIS AND CHRONOLOGY

Over the four years from the end of 1802 to the end of 1806, Beethoven entered into a surge of creativity unsurpassed in his lifetime. Moving into his "middle period," or, as I prefer to call it, his "second maturity," he transformed the symphony as a genre and also produced a series of works that rank among the best-known masterpieces of tonal music. They include the "Waldstein" and the "Appassionata" sonatas, the Triple Concerto, the oratorio *Christus am Ölberge* (*Christ on the Mount of Olives*), the opera *Leonore* in its first two versions, and the Fourth Piano Concerto. In 1806 he composed the Op. 59 quartets, the Violin Concerto; the *Leonore* Overture No. 3—and the Fourth Symphony, of which the autograph score is dated "1806."

Accordingly, the standard, final order of the four symphonies of this period—the Third, Fourth, Fifth, and Sixth—is the order in which they were completed and performed; the Fifth and Sixth were not actually published until 1809. But, as we saw, the surviving sketchbooks and other evidence suggest a different order for his initial ideas for these works. This genetic evidence is not fully conclusive owing to the partial loss of sources, but what we have suggests an order of initial creation that reshapes our view of the conceptual chronology of these works. Even as we accept the risks that come with the close interpretation of a great artist's sketch material, including material as rich and complex as Beethoven's sketchbooks, the following chronological sequence seems to emerge:

1. The *Eroica* Symphony, begun in late 1802, fully sketched in 1803 and completed by October of that year.[3]
2. Beethoven's initial ideas for two movements of what became the Fifth Symphony—the Scherzo and the first movement, the latter explicitly marked "Sinfonia"—which he entered on leaves of his *Eroica* Sketchbook that are otherwise devoted to the first three numbers of *Leonore* and thus belong to the first months of 1804.[4]

3. Several sketches in the same *Eroica* Sketchbook prefigure passages in the Sixth Symphony (the "Pastoral"). They include an idea for "Murmurs of the Brooks" that anticipates the "Scene by the Brook" that later became the slow movement of that work. In the same sketchbook we also find an entry for a "lustige Sinfonia" (joyful symphony), written down shortly after the entries for the Fifth Symphony. The "lustige Sinfonia" sketch is not related thematically to the Sixth Symphony, but it shows that in the first months of 1804, Beethoven was considering the idea of two symphonies of sharply contrasting character, one tragic, the other "joyful."[5]

For the Fourth Symphony we have no extended sketches and no indication of any sustained work on the symphony before 1806. The apparent loss of a major sketchbook from 1806 explains the absence of early drafts for all movements of the Fourth, as well as for the other major works of that year.[6] Admittedly, two tiny scraps of sketches for the finale survive on paper that has been dated to 1804, but they are nothing like sustained evidence of his work on the Fourth in that year, and it is entirely possible that he came back to put down these short random ideas at a later time. The few other surviving sketches appear to be from 1806.[7] Moreover, all of the circumstantial evidence suggests that the Fourth was composed in a fairly short time in the summer and fall of 1806, after his completion of *Leonore* and after the Opus 59 Quartets.

Within the flow of creativity that brought so many important works to completion in these years, the initial conception of the Fourth Symphony thus falls not directly after the Third but rather after *Leonore* in its first two versions and after the Op. 59 quartets that opened a new chapter in the history of chamber music. As we have seen, the sketch evidence also suggests that when Beethoven launched the composition of the Fourth, he had already at least envisaged, and made brief sketches for, the powerful C-minor themes that went into the first and third movements of the eventual Fifth, as well as his few ideas for a "joyful symphony" and an idea for a piece that could portray a brook in the countryside. It was only after the achievements of 1806 that Beethoven returned to work in 1807 and 1808 on the Fifth and Sixth Symphonies, bringing both to completion and performing them at his famous Akademie of December 1808.

BEETHOVEN'S PATRONS AND
THE DEDICATION OF THE FOURTH

The external evidence concerning the origins of the Fourth is partly documentary, partly anecdotal. In the late summer or early fall of 1806, Beethoven paid an extended visit to his long-time patron, Prince Karl Lichnowsky, in his country seat at Grätz in Silesia, near Troppau (now Hradec, in the Czech Republic). Ever since Beethoven's arrival in Vienna in 1792, Lichnowsky had been one of his strongest supporters, a prime mover in Beethoven's rise to fame. He had been a patron of Mozart during the composer's last years, and he was remarkably generous to the gifted young man that he and his fellow music-lovers saw as Mozart's emerging successor. As Lichnowsky had done with Mozart in 1789, he accompanied Beethoven on a journey to Prague and Berlin in 1796, gave him a gift of four string instruments to encourage him to write quartets, and bestowed an annuity on him in 1800 that lasted until Beethoven's breach with him in 1807.

But none of Beethoven's patrons (except the Archduke) could adequately deal with his tempestuous sense of entitlement, his rock-like belief that his stature as an artist stood high above their social pretensions. Arriving at Lichnowsky's family seat in Grätz, Beethoven was evidently working on the Fourth Symphony when an episode exposed their differences.[8] According to various accounts by contemporaries, Lichnowsky asked Beethoven to improvise at the piano for some French officers who had been invited as dinner guests. Beethoven refused. Then Lichnowsky, who might by now have known better, did not give in but insisted that he play—whereupon Beethoven left Grätz in a rage and walked to the nearby town of Troppau. Though reports of the episode differ, they have the ring of truth. It was in connection with this incident that Beethoven is said to have written a letter to Lichnowsky with the remark, "Prince, what you are you are through the accident of birth; what I am, I am through myself."[9] From 1807 on, their relationship was irreparably broken, and it may be that the loss of his annuity from the Prince helped motivate Beethoven's attempt to secure a post with the Court Theater in 1807.[10]

The eventual dedication of the Fourth to Count Franz Oppersdorff, a Silesian country squire, apparently stemmed from this same visit to Lichnowsky. Opperdorff's estate was situated at Oberglogau, about fifty kilometers from Lichnowsky's castle. The Count liked to have musicians as his servants and hired them if they could play orchestral instruments, as it appears they did when Beethoven and Lichnowsky visited Oppersdorff and heard them play his Second Symphony.

This performance must have been prior to the angry incident at Lichnowsky's with the French officers, at which Oppersdorff may have been present. In view of Beethoven's seemingly perpetual need for money or at least the promise of support, this would have been the time when he accepted a commission from Oppersdorff for "a symphony, which I have written for him." A receipt Beethoven wrote to Oppersdorff in late January or the first days of February 1807 shows that he had accepted a handsome fee of 500 florins for this work.[11]

It was typical of Beethoven to negotiate with publishers and demand a fee for the publication of his works—in this period, lacking all copyright, a one-time fee was all he could count on—but at the same time to offer the dedication of a work to a patron who could have it exclusively for six months, after which Beethoven was free to publish it. As early as 3 September 1806, writing from Grätz, Beethoven offered Breitkopf and Härtel in Leipzig three quartets (clearly Op. 59), a new piano concerto (the Fourth, Op. 58), his new opera (*Leonore*), his oratorio *Christus am Oelberge*, and a "new symphony" which must have been the Fourth.[12] As was often the case, not all were really ready, though some were in progress, including the symphony. On 18 November he wrote again to Breitkopf, this time telling them, "I cannot yet give you the symphony I promised you because a distinguished gentleman has taken it from me. But I still retain the freedom to publish it after six months."[13]

However, the distinguished gentleman was not Oppersdorff. Between February 1807 and November 1808, Beethoven had accepted payments from Oppersdorff for one or more symphonies, then wavered as to which works he might eventually dedicate to him and which he might reserve for more prominent dedicatees. In March 1808, in one of his two surviving letters to the Count, he made an unmistakable reference to the Fifth Symphony by writing that "the last movement has three trombones and a piccolo" and promising to send it to him.[14] In November of 1808, he wrote again to Oppersdorff to explain to him that, "You will probably see me in an unfavorable light, but necessity drove me to hand over the symphony written for you to someone else, and also another symphony—" [he is referring here to the Fifth and Sixth, which now were to be dedicated to Prince Lobkowitz and Count Razumowsky] "but be assured that you will soon receive the symphony that is intended for you."[15]

The upshot of all these dealings, reflecting Beethoven's habit of treating his dedicatees as imperiously as he liked, was that Oppersdorff had paid him for two symphonies but only received the dedication of one—the Fourth, when it was published in 1808.[16] Oppersdorff apparently never surfaced again in Beethoven's thoughts, as he does not appear in his correspondence or other documents.[17] We do know that during this period, probably in 1807, Beethoven was thinking of switching some of his dedications of major works (from the Fourth Piano Concerto to the *Coriolanus* Overture inclusive) from one patron to another, rewriting some draft title pages that had been sent him by his main Viennese publisher.[18] But Oppersdorff's name remained on the Fourth Symphony, securing a place for this distant figure among the more prominent aristocratic patrons to whom Beethoven dedicated one work each during his lifetime. After all, Oppersdorff had paid in advance.

THE FOURTH SYMPHONY:
FORM, CHARACTER, AND SIGNIFICANCE

The special qualities of the Fourth Symphony have fascinated many a commentator, whether the focus is the place of the work within the nine symphonies or the subtlety and beauty of the work in all four movements.[19] The key of B-flat major had a special appeal for Beethoven throughout his life. Previous works in this key included his Piano Concerto No. 2 and the Clarinet Trio, both stepping-stones of the early years. Thereafter, he used it for works of personal importance and high craftsmanship, such as the String Quartet Opus 18, No. 6, with its finale entitled "La Malinconia," and the Piano Sonata Op. 22, about which Beethoven wrote to his publisher Hoffmeister, "dear brother, this sonata is really a beauty."[20] And in later years, after the Fourth Symphony, we see it in such significant works as the Piano Trio, Op. 97 ("Archduke"); the "Hammerklavier Sonata" Op. 106; the slow movement of the Ninth Symphony, Op. 125; and the String Quartet Op. 130, with its original finale, the "Grosse Fuge."

The First Movement: Adagio Introduction

Opening with a soft and sustained B-flat in the flute, clarinets, bassoons, and horns, there emerges in the strings a soft and gradually descending theme, slowly shifting from half-notes to quarter-notes, as if quietly gaining rhythmic life. The harmony of the opening phrase is not B-flat major but B-flat minor, a dark key that dominates the opening through its first two large utterances before moving on to an even more distant new tonal center, B minor, reaching it by way of the pitch G-flat (which Beethoven then respells as the more playable F-sharp). A breathless succession of soft chords further extends the harmonic range of this strange opening. Only at the very end of the whole slow introduction does the harmony burst out in *fortissimo* with the true dominant of the real home key, B-flat major, preparing for the outburst of the Allegro to follow.

Looking back, we see that though the basic key of the whole first movement is B-flat major, Beethoven has delayed the arrival of this key throughout the whole Adagio introduction, while along the way he has planted exotic figures and motions to unusual keys (above all G-flat = F-sharp) that will bear fruit later in the Allegro. These methods—setting up a slow introduction that dramatically avoids the home key, delaying its arrival that comes only at the beginning of the subsequent Allegro—were precisely what he had done in 1806 in the first movement of the Quartet Op. 59 No. 3 and in the two *Leonore* overtures Nos. 2 and 3, each in its own way but using the same basic means.

The First Movement: Allegro vivace

From the very outset, the first movement rushes forward in rapid motion, as the balance between melody, harmony, and rhythm in the articulation of the larger form is weighted towards rhythmic action and rapid pacing. Of course the melodic and motivic elements of the opening theme of the Allegro provide a firm basis for all that follows, either by elaboration or by contrast. The opening theme contains two types of melodic motion—the triadic and the linear in immediate contrast. The first phrase is a succession of arpeggiated chord tones, the second is a flowing downward line in the woodwinds from G down to B-flat.[21]

From here on, the sense of urgent forward motion, what Tovey called "spin," is irresistibly present. In every thematic segment that follows in this exposition, newly defined rhythmic figures clearly emerge, as in the syncopated measures of the transition and in the main second group, where solo woodwinds (in the order bassoon, oboe, flute) begin the thematic succession that will enliven the exposition all the way to the end. It turns out that, as in the *Eroica* first movement, after the first long segment that establishes the tonic key area, there are six remaining clear-cut thematic segments in the later part of the exposition, each possessing a strong rhythmic identity.

In the development section, the two elements of the original first theme appear in new but recognizable guises as the sequential modulation pattern of this section unfolds. The arpeggiated figures of the opening of the first theme dominate in the first part of the development and pass through metamorphoses that include an apparent "new theme" that has its own intrinsic connection to earlier figures—again, astonishingly, as in the famous "new theme" in the *Eroica* development section.[22]

But most striking in this development section is the sense of drama created by the tone-color and dynamics that dominate whole segments, as in the striking diminuendo passages, at the end of which a strange new sound appears in the orchestra. This is the sound of *pianissimo* drumrolls in the timpani on the tonic pitch B-flat (= A-sharp) while the basic harmony of the passage is that of an F-sharp-major chord (F-sharp–A-sharp–C-sharp)—which, we suddenly remember, is the same as the G-flat major we heard in the slow introduction. Here Beethoven plays a seemingly simple but beautiful gambit, one of the most telling moments in all his symphonic writing. He moves directly from this seemingly remote key of F-sharp major on to an F-natural in the bass. The harmony thus returns to the home tonic of B-flat major, not the tonic chord in stable form but rather a form that needs resolution, which is to come at the recapitulation. Preparing for this resolution, the timpani emerges as a binding force, holding its drumroll B-flat steady for 22 measures while the strings gradually whip up momentum in a long crescendo that intensifies the sense of impending arrival, using the short rising figures that we remember from the end of the original introduction as it gave way to the Allegro. Among the many dramatic passages in Beethoven's orchestral music in which a vast crescendo grows from *pianissimo* to *fortissimo*, this is one of the most extraordinary.

The Slow Movement

The Adagio, one of Beethoven's most beautiful slow movements, is suffused with sustained lyricism from start to finish. Yet it begins with a simple two-note rhythmic figure that has an independent life of its own, and that runs through the movement as a pulsating ostinato that always accompanies the long lyrical line of the expansive opening theme.

Thinking about the Beethoven of late 1806, we can see that this dotted figure closely resembles the two-note timpani figure with which Beethoven had suggested Florestan's beating heart in the great F-minor orchestral introduction to the dungeon scene that opens Act II of *Leonore*. And at a later stage of this intricate Adagio movement, the two-note dotted figure indeed appears twice in the timpani: the first time as the mysterious middle section is about to reach the reprise of the main theme in elaborated form, and then again at the very end, in *pianissimo*, just before the final *fortissimo* close.

The opening theme is in a class by itself among Beethoven's long-line melodies of this period. Marked "*cantabile*," it covers a full eight bars in each of its first two statements, which appear first in the strings, then in the winds in higher register. Unlike so many other Adagio themes of Beethoven's early and middle years, it is not set up in parallel phrases of the same length (as in the famous slow movement of the Second Symphony), nor do its component phrases come to intermediate moments of pause, as in the Funeral March in the *Eroica*. Instead the line remains sustained over a full eight bars without a break, gracefully moving from its first three descending quarter-notes to the shorter note-values that animate the remainder; then the whole theme is repeated in the woodwinds with the inexorable dotted figure softly remaining at its side in the strings.

What emerges is a vast rondo, a form that Beethoven used for a fair number of slow movements in these years. In this one he achieves a degree of rhythmic complexity that is rare in his works before the last period (the slow movement of the Ninth Symphony comes to mind) and is more common in the rich, intimate world of his string quartets than in his symphonies. And yet the variety of rhythmic figures, the delicate tracery that abounds here more than in any other of his symphonic slow movements until the Ninth, remains in perfect equilibrium with the lyrical, song-like quality and its dialectical opposite, the two-note dotted figure that returns again and again.

In the absence of sketches we cannot know whether this Adagio could have been a generating element in Beethoven's formation of the whole symphony, but there is no doubt that among his orchestral slow movements it is the one that most fully anticipates the world of the Romantics four decades later. Robert Schumann certainly felt the connection when he came to write his First Symphony, the "Spring" Symphony, in 1841. Eight years earlier, in 1833, he had actually made a piano reduction of the opening section of this very movement by Beethoven, as well as of the *Leonore* No. 3 Overture.[23]

The Scherzo

Nowhere is Beethoven's fertility and strength of imagination more evident than in the Scherzo movements of his symphonies, especially when we compare them to those of his string quartets, the other major genre in which the classical four-movement scheme ruled. Piano sonatas and keyboard chamber works could have three movements, as many of his do, though occasionally he expanded them to four as well. The term "Scherzo," as an alternative to "Menuetto," appears as early as 1795 in his piano sonata in A major, Opus 2, No. 2.[24] From then on, his creation of this new, rapid, and vigorous type of dance-derived movement became a primary feature of Beethoven's "personal style," as it was called by Gustav Becking, the author of a classic book on this subject.[25] One reason why these Scherzo movements stand as main exhibits of Beethoven's grand development over the years lies in the rigid structure of the form, which remained a basic two-section binary form with the first section fully repeated by means of the sign "d.c." (*da capo*). But Beethoven's dynamic innovations, though they maintained the outer shell of the formal structure, put the whole movement-genre on a new basis.

The Fourth Symphony Scherzo exemplifies Beethoven's search for new ways of shaping this movement, and in both form and content he makes it new. Instead of mechanically repeating the opening large Scherzo section after the Trio, the movement is expanded to a full five-part form: Scherzo–Trio–Scherzo–Trio–Scherzo, with all sections fully written out. He had used this format for the first time in the E-minor Quartet Op. 59, No. 2, and he used it again in other middle-period works, including the A-major Cello Sonata Op. 69, the Quartet in E-flat major, Op. 74, the Seventh Symphony, and the "Archduke" Trio, Op. 97. One result of this formal extension is that the Scherzo, with all sections written out, now stands up handsomely to the other large movements in its weight and length, rather than serving as a point of relaxation before the finale. Another result, on which Beethoven capitalizes in the Fourth, is that he can abbreviate the last statement of the Scherzo and then at the very end of the movement can write a short additional coda that brings the whole movement to a firm and striking close.

Opening a Scherzo with a theme in syncopated rhythm, with two-beat figures inside the metrical three beats to a measure, is not wholly original with Beethoven, as Haydn and Mozart had done it before him, and he himself had done it in less radical form in the *Eroica,* not to mention the cross-rhythms of the Scherzo in the quartet Op. 18, No 6. But this initial statement is strikingly new in his symphonies, and all that then flows from this first theme grows from the rising and falling elements that make up the two portions of the theme. The Trio—"*un poco meno Allegro*"—is smooth, *dolce*, and dominated at first by the winds, in slowly rising sequences with short interjections in the strings.

The Finale

Main themes in running sixteenth-notes in duple meter had been fairly familiar in the classic era, as Haydn had shown, but up to now Beethoven had used them sparingly, as in the Allegro section of his *Prometheus* overture. More commonly, his themes of this type in Allegro movements combined the steady pulsating note-values with other rhythmic motives that have sharply defined profiles, motives he could then use for development throughout the movement.

And so the first paragraph of this movement is highly distinctive among his many 2/4 finales of this or any period of his career. Its opening thematic fragment in the first violins in running sixteenth-notes breaks off abruptly in the second bar, and the thematic action then continues in the lower strings while the violins and winds break in suddenly with short eighth-note exclamations that are distant reminders of the clipped eighth- and quarter-notes in the Adagio introduction to the first movement. The opening bars contain the seeds of all that follows, but what now persists throughout, and especially in the development section, is the steady pulsation of a *perpetuum mobile*, often using the opening figure of the first measure as a recurrent motif. A lyrical contrasting theme will enter as the principal second subject, accompanied by triplets instead of sixteenth-notes, but the insistent four-note motif will soon return in paired phrases that alternate *fortissimo* and *pianissimo*, and the opening motif regains the foreground right to the end of the exposition and through the development.

Surprises of all kinds abound, not least the appearance of a solo bassoon with the main theme at the recapitulation, giving this structural juncture a special tone-color like no other in Beethoven's symphonies. And for the coda he reserves the last and most effective of the many playful ideas that crop up in this amazing movement: the opening theme, which has been rocketing forward in sixteenth-notes from the very beginning, now appears in quiet legato eighth-note motion, then suddenly stops with a fermata after its first three motifs. The well-favored bassoons bring the next four-note phrase but again come to a full stop, whereupon the strings pick up the continuity but again come to an extended pause, now for the third time. This whole succession of cut-off phrases has been in *pianissimo*. But now, as if the manic energy of the movement has been dammed up to the breaking point, the full orchestra crashes in, *fortissimo*, with the descending scales and rising clipped eighth-notes that had originally sent the whole colossal movement into action—and the whole symphony closes with a decisive three-chord final cadence that brings down the house.

Page from Beethoven's autograph manuscript of the Fifth Symphony
showing the four-note opening theme
(Staatsbibliothek Berlin, Stiftung Preussischer Kulturbesitz / Art Resource)

5

THE FIFTH SYMPHONY

"FATE"

The primal force of the opening gesture has never faded. "Thus Fate knocks at the door" was the remark attributed to Beethoven by Anton Schindler, his sometime factotum and biographer, afterwards endlessly repeated by commentators.[1] If Beethoven did utter these words in Schindler's presence, which is possible, he did so long after the work had been composed, perhaps in 1822 or 1823, when Schindler was a member of his immediate circle. And yet, portentous and rhetorical as they sound, these words have the ring of plausibility, despite Schindler's notorious reputation as a falsifier of Beethoven documents. We know from Karl Holz, a more trustworthy witness and Beethoven's close associate from 1825 on, that in his later years Beethoven tended to talk in a grandiose manner.[2] And surely the reference to "Fate" (*Schicksal*) resonates with Beethoven's letter to Franz Wegeler of November 1801. Opening his heart to his old friend from Bonn, Beethoven described his increasing deafness, his psychic pain and depression, and his tremendous resolve to fulfill his destiny as an artist. He wrote, "I will seize Fate by the throat; it shall certainly not bend and crush me completely."[3]

At the beginning of this symphony, we hear the virtually physical enactment of this sentence, an auditory embodiment of Beethoven's gesture of resistance to the frailty of his own being and of the human condition. With this opening passage, and in all that follows in the first movement, both the thematic content and the range of harmonies within the larger tonal space are stripped down to their essentials. By this means, Beethoven builds a work that seems to symbolically confront fundamental issues of life and death. It is no surprise to find that its performance history includes later occasions on which people living under conditions of mortal duress have felt in this work a revelation of tragedy that ends in a vision of hope. Many years later, when Beethoven came to write the Ninth Symphony, his only other symphony in a minor key and ending with a vast major-mode finale, the Fifth stood as a partial structural model. It conveys meanings that lie beyond words yet are emotionally clear, meanings to which listeners have unfailingly responded from his time to ours. The mode of understanding that I am referring to is essentially visceral, spiritual, and deeply emotional, and it beggars all attempts to attach the work to a particular descriptive model or narrative, despite the many attempts to do so that populate the literature. At the level I am now speaking of, the same is actually true for all his other symphonies, even the Sixth, although it is overtly programmatic. In fact, in ways that may not be apparent to casual listeners, the "Pastoral" Symphony is really a structural counterpart to the Fifth that is conceived in a drastically different aesthetic mode.

THE "C MINOR MOOD"

The idea of a C-minor symphony had comparatively few antecedents, and in the late eighteenth century the minor mode in general was rarer than major, certainly so in symphonies. In the 1790s Beethoven would have known Haydn's Symphony No. 95 in this key, which Haydn composed for London in 1791, a year or so before

Beethoven's arrival in Vienna, nominally as Haydn's pupil. As Douglas Johnson pointed out, this is the only one of Haydn's London symphonies that lacks a slow introduction, and it also begins with a short five-note motif with a decisive rhythmic form that closes with two quarter-note downbeats in 2/2 meter.[4] It is also the only late Haydn symphony in a minor key. Although Haydn had written two earlier ones in C minor (No. 52, from the 1770s) and No. 78 (perhaps from 1782), we cannot be sure that Beethoven would have known them. In Mozart's world, C minor is clearly a significant key—witness his C-minor Mass, his Masonic Funeral Music, and other works, including the wonderful Piano Concerto K. 491 of 1786—but Mozart never wrote a C-minor symphony. Yet, the G-minor Symphony (No. 40, of 1788) was clearly well known to Beethoven, and its finale theme has a close structural affinity to the rising C-minor arpeggio that begins the Scherzo of the Fifth Symphony. We can be sure of this connection because Beethoven himself wrote out an extended passage from the finale of the Mozart G-minor on leaves in which he sketched his own Scherzo, probably in 1808.[5]

Though Beethoven shared the belief that individual keys have their own affective associations, there was nothing dogmatic about his choice of a particular key for a given work. The critic and editor Friedrich Rochlitz reported Beethoven's saying about the poet Klopstock that his style was always "*maestoso* and in D-flat major."[6] In a sketchbook entry of 1815–16, Beethoven wrote a short passage in B minor and added the words, "B minor—dark key."[7] That he felt a special affinity to C minor in early years is by now well known and has even been diagnosed as a "mania" that took hold most strongly in works written between 1793 and 1802.[8] In many of these works, capped by the great C-minor String Trio Op. 9 No. 3, there are dark, stormy Allegro themes, strong and even violent dramatic contrasts, sudden *forte* and *piano* accents, rich figurations and hurtling rhythmic effects. These occur not only in first movements but in

finales and even in his Scherzo movements. Some of these qualities
are prefigured in C-minor chamber works by Haydn and Mozart,
but in Beethoven's hands they take on a new dramatic intensity. And
he was still under this spell when he wrote the C-minor Scherzo of
the "Harp" Quartet, Op. 74, of 1809, and the first movement of the
piano sonata Opus 111 of 1812.

Shortly before resuming and completing the Fifth Symphony in
1807–8, Beethoven had unleashed comparable power in his overture
for Collin's drama *Coriolanus* (1807). Here the opening two-note
gesture is an aggressive fraternal twin to the Fifth and the entire
work holds affinities with the first movement of the symphony.
Beyond the aesthetic associations we can also see that when writing
for strings in C minor (and also in C major, of course) Beethoven
could exploit the resonant sonorities of the open C strings of the
violas and the cellos, typically near the beginning of a movement
and unquestionably at the end.

The Fifth symphony gripped its early listeners with emotions
they had never experienced in concert music. As E. T. A. Hoffmann
wrote in his famous review of 1810, which may have been written to
influence readers on behalf of the new aesthetic aims of the German
Romantics, this work evoked "terror, fright, horror, and pain, and
awakens that endless longing which is the essence of romanticism."[9]
In his long essay, with its detailed descriptions of all four movements and its many music examples, Hoffmann captured the feeling
of raging momentum conveyed by the opening and gave a step-by-
step account of the first two phrases and their continuation up to
the point at which a third fermata frames the first large paragraph.
He continues: "A presentiment of the unknown, of the mysterious,
is instilled in the listener. The beginning of the Allegro up to this
pause determines the character of the entire piece."

This much-quoted review initiated a line of Romantic criticism
of the symphony that has never flagged, even in the modern age
of structural analysis for which the standard-bearer for the past

century has been Heinrich Schenker, though not without much development and transformation of his views of tonal structure.[10] But whether we follow the critical tradition that leads from Hoffmann to Wagner and beyond, the form-analytic tradition generated by A. B. Marx that has recently been elaborated in new theories of sonata form, or Schenker's deeply perceptive layered analytical approach, one central insight seems to dominate in the reception of this work. That is the feeling that in this symphony Beethoven is speaking to the world not in high rhetoric or in the grand and epic manner, as in the *Eroica*, but rather that he is speaking from deep within himself, creating music that arouses the most basic emotions with an intensity unparalleled in symphonic music before his time and rarely equaled afterward. These emotions include what Hoffmann felt—terror, horror, and pain—and, at the end, when all was done, a vision of triumph.

THE EARLIEST KNOWN STAGES

Early in 1804, Beethoven wrote out his first ideas for two movements of a C Minor "Sinfonia." These are abbreviated but meaningful sketches that clearly present early versions of the principal themes of his third and first movements, in that order, with the first movement sketches marked "Sinfonia." They appear in his primary sketchbook for that year, the so-called *Eroica* Sketchbook, which contains all his compositional work on the early stages of the *Eroica* Symphony and other works of 1803 and early 1804.[11] These entries that prefigure the Fifth Symphony appear on the lower portions of pages devoted to sketches for the opening duet in the first act of *Leonore,* which he began to compose in January and February of 1804. Since these concise Fifth Symphony entries do not show the usual revisions and changes of mind, it has been thought by some that they may have been entered much later, perhaps after the sketchbook was filled. Evidence contrary to this assumption is the fact that the first movement sketches are immediately followed by fragmentary jottings that seem clearly to be intended for later portions of the first movement, plus some annotations for a C-major slow movement and a very early idea for a possible finale, not at all resembling his eventual finale for the finished work. It's clear that they belong to a primordial stage of his conception of the work, and they are corroborated by some other sketches that have been dated to 1804.

These earliest sketches appear in this order:

1. First, an extended concept sketch of the opening section of the third movement with its two main themes, followed by a similar concept sketch for the "Trio" (so marked; see Web Example F).

2. Second, and significantly marked "Sinfonia," we find a précis of the exposition of the first movement. The sketch begins with the two-fold statement of the opening motif in its final form, then continues and leads to an early version of the horn fanfare that prepares the main second theme. Then comes the lyrical second theme, twice in succession, first in the relative major, E-flat major, then in C major, the key of the recapitulation (see Web Example G).

There is no sign here of the slow movement in A-flat major, nor of the triumphant finale. Accordingly, it seems likely that the first and third movements could have been the generating elements on which Beethoven could later build the rest of the symphony. With his basic ideas for the two C-minor movements firmly in view, he could then turn to the slow movement and the finale.[12]

When did he begin to work on the slow movement and finale? We can't be sure, but it is possible that he might have turned to the G-major 3/8 entry marked "Andante sinfonia" written about three years earlier, discussed earlier in connection with the Second Symphony. This theme could have been in his memory and even in view as he began to conceive the 3/8 slow movement of the Fifth. He could easily have found it near the beginning of his main sketch-book for 1801–3, where it seems to have been intended for the slow movement for the Second.[13] It begins, as we saw, with a duet for two horns ("*Corni soli*") and its melodic and rhythmic contour foreshadows the great second theme of the Fifth Symphony slow movement, with its dotted two-note upbeat and then three steady eighth-notes leading to a downbeat—it is a rhythmic formulation that in the Fifth partly echoes the famous four-note motto of the first movement, but now in triple meter.

Some clarification of the slow movement's emergence is provided by the collateral sketches that have been dated to 1804, referred to above.[14] Here we find an early idea for the slow movement of the Fifth in its final meter and key (A-flat major, 3/8 meter), with an opening theme that prefigures the final version but is far less musically developed. Known and quoted ever since the late nineteenth century, the theme consists of two simple phrases, with the second a simple elaboration of the first (see Example 5).[15]

Example 5. Sketch for the Fifth Symphony, slow movement

Source: MS Aut 19E.

The heading of this sketch is quite striking. Beethoven writes, "Andante quasi menuetto," and then "Trio" for the next section, where the four-note motto reappears in its slow tempo version, as in the finished movement. It looks as if Beethoven was either thinking of a slow movement "in the manner of a Minuet," or possibly that he was thinking about a movement that might combine the features of slow movement and Scherzo, imagining that the symphony might have three movements. But any such plan would seem to have been entirely negated by the Scherzo sketch in the *Eroica* sketchbook, which is a true harbinger of the fully realized demonic Scherzo that he achieved in the final version.

We come now to the finale. That this symphony, unparalleled in the directness of its emotional expression, should end with a vision of fulfillment and hope, turns out not to have been Beethoven's earliest plan. In the movement-plan in the *Eroica* sketchbook, he tries out an idea for a rapid C-minor movement in 6/8 meter, beginning softly and expanding. This sketchbook version (Web Example H) is marked "Presto," "*letztes Stück*" [that is, "Presto," "last movement"] and the sketch presents six measures of the opening theme. At the end of this entry he writes, "it could close at the very end with a March" (*konnte zuletzt endigen mit einem Marsch*).[16]

In the collateral sketch bundle of 1804, he tries out another idea for a 6/8 Finale ("*l'ultimo pezzo*") but still in C minor, and with a further continuation in the form of a rising figure (see Web Example J).[17] This last idea does not bear fruit in the Fifth Symphony, but he also tries it out in D minor on a later page of the *Eroica* Sketchbook, and there this short D minor theme is also marked "Sinfonia." This D minor jotting will later re-emerge in an entirely different context. But it is of the highest interest to note that very early in 1804, Beethoven already had the fleeting idea of a symphony in D minor (see Example 6).

Example 6. Sketch for "Sinfonia in D moll"

Sinfonia in d moll

Source: *Eroica* Sketchbook, 177, st. 9.

THE LATER STAGES

Beethoven's further steps are difficult to trace. Some later sketches and the heavily revised autograph exist, but the presumed score sketches that must have preceded the full autograph score are missing, as they are for so many of his works. And since his heavy revisions in the autograph itself have not yet been fully deciphered and elucidated, a more complete understanding of his late-stage revisions remains to be undertaken. Nor does there yet exist a full-scale modern study that brings all the known sketches and the autograph revisions together and shows the stages of the genesis of the work between 1804 and 1808.

As of now we can say this much: Beethoven conceived the first and third movements early in 1804 and experimented with the slow movement. He then let the whole project stand while he attended to other important compositional projects. It looks as though he came back to the first movement sometime in 1806, but his main work on the last three movements took place in 1807, which we can date from a scattered group of sketches that were originally part of a home-made sketchbook of that year. The full autograph was completed by around March of 1808.

We also know that in February and March of 1808, with the Fifth Symphony near completion, he took time off to write the A-major Cello Sonata, Op. 69, a masterwork as unlike the Fifth Symphony in character as any we can imagine. No examples better illustrate a great artist's ability to hold entirely different aesthetic conceptions in mind and to shift attention to the different demands that each project made on his imagination.

At some point in developing this symphony, certainly by late in 1807, Beethoven arrived at a completely different idea of the last movement from the one he had sketched in 1804. The dark C-minor initial theme in 6/8, beginning pianissimo, would have partially paralleled the first movement. Now Beethoven completely reconceived the idea of the finale, arriving eventually at the great C-major first theme—"magnificent, jubilant" as Hoffmann called it—replete with piccolo, contrabassoon, and trombones. This movement has stood ever since as the great Beethovenian example of emotional fulfillment at the end of a tragic journey, foreshadowing the comparable role of the finale of the Ninth Symphony.

THE SYMPHONY AS A WHOLE

We turn now to the finished work. The layout is as follows:

Movement	Meter	Key
1. Allegro con brio	2/4	C minor
2. Andante con moto	3/8	A-flat major
3. Allegro [Scherzo]	3/4	C minor with Trio in C major
4. Allegro, with partial return of the Scherzo	4/4	C major

THE FIRST MOVEMENT

Familiarity and the Opening Motif

The opening motif (Example 7), with its pattern of 3 + 1 beats, the last prolonged by a fermata, remains imprinted in modern musical and cultural memory and has been endlessly discussed in the popular literature. Over time this four-note motif became an auditory icon that generated endless associations and citations. It was used during World War II as the symbol of the Allies' "V for Victory" because its rhythmic shape by chance is the same as that of the letter "V" in Morse code. Quotations of the motif dot the landscape of popular culture from films to comic strips. And yet, as with other artistic symbols that have attained this level of notoriety, the context in which it originated—not just the opening phrase but the whole symphony as a work of art—has been ignored or neglected, and the few attempts to broaden knowledge of the compositional background of the work have had to rely on the incomplete evidence available thus far.

Example 7. Opening phrase of the Fifth Symphony, first movement, showing the two paired four-note motifs, the second prolonged by a fermata, and the two-note motif E♭–F, consisting of the last note of the first motif and the first note of the second.

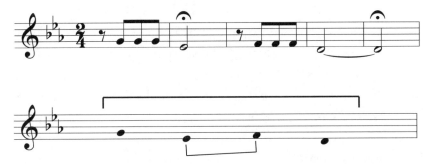

Attending not just to the beginning, but to the symphony as a whole, Schenker observed that the opening four-note unit is best understood as the first half of an eight-note pair, with a fermata prolonging the second unit, and that the double statement is consequential for the way the movement unfolds.[18] Though Beethoven had not yet written the additional measure with fermata to the second statement when he wrote out his autograph manuscript of the symphony, it was added in the earliest performing parts made in 1808 for the first performance by his copyist Joseph Klumpar, parts which were corrected by Beethoven. Accordingly, the authenticity of the fifth bar with fermata appears to be rock solid. By extending the second statement of the motto by a full measure, Beethoven made it clear that he conceived the opening as consisting of two 3 + 1 units, not one, and that the whole phrase is to be heard as moving downward from the first four-note motif to the second, with a dramatic pause at the end of the whole phrase on an implied dominant harmony that demands resolution. The first resolution to the C-minor tonic harmony then arrives quietly, but it is hardly a resolution since the passage that follows the *fortissimo* opening brings a completely different emotional atmosphere as the movement proceeds in *piano* and opens the way to the full Allegro sonata-form first movement.

Just as important—and rarely noticed in the general Beethoven literature since it was first pointed out by Schenker—is that a rising two-note stepwise motif from E-flat to F is concealed within the two-phrase opening.[19] Because this two-note motif is made up of the E-flat that ends the first motto and the F that begins the second— and thus the two notes are separated by a rest—it will not be immediately recognized as a motif by most listeners. But, as with other comparable subtleties of musical thought, once auditors become aware of it they will realize that it plays a vital role later in the movement. Such a motif, made up of two notes that were originally disconnected, has no precedent in Beethoven's earlier works, so far as I know. It is one small but telling indicator of the unorthodox patterns of imagination that underlie this work.

This rising two-note motif first becomes an entity as part of the horn fanfare that announces the lyrical second subject.[20] Later in the development section it reappears as an independent motif and becomes a basic element in the continuity of the whole section, acquiring a mysterious life of its own in the quiet, breathless passage that precedes the recapitulation. Finally it re-emerges in the coda, where this figure appears in march-like quarter-notes as the tragic narrative nears its end.

The relationship of content to form in this movement is like that of no other Beethoven first movement. The layout is that of a four-part sonata form, with an ample coda, and the four sections are of about equal length. How different this is from the *Eroica* first movement, with its enormous development section. But the special character of the first movement of the Fifth obviously derives from the relentless repetitions of the rhythm of the initial motto. It seems clear that Beethoven's imagination was riveted on a stark dualism of primary elements and on making the strongest possible contrast between his demonic opening in C minor and the song-like second subject in E-flat major. Yet even as the second subject arrives, offering relief from the hammering repetitions of the first part of the exposition, the 3 + 1 motif is heard as a quiet presence in the cellos and basses, reinforcing each cadential motion within the theme and its continuation over the next long paragraph.[21] Then the next powerful fortissimo attacked chord launches the next portion of the exposition. And it is a foregone conclusion that the motto will dominate the rhythmic life of the movement all the way to the very end.

Some special features of the first movement call for brief comment.

The Character of the Development Section

The exposition ends punctually in the key of the relative major (E-flat major) as would be expected in a sonata-form movement in a minor key, but what surprises thereafter is the virtually complete containment of the whole development section within a chain of minor keys, as follows:

F minor–C minor–G minor–C minor–F minor (unstable)–G major
–F minor–C minor

This modulatory path is remarkably restricted, and it stands apart from Beethoven's usual patterns in formulating his development sections.[22] In the whole development section there are only a few brief measures in the major mode and even this momentary gleam is short-lived.

The development discloses another aspect of dualism along different lines. After the first part of the development has elaborated the four-note motif with growing intensity, the action culminates with the horn call figure from the exposition that had introduced the second subject. Beethoven then creates a long passage in which the four-note motto is finally abandoned, replaced by the rising two-note motif in half-notes that grew out of the original double statement of the motto at the opening of the whole work. He then deploys the two-half-note motif to dramatic effect throughout the second half of the section.

For more than thirty bars, this two-half-note rising figure fills the musical space, alternating between winds and strings, groping forward through unstable harmonies, shifting the meter in a very surprising way, and gradually growing softer until it reaches *pianissimo*.[23] In its last phrase the two notes of the motif are further divided, now appearing as single measures alternating high and low. It is a moment of ultimate strangeness, as if signaling a psychic collapse after the immense expense of energy that has come before. Beethoven had used similar alternations of high and low single chords twice before to convey uncertainty and mystery—in the finale of Op. 18, No. 6, "La Malinconia," and as a striking passage that occurs three times in the first movement of the F-major Quartet Op. 59, No. 1.[24] The breathless half-notes are interrupted at last by renewed blasts of the horn-call figure, now modified, that leads on to the recapitulation.

The Oboe Cadenza in the Recapitulation

The oboe solo early in the recapitulation, a lyrical pause for reflection, is the most poignant moment in this astonishing movement. It is a short cadenza, marked "Adagio," in which the solo oboe stops the incessant forward momentum to bring a single phrase that moves down stepwise from G to D—a choice of notes that cannot help being heard as a re-ordering of the original notes that made up the initial eight-note pair of motifs—G–F–E-flat–D—now in scalar form. Beethoven prefers the oboe for passages of special emotional expression in his symphonic writing—witness its use as the melody-bearing instrument in the *Eroica* Funeral March for the consoling C-major middle section and for the subsequent return of the C-minor funeral march theme. At the solo cadenza in the Fifth Symphony, one commentator has put it, this oboe solo emerges like a voice "from another world."[25]

The Coda

As in many another Beethoven first movement in sonata-form, the coda is a richly developed section in its own right. It balances the development section and gives the whole movement not three principal sections but four—in this case four sections of just about equal length. Beethoven's sense of proportions trumps all other considerations in determining how the movement should end, but it appears that at a very late stage of composition he had still not made up his mind about the way to end, for in the autograph manuscript we find a lengthy closing segment of more than twenty measures that he first wrote out in full score—and then crossed out completely, replacing this long closing passage with the brief three bars that end the movement with its powerful final cadence. The cancelled segment would have extended the assertion of the tonic C minor and would then have hammered home the four-note motif once more, just before the last three-chord cadence. But in the final version we see that Beethoven stripped down the last segment to the minimum, omitting the motto at the very end.

THE SECOND MOVEMENT

Easing into A-flat major after the storm of the first movement, one has the feeling of settling in comfortably to a place of shelter. The shelter is nearby, because the tonic pitch C of the first movement is now the third of the tonic chord of the new key, A-flat major. And so in this Andante Beethoven proceeds to exploit the contrast of A-flat major and C major to shape the formal dynamics of the whole movement, employing two basic contrasting themes that identify each section and enabling him to elaborate both themes freely and expansively.[26] The basic outline of the movement is as follows:

Section	Key	Comments
A	A♭ major	The "A" theme in piano, *dolce*; at first a beautiful and intricate 8-measure period, deftly foreshadowing C major within its A-flat major framework. After the theme, soft exchanges between winds and string bring the closing segment.
B	A♭ major– C major– A♭ major	The "B" theme, first in clarinets and bassoons with soft string accompaniment (the theme may have been borrowed from a sketch of 1801, see above); the whole theme then repeated "*sempre ff*" in C major, reinforcing its use of the 3 + 1 rhythm from the first movement. This section closes with a lingering phrase that prepares the return to the home tonic, A-flat major.
A1	A♭ major	Section A in a varied repetition, the theme now in sixteenth notes, the closing section identical.

Section	Key	Comments
B1	A♭ major–C major	The B section repeated with rhythmically intensified accompaniment; the closing segment now with mysterious repeated-note figures in the cellos.
A2	A♭ major E♭ major– A♭ major	A further elaborated and extended variation of the "A" theme. The opening motif of the "A" theme in the winds.
B2	C–A♭ Transition	The "B" theme crashes into the texture, again in C major, *ff*. Opening motif of "B" theme developed.
A3	A♭ minor A♭ major	"A" theme in new form and articulation. "A" theme in canonic imitation at 1 bar.
Coda	A♭ major	Più moto; Tempo 1. After a new variant in the bassoon, the extended closing of the original A section returns and prepares the final triumphant ending.

THE THIRD MOVEMENT:
A THREE-PART OR FIVE-PART SCHERZO?

We saw that the third movement may have been one of the generating movements for the whole symphony, as it preceded the first movement when both were drafted in the *Eroica* Sketchbook. Beethoven's original plan, even in short form, brings forward the two essential themes on which the Scherzo is built:

1. The first theme (though originally without upbeat, with a slightly different rising arpeggio, and with continuation as in the final version);

2. The famous 3 + 1 motif, exactly as in the final version though with a continuation different from what he later wrote (the theme in the final version occurs first in the horns, then the full orchestra).

Thematic dualism is thus clear from the outset, as in the slow movement. In the initial movement-plan in the sketchbook, the Trio shows no sign of the contrapuntal writing that so clearly marks the final version, but it does have running eighth-note patterns in C major and its *forte* marking shows that the emphatic solidity of the Trio, in contrast to the *misterioso* opening of the Scherzo, was planned from the first, even if its contrapuntal texture emerged later.

The original form of the movement has been a source of controversy in modern times, owing to major discrepancies among the earliest sources. But this much is clear: at the stage of writing out the autograph score of the symphony, Beethoven intended this movement to be in five parts, as follows (following Jonathan Del Mar's extensive summary of all the evidence and current interpretations):[27]

Scherzo ||: Trio Pt. 1:|| Trio Pt. 2 || Scherzo ||: Trio Pt. 1:|| Trio Pt. 2 || Scherzo & Coda

As we saw in discussion of the Fourth Symphony, the five-part Scherzo form was one of Beethoven's innovations. It appears in works from between 1806 and 1810 and in one late work, the C-sharp-minor Quartet Op. 131. But a close look at the Fifth Symphony sources—the autograph score of the symphony, the earliest copies of the score and the parts, and the first editions—shows that in the course of making his final decisions Beethoven altered the Scherzo to the three-part form that is found in the most reliable modern editions. Yet the five-part version seems to have survived for many years after the first performance in 1808, as we know from remarks in one of Beethoven's Conversation Books from 1820. Here his confidante Franz Oliva tells Beethoven that yesterday the amateurs shortened your symphony—in the third movement they left out nearly half of it—the fugato middle section happened only once, then came the bit where the violins have pizzicato, and the transition to the finale . . . it made a very bad effect.[28]

Evidently, various sets of performing parts used between 1808 and 1820 still had the repeats, and in some cases had them crossed out but then restored by written-in performers' markings. Beethoven himself, busy in his work in Vienna or in the country, probably knew nothing of such practices.[29]

Beethoven's final intention, then, was to shorten the movement to its three-part version, to transform the return of the Scherzo into an extended *pianissimo* section with *pizzicato* in the strings, and to link the Scherzo directly to the Finale by means of an extended coda with the four-note motto in the timpani, with long-held notes in the lower strings, and with a crescendo that quickly erupts into the final Allegro. The truncation of the Scherzo hangs together with his further idea of bringing the *pianissimo* version of the Scherzo back within the Finale as the lead-in to the Recapitulation, now re-orchestrated and with another oboe solo that is joined by flute and bassoon as it nears the climactic arrival.

This return of the Scherzo in the last movement is one of the most famous moments in the symphonic literature. It marks another way in which this symphony breaks new ground in its cyclic integration not only of its thematic material (using the motto in all its guises but always maintaining its basic rhythm), but also in the connecting of movements to form a multi-sectional whole in which the last two movements are joined. We know that Haydn, in his "Farewell" Symphony No. 45, and in his No. 46 in B major, had anticipated the idea of cyclic integration, but we cannot be sure that Beethoven knew either of these works.[30] It seems more likely that he may have conceived the cyclic integration of the Fifth along the lines of the "Fantasia"—a freely developed sectional form as understood in the late eighteenth century, with which Beethoven had experimented before and to which he turned again in his Choral Fantasy Op. 80 and his piano Fantasy Op. 77.

As we saw earlier, in the genre of the "fantasia," one section followed another without pause, *attacca*, and we also see that in more than one of Beethoven's fantasias, and related works, an opening section returns before the end. This was what he had done in the first of his two piano sonatas of Op. 27, both significantly called "*quasi una fantasia*." In the first sonata of this pair a substantial portion of its Adagio slow movement returns near the end of the Finale; similarly, in the piano sonata Op. 101 and the cello sonata Op. 102, No. 2, he brings back the initial Andante just before the rousing 2/4 finale.

THE FINALE

From the very opening, as its rising march-like theme in pure C major blazes forth in the full orchestra, a new landscape opens up before us. Both the tragic and lyrical qualities of the earlier movements now give way to the glory of a triumphant ending. This finale is sometimes linked to the "*éclat triomphale*" of the French Revolution, with which it may have had associations for listeners in Beethoven's time. But what is certain is that in later times, and now just as much as before, this opening transports the listener's imagination on to a higher plane of experience, encompassing and going beyond all that has passed.

On closer listening, we notice that this finale maintains inner contact with aspects of the preceding movements, now transforming them in the new context. Of these the only formal recall—and it is only partly literal—is the return of the Scherzo just before the recapitulation. But other connections are audible as well. Though the primary themes of the finale are independent and new, they also have links to the earlier movements, which they bring to a final stage. These thematic connections emerge within the larger tonal organization of this movement and of the symphony as a whole, for we can now see that from the first movement onward there has been a dialectic between C minor and C major that now ends with the triumph of C major. This is not simply a matter of supplanting the minor mode with the major. The return of the Scherzo in the finale, leading back to the first theme, is the last stage of the process by which the minor/major antithesis is resolved. A diagram will make this clear:

Movement	Keys
1.	C minor–E♭ major
	F minor–C minor–C major–C minor
2.	A♭ major–C major–A♭ major
3.	C minor–C major–C minor
4.	C major–G major
	C minor–C major

To give this movement the range and space required to fulfill its purposes, Beethoven needs more than the two basic contrasting themes that have dominated in every previous movement. There are at least four primary themes in the exposition:

Theme A March-like phrases in pure C major, full orchestra;

Theme B A second principal theme in the tonic C major, then developing in the strings as the harmony moves towards the dominant area of the exposition;

Theme C Triplet upbeats to a firm downbeat define this new theme, clearly reminiscent of the motto rhythm of the earlier movements;

Theme D Beginning *fp*, with a two-measure phrase descending a fourth, its second and third measures again evoke the motto rhythm; the exposition closes *fortissimo* with rising arpeggios and sustained chords in winds and brass.

The full consequences of this multi-thematic exposition, besides its being fully repeated and then amplified in the lengthy recapitulation, are found in the coda. The coda is one of the longest Beethoven ever wrote and is the one large segment of this symphony that has been criticized for its length and, by some critics, for the excessive repetitions of its tonic hammer-blows at the very end. Hoffmann thought that the final chords "are strangely positioned" and went on to describe the final bars as a disruption of the feeling of closure: "the perfect calmness which the heart feels as a result of the several closing figures . . . is destroyed by these single struck chords and pauses." To which Tovey replied, with a classic assertion of belief in Beethoven's sense of proportions, that "these forty bars are meaningless without the rest of the symphony, but the symphony ends as truly within its own length as the *Et in terra pax* of the B-Minor Mass."[31]

A look at the larger structure of the coda can help to clarify the situation. First, there are really two codas, and it is crucial to note that the tempo speeds up from Allegro to Presto for the final peroration. The complementary relationship between Beethoven's codas and his development sections is familiar, but the inordinate length of this double coda, or of these two codas placed together, even with the change of tempo to Presto for the second section, needs some explanation. The first lies with Beethoven's choice of dominating themes.

Coda I

In the first coda, Beethoven begins with two statements of Theme "B," thus immediately referring back not to the development (where "B" had played no role) but to the exposition and recapitulation. Since he had left this "B" theme without elaboration up to this point, he can now give it the full treatment, in a succession of large phrases.

Coda II

We are now ready for the second and final coda, with its Presto tempo that will prevail to the end. The approximate length of this second coda, in Presto, is about the same as that of the first coda, if we accept the metronome marks that Beethoven appended in 1817 to his earlier symphonies and quartets (Coda I = Allegro, half-note = 84; Coda II = Presto, whole note = 112). Coda II begins its confirmation of the tonic harmony with Theme "D," alternating tonic and dominant harmonies in each full bar. A marvelous feature of this Presto opening, little noted in the literature, is that this rising triadic motion in C major repeats, in the large, the same rising motion that had started the Finale altogether (Theme "A") and that it adds to this the basic rhythm of 3 + 1 that has saturated this symphony from the first measure of the first movement.

From here on the great final outpouring continues, with a compact version of Theme "A" starting off a magnificent rising pattern that sparks the last phase of the movement in all its glory. This sequence can be seen and heard as a large-scale three-part structure, with symmetry between its first and third parts and a slightly shorter middle part.

And so the second coda, with all its repetitions of the tonic, emerges as a balanced larger section, and its lengthy reaffirmations of the tonic harmony form part of the greater formal structure of the symphony as a whole. Coming to the end of this colossal finale, we remember Beethoven's original thought, years earlier, as he first laid out his sketches for this symphony—"it could conclude at the very end with a march." As indeed it does.

THE FIFTH AND THE *EROICA*

When Beethoven played the *Eroica* for Ferdinand Ries in the fall of 1803, Ries said it was "the greatest work that he [Beethoven] has yet written." And it was just a few months later that he wrote down his first ideas for this C-minor symphony that became the Fifth, leaving us to wonder what he might then have said to Ries, even at this incipient stage. The *Eroica*, after all, is the primary work through which Beethoven had revolutionized the symphonic genre and, in a sense, the world of musical experience of his era. The Fifth, when completed, enlarged that world still further with its unforgettable representation of tragedy and salvation. So a few words on the two works are in order.

In scope and breadth the *Eroica* stands alone, and its plenitude of content is in proportion to its size. The great length of the first movement, above all of its development section, enables Beethoven to present the widest range of material that he ever included in a sonata-form movement. He gives the development section a number of special features that do not appear in this magnitude in any other symphonic first movement by him or his predecessors. One is the introduction of its new theme in the distant key of E minor; another is the long and intense dominant preparation for the return to the tonic; and a third is the celebrated "wrong-measure" horn entrance just before the recapitulation. The same great size is shared by the other movements, whose wide emotional range includes the mourning of a fallen hero, followed by the dynamic Scherzo and the evocation of battle sounds in the Trio, and at last the expanded variations of the finale. The whole is clearly conceived on a vast scale, something like an epic narrative on the theme of heroism.

The Fifth, by comparison, is a lean and tightly knit drama in which a generating rhythmic motif—the relentless 3 + 1 figure in its initial and then later forms—binds together all the contrasts that follow, from the first movement's intensity through the consoling Andante (within which the motto plays a major role); the renewed darkness of the third movement, with the motto now strongly proclaimed in undisguised form; and the triumphant Finale, in which the motto is subsumed within the array of themes.

It is especially in their finales that the two works differ most sharply.[32] Again, their diverse points of origin can guide us. Because the *Eroica* finale is derived from a set of piano variations and combines a set of linked variations with a large-scale three-part form and fugal episodes, it could never have been shaped along the dramatic lines of a sonata-form movement. A sonata-form finale in the *Eroica* would have included a large-scale structural repeat of the exposition, a propensity to motivic development along modulatory paths, and a dramatic return to the opening theme in the tonic at the recapitulation. Instead, the *Eroica* finale is built up, literally, from its introductory bass and theme to form a grand new type of symphonic variations form—but it does not and cannot have the dramatic intensity that Beethoven brings to sonata form in so many of his works. Nor does the *Eroica* finale have the overwhelming force that breaks through all barriers, as in the last movement of the Fifth. It feels more nearly like an immense meditation on the theme of heroism than a direct representation of the emotions themselves, which is what we feel in the Fifth.

It seems apparent, then, that Beethoven did not conceive the *Eroica* finale as the emotional summit of the symphony as a whole, but that it was from first to last a variations finale on the grand scale, a fitting conclusion to the great work but not its dramatic culmination. The return of the main theme in the tonic at the Poco Andante and the coda that follows gives the *Eroica* finale the character of an epic conclusion, not one designed to relieve latent tensions that have been left unresolved. It is not meant to rival the first movement by providing a heightened drama of thematic and motivic growth, let alone explore a vast tonal space in the way that the first movement does; its emotional tone is more nearly that of a vast panorama than a tightly plotted play.

In the Fifth, on the other hand, we have the strongest example in Beethoven of a finale that fulfills and transforms the emotional implications of all that has come before, a last movement that weights the symphony decisively towards its ending. It relieves the pain and fear we feel in the three earlier movements by bringing them into the full light of day. Insofar as we may ascribe its special features to Beethoven's personal issues, as many have done, we can relate it to Beethoven's own torment and his will to overcome it—in that sense it might be heard as the equivalent of the "one day of pure joy" that he longed for in the Heiligenstadt Testament. But if we take it as an artwork that transcends the personal and speaks to mankind on universal terms, we can understand the finale as the completion of an artwork on the highest level and can understand the symphony as a powerful message to the future about the courage and resilience of the human spirit.

6

THE "PASTORAL" SYMPHONY

BEETHOVEN AND NATURE

In May of 1810 Beethoven wrote to his boyhood friend Franz Wegeler, addressing him as "Good Old Friend":

> For about two years I have had to give up my rather quiet and peaceful way of life and have been forced to move in society. So far I have noticed no beneficial result; on the contrary, perhaps, a rather unfavorable one—but who can escape the onslaughts of tempests raging around him? Yet I should be happy, perhaps one of the happiest of mortals, if the demon had not settled in my ears— If I had not read somewhere that a man should not quit this life so long as he can still perform a good deed, I would have left this earth long ago—and, what is more, by my own hand—Oh, this life is indeed beautiful, but for me it is poisoned forever.[1]

The importance of this letter of 1810 has not been fully recognized by Beethoven biographers. It tells us that the emotional crisis he had undergone at Heiligenstadt in 1802, almost eight years earlier, had not been healed or truly mended. It tells of Beethoven's ongoing

Beethoven composing in the countryside, engraving by Franz Hegi, ca. 1838.
(Beethoven-Haus, Bonn / Bridgeman Images)

despair, his deafness and social isolation, and his recurring thoughts of suicide. Coupled with evidence of a parallel depression in 1812, it enables us to realize that his physical and psychological infirmities did not crest with one major crisis in 1802 and then improve, but that his pain continued unabated over many years. It reached into his last period, when his deafness, illnesses, and isolation became even more debilitating.

In the light of this letter, it is heartening to realize that by 1810, Beethoven had passed through some of his most productive years, had produced a stream of major works, and was by now the acknowledged master composer of his time—acclaimed for his orchestral, keyboard, and chamber music as well as for vocal works such as the *Christus* oratorio and the Mass in C. Yet the wounds of his inner life remained open and painful, and he attributed at least some of them to "evil persons."[2] In 1810, his inability to find love in marriage to Teresa Malfatti (a hope that indeed failed within a month of his letter to Wegeler) would only have intensified his feelings of loss and deprivation.

If we regard Beethoven's love of nature not only as a trait of character—one that was both highly personal and typical of the German Romantics—but as a release from his persistent loneliness and deafness, it gives us a new perspective on his impulse to create a musical portrayal of the experience of country life, an impulse that attains its highest artistic form in the "Pastoral" Symphony. Having grown up in Bonn, directly on the Rhine, he remembered the hills and valleys of the Siebengebirge across the river to the south. As early as 1801, revealing his deafness to Wegeler for the first time, he had made the quixotic suggestion that, "if my situation continues," Wegeler might

rent a house for me in some beautiful part of the country and then for six months I will lead the life of a peasant—perhaps that will make a difference. Resignation—what a wretched refuge! Yet it is all that is left to me.[3]

In later years, Beethoven longed for nothing more than to leave the city and tramp through woods and fields in the countryside outside Vienna or near one of his summer abodes—Baden, Mödling, Döbling, Hetzendorf, or Heiligenstadt. He eloquently described these feelings in a letter to Teresa Malfatti, again in May 1810:

> How fortunate you are to be able to go into the country so soon . . . I look forward to it with childish excitement. How delighted I shall be to ramble for a while through bushes, woods, under trees, over grass and rocks. No one can love the country as much as I do. For surely woods, trees, and rocks give back the echo which man desires to hear.[4]

These sentences are virtually an extended paraphrase of the heading of the first movement of the "Sinfonie Pastorale," the title that he had given to his Sixth Symphony when it was published in May 1809, about a year earlier—"The awakening of happy feelings on arrival in the countryside."[5] We are struck by his heady anticipation of unspoiled pleasure, the "childish excitement" he feels at the prospect of being in the country, the release it must have promised from all the personal, social, and professional entanglements of his daily life in the city, which he wants so much to leave behind, hoping to find solace in nature. In other references to his forays into the countryside, a strong religious strain is intermingled with his experience of the outdoors. Thus, on a sketch sheet of 1810 he wrote:

> My unhappy ears do not torment me here. It seems as if every tree in the countryside spoke to me, saying, "Holy! Holy!" In the forest, enchantment! Who can express it all? If everything else fails the country remains even in winter—such as Baden, Lower Brühl—easy to hire a lodging from a peasant, certainly cheap at this time.[6]

And elsewhere: "Without the company of some loved person it would not be possible to live even in the country."[7]

Sometime after 1811, likely in 1816, he wrote extensive annotations into a copy of Christoph Christian Sturm's *Reflections for Every Day in the Year on the Works of God in the Kingdom of Nature and Providence*, a popular tract on nature and religion.[8] The intertwining of his love of nature, his religious faith, and his quest for a beloved are essential themes in Beethoven's longing for personal salvation, a dream that remained unrealized in his daily life. It remained the elusive "inner peace" that he later mentioned in his inscription on the "Dona nobis pacem" of the *Missa Solemnis*.[9] This multiple quest is a key to understanding the "Pastoral" Symphony as the central work in which these tendencies coalesced. I construe this work, then, as not merely a programmatic representation of the experience of being in nature, but also that it is something like Beethoven's "dream-time," a vision of the healing experience of Nature. Beneath the surface of the work lies his deep personal need for such healing; and both these levels of consciousness were rooted in his belief that all that is good in nature is a manifestation of God.

It does not seem accidental that the Sixth Symphony followed the Fifth as Beethoven's next major project of the year 1808. Both were given their first performances at a concert held by Beethoven on 22 December 1808 at the Theater an der Wien. The concert began with the "Pastoral" Symphony, which was listed on the program as No. 5, and the second part began with the "Grand Symphony in C Minor," correspondingly labeled "No. 6."[10] Then came the aria "Ah, perfido" (composed in 1796 but now recently published as Op. 65); the "Gloria" from his Mass in C of 1807; and the premiere of the Fourth Piano Concerto, Op. 58, with Beethoven as soloist. The second half began with the C Minor Symphony, followed by the Sanctus from the Mass in C; then Beethoven improvised alone at the keyboard, and the long evening ended with his hastily composed Choral Fantasy for piano, orchestra, and chorus.[11]

EARLY IDEAS RELATED TO THE "PASTORAL" SYMPHONY

In the same sketchbook in which Beethoven worked out the early stages of the *Eroica* and also entered his first ideas for the Fifth, he also wrote out several short musical entries that later bore fruit in the Sixth Symphony. Unlike those for the Fifth, these individual ideas are separated from one another, are not marked "Sinfonia," nor are they laid out in the form of a movement-plan or as continuity drafts. Some of these early sketches that have been claimed as antecedents to the "Pastoral" are doubtful, and some that we can readily accept as antecedents to the symphony are only partially related to it. But, as we saw earlier, we can certainly attach some importance to Beethoven's brief jotting of an idea for a "joyous symphony" (*lustige Sinfonia*) in this same sketchbook, directly after his first ideas for the C-minor symphony that became the Fifth.[12] We should remember that it was about four years later that Beethoven went to work full-time on the Pastoral Symphony, after his completion of the Fifth.

The two sketches of 1803–4 that are most closely related to the "Pastoral" are these:

1. A sketch for the Trio of the Scherzo. The first item is a four-measure concept sketch for the 2/4 phrase that he later employed for the Trio of the Scherzo of the "Pastoral," the "country-dance" associated with the peasants whose "merry gathering" is the programmatic subject of the third movement of the symphony.[13] It appears in the midst of his early work on the Trio of the Scherzo of the *Eroica*, where it was soon displaced by the three-horn fanfares that captured his imagination how to frame the Trio section in that Scherzo. In the 1803–4 sketch, the key of the 2/4 passage is E-flat major, which fits the *Eroica*, and we can speculate that Beethoven might have imagined that if he did not make use of it in

his heroic E-flat major symphony, it would find a place in a later context that better suited to its slightly modal "country-dance" features. Such a possibility can never be proved, but it gains plausibility from other cases in which Beethoven went back to his sketchbooks years later to find ideas that he could use in new and different contexts; there are more than a few.[14] And indeed, on another page of his sketches for the *Eroica* Scherzo, a passage turns up that was clearly designed as a possible ending for that movement—in E-flat major and in 3/4—but which served later as a model for his ending of the finale of the Sixth Symphony, there of course in F major and in 6/8 meter.[15]

2. A preliminary idea for the "Scene by the Brook." By far the most important and suggestive early musical idea that prefigured the "Pastoral" is an entry of late 1803 that bears the heading "Murmeln der Bäche" (Murmurs of the Brooks; see Web Example K).[16] In its equivalent of 12/8 meter and "Andante molto" tempo, it anticipates the slow movement of the symphony (see Web Example L), which in final form is one of Beethoven's very few movements in this meter and is marked "Andante molto moto."[17]

The "murmurs" sketch consists of two phrases, each three bars long, marked "Primo" and "Secundo;" this looks at first like the upper and lower parts of a four-hand keyboard idea, but it may mean something like "First section" and "Second section." The first phrase, in C major, presents a succession of triplets that suggest the quietly rippling waters of a brook. Below both phrases Beethoven writes: "je grosser der Bach je tiefer der Ton" (the greater the brook, the deeper the tone).

In its meter, tempo, rocking motion, and character, this sketch directly anticipates the initial accompaniment figures of the slow movement of the symphony. The inscription does so in a still higher degree, as it does nothing less than predict the larger structural organization of the whole movement. Beethoven says that the brook becomes "wider" (literally "greater" but for a stream that should mean "wider" and, most likely, "deeper"). Accordingly, as it does so, the "tone" of the movement becomes "deeper." The words show Beethoven imagining a meandering brook as it moves forward, gathering strength, and becomes a river, gradually gaining in width, depth, and flow. Later, when he comes to the composition of the "Scene by the Brook" in the symphony, this is exactly what happens in the course of the movement, namely that he establishes a correlation between the image of the widening and deepening brook and the orchestral forces that develop the form of the movement.

We will come back later to the relationship between the pictorial elements in the movement and its formal structure. But for now, the important point is that in 1803–4, the year of the *Eroica* and the "Waldstein" sonata, Beethoven not only envisioned some basic ideas for his powerful C-minor symphony, but also some that he could use for a work in the pastoral tradition—which he then held in abeyance until at least the summer of 1807, when he was working on the Mass in C. He really only came back to complete this symphony in the summer of 1808, after he had completed the Fifth and had also finished the A-major Cello Sonata Opus 69.

"MORE THE EXPRESSION OF FEELING
THAN TONE-PAINTING"

This symphony has spurred a vast amount of commentary, exceeded only by that on the Ninth, mainly because of its programmatic elements. In a letter to Breitkopf of March 1809, Beethoven told them that "the title of the symphony in F is *Pastoral Symphony or Recollections of Country Life: More the Expression of Feeling than Tone-Painting*."[18] The first publication was entitled "Sinfonie Pastorale," without the addendum, but the words "More the Expression of Feeling than Tone-Painting" did appear on an early violin part, along with the titles of the individual movements, as expressly requested by Beethoven.

The movement-titles, tempo markings, meter and key of each of the five movements of the symphony, as they appeared in the first edition, are these:

Movement	Meter	Key	Heading
1. Allegro ma non troppo	2/4	F major	"Erwachen heiterer Empfindungen bei der Ankunft auf dem Lande" (The awakening of joyous feelings on getting out into the countryside)
2. Andante molto moto	12/8	B♭ major	"Scene am Bach" (Scene by the brook)
3. Allegro	2/4	F major	"Lustiges Zusammensein der Landleute" (Joyous gathering of country folk)
4. Allegro	4/4	F minor	"Gewitter. Sturm" (Thunderstorm)
5. Allegretto	6/8	F major	"Hirtengesang. Frohe und dankbare Gefühle nach dem Sturm" (Shepherd's song. Happy and thankful feelings after the storm)

These headings underwent changes in wording as the symphony developed in Beethoven's hands, and those he sanctioned even as late as the 1808 concert were not quite final. Nor are we surprised to find that he tried out some of them as he worked on the composition in his sketchbooks. His vision of what each movement should be, what it "represented" or "depicted," was fully informed by his experience of country life and the emotions it evoked in him—how it felt to arrive among woods and streams; the way the brook flowed and the birds sang; his image of how peasants enjoy gathering together, dancing and reveling, their festive day that was marred by a storm; and at last a song of thanks to God for the return of peaceful life after the storm.

It is well known that a similar set of movement-titles had been used by Justin Heinrich Knecht (1752–1817), a minor German composer, in a five-movement symphony entitled *Le portrait musical de la Nature*. Knecht's five movement-titles partly resemble those of Beethoven, and Beethoven might well have known the work, or known about it, in his teenage years, since it was advertised by the same publisher, Bossler of Speyer, who brought out Beethoven's precocious little piano sonatas, the "Electoral" sonatas, in 1783. But beyond Knecht's titles and its storm that breaks in upon a bucolic landscape, it is improbable that it meant anything more to Beethoven than other minor products of the genre. Works with programs similar to those of the "Pastoral" Symphony were fairly plentiful at the time; Richard Will lists 27 such works from between 1773 and 1797 by thirteen composers, among them Dittersdorf, Haydn, Rosetti, Carl Stamitz, and the brothers Anton and Paul Wranitsky. The latter two were in the service of Prince Lobkowitz, one of Beethoven's major patrons, and Beethoven knew both personally.

DEPICTION AND REPRESENTATION

That music can imitate natural sounds, can "depict" elements in nature or in other surroundings, had been evident for centuries. In late medieval and Renaissance music, the songs of birds or the clash of arms in battles had been used by composers for programmatic works, and they continued to be exploited down through the eighteenth century. Though around 1800 European interest in music of earlier ages was beginning to strengthen as collectors of "ancient" music were beginning to assemble works of polyphonic masters in private collections, it's likely that more recent works in the pastoral tradition would have drawn Beethoven's attention. Foremost among them would have been Haydn's great oratorios, *The Creation* (composed 1796–98, first performed publicly in 1799) and *The Seasons* (composed 1799–1801, first performed publicly in 1801). Not only were these oratorios immensely popular with Viennese audiences in the years leading up to the "Pastoral" Symphony, but both combined pictorialism with praise of the Creator; and, at least equally important, both were crowning achievements by the aging master who remained one of Beethoven's revered models, no matter how different their aesthetic aims. What these two great oratorios had shown was that what Beethoven called "the situations," i.e., the visual and aural subjects of musical tone-painting, could be integrated into music of the highest caliber.

Beethoven used the term "characteristic" for works with specific subjects, like this symphony and the "Lebewohl" (Farewell) Piano Sonata he wrote in 1809 for the departure of the Archduke Rudolph, his patron and pupil. He disdained much current program music, because as he put it, it pushed pictorialism "too far." Nonetheless, his ambivalence did not deter him from writing such works as long as he could feel that he was working on the higher levels of musical structure and originality. Clearly, his conception of this symphony was that it should satisfy the higher artistic criteria yet also express his joy in nature and his reverence for God the creator. He aimed to render the sounds and images of nature as literally as necessary, but also to amalgamate them into the framework of the new symphonic genre that he had fashioned since the *Eroica*. There is no doubt that he also intended to show his contemporaries how such illustrative music could be written, and that in his hands, the pastoral genre, with its familiar topics—brooks, birds, storms, peasant dances, etc.—could be raised to an artistic level that his fellow musicians, however competent, were not likely to reach.

His ambivalence is writ large in the entries he wrote into his current sketchbook as he wrestled with the right way of characterizing this work and hunted for a suitable subtitle. He wrote down the following entries, among others that express the same thoughts:

1. "One leaves it to the listener to discover the situations";
2. "Each act of tone-painting, as soon as it is pushed too far in instrumental music, loses its force";
3. "Even without a description the whole will be understood, as it is more feeling than tone-painting";
4. "Sinfonia pastorella. Whoever has any idea of country life can imagine for himself what the composer has in mind without a great many titles";
5. [As possible title] "Sinfonia caracteristica—or Recollections of Country Life"—[or] "A Recollection of Country Life."

The first four entries show his skepticism about movement-titles, and the second is an implicit rejection of much of the program music of his time. We would like to know what were his prime examples of compositions in which tone-painting was "pushed too far," but they probably included some popular works that titillated audiences with sounds of battles, storms with thunder and lightning, the howling of the winds, and other topics. For him they must have been "pushed too far" because they were not redeemed by sufficient command of form and expression.

Yet Beethoven himself was vulnerable to the same temptations, and five years later, in 1813, it was he himself who pushed pictorialism too far. In that year Beethoven succumbed to rampant anti-Napoleonic patriotism and the blandishments of Johann Nepomuk Maelzel, the promoter and popularizer of the metronome, and agreed to write his "Battle Symphony," also called "Wellington's Victory," to celebrate the British victory over the French at Vitoria in Spain. The work, at first written for Maelzel's mechanical "Panharmonicon" and later transcribed for orchestra, carries the title "symphony" only by courtesy. It is a battle-piece pure and simple, which represents the British and French armies and quotes "Rule Britannia" and "Malbrouck s'en va-t'-en guerre" as their marching songs. Its noise-making accouterments include a battery of percussion instruments that can fire cannon shots, which are marked in the score, and the whole thing ends in a "Victory symphony," that is, a triumphant finale. That this showpiece made Beethoven a great deal of money is not irrelevant; he would never have counted it among what he called his "great works." But there was always a side of him—no matter how fervently he believed in the higher values—that craved contemporary fame and glory not only among the nobility and the bourgeoisie but at the broadest popular levels. For those audiences, this sensational piece of program music—a "frolic" as Thayer called it—was his calling card.

When it came to musical aesthetics and comments on other musicians, Beethoven's writings—mainly his letters, but also his diaries and the little we can make out of the later conversation books, in which he is pre-eminently a listener not a speaker—these are laconic in the extreme. The few remarks we do have show his awareness of being far above the level of most of his contemporary composers, with few exceptions: a self-made artist pursuing a mission in the world.

This way of thinking about his role as a composer—a visionary artist in advance of his times—was built deep into his creative character. It resonates with other remarks that show his lifelong ambition to keep his aesthetic aims and creative work as fully focused as possible on the higher planes of achievement to which he aspired—typically complaining that the "wretched necessities" of life, earning a living, and the need to publish and disseminate his works, was a nagging interference. He never lost the feeling that in a better world a true artist would not have to carry out such demeaning tasks—yet at the same time he carried them out with energy and concentration. The "empire" metaphor recurs in his writings, as we saw earlier in his letter of 1814.

THE "PASTORAL" SYMPHONY AS
A UNIFIED ARTWORK

In a much-criticized passage, Donald Francis Tovey wrote that "not a bar of the 'Pastoral' Symphony would have been different if its 'programme' had never been thought of."[19] Thus spurning the idea that tone-painting in a symphony could have any intrinsic value of its own but must be seen as a mere concession to the public—who might enjoy the birdcalls and other sounds of nature but could not be imagined to perceive the formal structures within which they were embedded—Tovey's view goes far to the formalistic side, denying that the "program" of the work is of any importance. Tovey remained unconcerned by the circularity of his argument. For if Beethoven had really "never thought" of the idea of a "pastoral symphony," he would obviously not have produced this work, let alone as artfully as he in fact did. To the contrary, all the evidence about his thinking tells us that writing a work with this "program" was precisely what he intended to do, and the job of posterity is to try to understand what conditions this intention imposed on him as he did so.

As Richard Will pointed out in a salient article, Tovey was reacting to a long tradition of criticism that not only praised the pictorialism in the symphony but claimed it as evidence that Beethoven was the "father of nineteenth-century program music." The proponents of this view, admirers of Berlioz, Liszt, and Strauss, stood opposed to the "formalistic" view that the depictions of nature in the work were trivial when compared to its intrinsic musical and structural properties, and that only the latter should be attended to.

Though these divergent lines of approach can hardly be reconciled as part of a single experience, it is possible to argue, as Will has done, that one does not invalidate the other. As Will writes, the "Pastoral" Symphony "inhabits two generic worlds, that of the symphony and that of the programmatic symphony as it was practiced, not by Berlioz and Liszt, but by Beethoven's contemporaries and predecessors." In fact, I would go further, and claim—certainly for the slow movement but to some degree for the whole symphony—that Beethoven really wanted to have it both ways. On the one hand he aimed to write a symphony in the "pastoral" tradition that employs many of the time-honored pictorial devices known to the programmatic genres, and uses them in such a way that listeners could indeed delight in recognizing and enjoying his imitations of natural sounds within the fabric of the composition. At the same time, he aimed to write a work whose high level of expressive and formal cogency would match that of his recent path-breaking symphonies—the Third, Fourth, and Fifth—and which would use some of the time-honored "pastoral" sounds to give the work a highly individual profile and sound-world of its own, like his other symphonies up to this time. The two dimensions differ in importance and audibility from one movement to another, but the duality runs through the whole work.

THE FIRST MOVEMENT

From the opening measures, we are in a domain of sound as different from that of the Fifth as we can imagine—quiet, unhurried, with a drone bass fifth sustained in the lower strings while the violins above sing a graceful four-bar phrase that ends with a fermata on a dominant harmony—a phrase in which each of the first three bars contains an identifiable motif that Beethoven can later develop independently, as is his custom—as he said, years later about another work, "the motives are contained within the theme." From here on, the movement unfolds in sonata-form and with long passages of rhythmic and motivic repetition, but also with much use of harmonically static passages and with a remarkable restriction of its harmonic language—there are hardly any minor harmonies throughout the movement. Further, and directly connected to the prevalence of major-mode harmonies, the principal contrast to its tonic F major is not its dominant key, C major, as would be customary, but its subdominant, B-flat major. This use of B-flat major is especially telling at the beginning and end of the development section and at the beginning of the recapitulation. There is no explicit pictorial narrative in this movement but there is an unmistakable feeling of the sustained joy of being in the countryside, just as the movement-title tells us. This movement exemplifies what Beethoven meant when he wrote "More the expression of feelings than tone-painting."

THE SLOW MOVEMENT: "SCENE BY THE BROOK"

The choice of title is significant. We saw that in 1803, Beethoven had sketched an idea labeled "Murmurs of the brooks," with the words, "the greater the brook, the deeper the tone." And now Beethoven realizes both his conceptual and visual image of a rippling brook and his remark that the brook can grow in depth and force as the range of tone becomes deeper. Whereas the first movement had been presented as an "awakening," implying an abstract protagonist whose experience is in some way conveyed, he calls the second movement a "Scene" (in German a "Szene," equivalent of the Italian "Scena"), which evokes the idea of a theatrical situation. It may also allude to "Scena" in the operatic sense; that is, a unit of dramatic action that contains one or more musical numbers or even just one character singing an aria. Beethoven used the term in the normal sense of his time for the soprano aria "Ah perfido!" (that is, in German, the piece is called "Szene und Arie"), and it is the vocal work he included in the 1808 concert along with the Fifth and Sixth Symphonies. And so it is no surprise to find that this "scene" is indeed illustrative, that it can be heard as an auditory portrait of a bucolic landscape "by the brook," and that here Beethoven opens up his tone-painter's palette and uses it to the fullest, both in broad conception and in picturesque details. To do so, he devises ways to represent each of these elements:

1. The brook itself, with a well-formed melody in repeated triplet figures in the middle and lower registers of the strings, later subdivided into sixteenth-note patterns but always with the continuous rhythmic motion that conjures up the image of the running stream;

2. Distinctive melodic figures, phrases, and trills in the first violin part as the movement begins. As it unfolds, it becomes increasingly clear that the trills in high register are meant to be heard as the sounds of birds. These trills, at first on long-held notes, then chirping on short ones with grace-notes, create an immediate picture with the brook at ground level. We imagine the birds above, either perched or flying among trees that stand by the brook. From here on, trills in high register abound throughout the movement, later joined by a rising arpeggio in the high flute that Schindler said was the call of a "yellow-hammer" (claiming that Beethoven himself had so named it). Schindler's account has been dismissed by later commentators unwilling to believe that Beethoven could have been so literal-minded, but we can see that a new contrasting figure does occur at the opening of the development section, just as the movement moves into G major, and that this new figure adds to the motivic variety of the movement. As the stream rolls forward and gains in strength, the bird-sounds as trills and short figures increase in number and density; they do this notably at the end of the development section and late in the recapitulation.

The most famous bird-calls occur at the end, where Beethoven names the three individual birds—the nightingale (solo flute), the quail (solo oboe), and the cuckoos (two clarinets)—who combine in a passage that dominates the coda of the movement. In his autograph manuscript, Beethoven wrote a note to his copyist insisting that the names of these three birds be written into the score, and so he could hardly have made it clearer that his tone-painting intentions were fully serious. It has been wisely noted that these wind instruments had already been prominent in the development section and these two passages are "a perfect union of music and image." I would add that we can hear the three birds as nature's equivalent of a trio of solo voices who perform an ensemble cadenza at the end of the movement. This is a feature that Beethoven indeed used in other works from early to late, including his cello sonata Op. 5, No. 1, his Trio for two oboes and English horn, Op. 87; the Triple Concerto, Op. 56; the Violin Sonata in G major, Op. 96; the Adagio near the end of his *Fidelio* Overture in E major (the final overture, that of 1814); and, above all, the very ending of the Ninth Symphony. There, just as the finale is about to close, the four solo voices—now of course human, not instruments—sing as individuals for the last time, just before the Prestissimo brings the colossal work to an end.

That the movement can be heard, then, as a beautiful depiction of a scene in nature, is in complete accord with that part of Beethoven's imagination which aimed to produce a fully serious programmatic musical experience, with no embarrassment about "tone-painting." At the same time, no such piece or movement, in his hands, could fail to be governed by his primary artistic drive to create a dynamic musical structure. This movement is no exception. Ultimately, it is in the union of these two dimensions that gives this Andante, this "Scene by the brook," its richness of content. If we now consider it as a product of his form-building imagination, it can be heard as a four-part sonata-form, as follows:

Exposition

A1	Strings in middle and low register, rippling motion; theme in Violin I
A2	Violin I trills in high register; theme in winds; thickening texture
B	Strings and winds share B theme; new accompanying figures at 19–20
A3	New expansion of A theme, leading to the dominant
C1	C theme in bassoon, trills in Violin II
C2	C theme in violin and flute; B returns
Codetta	

Development (5 sections)

(1)	Return to the brook figures, now modulating
(2)	G major, arpeggio theme in flute; elaborated A in strings
(3)	B theme fragments; then the first hint of minor (G minor)
(4)	E♭ major: new elaborations of A1 and extensions of arpeggio theme then B fragment
(5)	G♭ major; C♭ major (= B major) modulating back to F; trills in violin I

Recapitulation

A2	Orchestral tutti; combines A themes with arpeggio theme;
C1	C theme in bassoon with trills in Violin II
C2	Theme now in violin and oboe; at end, B theme fragments
Codetta	Return of A1; then sustained harmonies in Violin I and winds

Coda (2 sections)

    (1)   Ensemble cadenza of individual birds: Nightingale;
                Quail; Cuckoos
    (2)   The bird ensemble repeats its cadenza; the orchestra
                closes with B theme fragments in *pianissimo*.

"The greater the brook, the deeper the tone."

We can now see that these words offer a direct clue to the mimetic and structural characteristics of the movement. They suggest a correlation between musical register—the depth and height of the musical events, within the tonal system—and the visual images. The brook begins as a meandering stream, with a few birds above; it grows in volume as the movement progresses and it becomes a river when it reaches the recapitulation, where the full orchestra is now in play. The recapitulation returns to the tonic B-flat major after a remarkably wide span of keys had been explored, and at this climactic moment it brings the full orchestra in the wide span that ranges from the low bass instruments to the high violins and flutes. All this is in keeping with Beethoven's habitual deployment of register to dramatize the developing patterns of his formal plans, especially in sonata-form movements; here it also symbolizes the enlargement of the brook from stream to river. At such a moment the two modes of perception intertwine—bringing together the formal, the expressive, and the pictorial dimensions.

THE SCHERZO, STORM, AND FINALE

That this symphony has five movements instead of four is exceptional but not surprising. The program of the later part of the work calls for a sequence of situations requiring, first, a gathering of peasants that is interrupted by a storm, then a song of thanksgiving as the weather clears and calm returns. Beethoven could have accomplished this with a full-scale Scherzo and the storm as a brief interlude or introduction, followed by his finale, each a separate movement. This scenario, very similar to the one used by Knecht, would have been possible, but Beethoven's dramatic instinct permits nothing of the kind. Instead he creates a continuous three-movement sequence in which there is no decisive final cadence until the very end of the whole work. The storm interrupts the Scherzo, and then eventually gives way to the shepherd's song that opens the finale.

The "Joyous gathering of country folk" as third movement gives him a programmatic pretext for a Scherzo that combines the atmosphere of peasant-dance music in two different meters (3/4 for the scherzo, 2/4 for the Trio) with rhythmic, harmonic, and orchestral effects that stand up handsomely to the first two movements in subtlety and imagination. The strong dualism of triple and duple time Scherzo and Trio has a kind of counterpart in the harmonic dualism of the Scherzo itself, in which the first theme, descending through the notes of the F-major triad, is followed immediately by the counter-theme in D major, thus setting up the two keys, F major and D major, in close contrast without any intermediate steps. And the regular patterns of phrase structure at the opening of the movement are equally well contrasted with the later section, in which the oboe and then the clarinet present rousing solo passages over repeated string chords. Schindler tells of Beethoven's reminiscing about country musicians who occasionally fall asleep while playing, then wake up, play a few short notes and then go to sleep again—perhaps this is what Beethoven is satirizing in the bassoon part where the player seems to be uncertain whether to play three or four notes in the cadences under the solos in the upper winds.

The 2/4 Trio, which has all the earmarks of a foot-stamping peasant dance of the type which Schindler says often alternated with triple-meter in Austrian country dancing, stresses the juxtaposition of F major and B-flat major, treating the latter as an alternative tonic in a way that twists the normal harmonic syntax. The heavily accented tune originated years earlier, again in the *Eroica* sketchbook of 1803–4, and now Beethoven had the opportunity to put it to use in the symphonic context.

This five-part Scherzo, resembling that of the Fourth Symphony and one of the original plans for that of the Fifth, suddenly shifts from its firm F major into a mysterious low D-flat tremolo in the cellos and basses, an ominous warning of the coming storm. And within a few measures the music has plunged into a succession of unstable harmonies within the realm of F minor—the first extended use of the minor mode in the whole symphony up to this point. From here the storm grows in strength and fury, rumbling figures in the low strings underpin tremolos and long-held chords in the winds. Subsequently a second phase emerges, with soft tremolos and running sixteenth-note passages in the lower strings, while sudden short figures erupt above—lightning flashes—until the whole eventually reaches a long climactic section that finally settles down in a *pianissimo* C major, signaling that the storm is over. A chorale-like descending phrase reminds the listener that behind this celebration is a strong religious strain, reflecting what Beethoven meant when he wrote on a sketch for this passage, "Herr, wir danken Dir" (Lord, we thank thee!).

The idyll of peace, serenity, and thanks to God that permeates the finale, which Beethoven labels "Shepherd's Song," has well been compared to passages from Haydn's *The Seasons,* as when the character Simon in the oratorio sings his aria, "The cheerful shepherd now gathers his joyous flock." The clarinet and horn passages that open the movement and bring the light of day after the storm's darkness resemble Alp-horns playing the *Ranz des vaches,* which Beethoven could have known about even if he had never ventured to such heights himself. And this opening duo is more than an introduction, it also serves as a sonorous marker of the return of the whole first theme when it returns at the beginning of the middle section of the movement (mm. 60–63) and again at the recapitulation (mm. 113–16).

The form of the finale has been construed as a modified sonata-form, but far more telling than its formal plan is the richness of feeling that emerges from its primary theme and its varied reprises, along with the gently contrasting themes that Beethoven devises in the course of the movement. In the later phases of this gradually unfolding portrait of serenity, the primary theme will reappear at the large recapitulation, where it is embedded within a sixteenth-note legato version in the first violins, but no one can mistake the sense of homecoming that this moment brings. And at the very end, a solo muted horn plays the *Ranz des vaches* for the last time, now without its clarinet companion, as the string sections bring a quiet lyrical running sixteenth-note figure in a descending pattern, one measure at a time, through three octaves, as if to confirm the sense of space and serenity in nature that has pervaded this symphony from its very opening. The experience of nature has now come full circle, and we now have an unmistakable feeling that the richness of experience accumulated over the whole symphony has reached its culmination. The ending seems to confirm the peace of nature and the peace of the soul that the work had promised from the beginning, the feeling for which the composer had been longing all his life.

Archduke Rudolph, Beethoven's pupil and later patron, as Cardinal Archbishop of Ölmutz in Moravia, painting by Johann Baptist Edler von Lampi, ca. 1825

(Historisches Museum der Stadt, Vienna / Bridgeman Images)

7

THE SEVENTH SYMPHONY

"THE WINGS OF DAEDALUS": BEETHOVEN IN 1812

In 1812, Beethoven completed the Seventh Symphony and then the Eighth—each so brilliant in its own way and so strikingly different from one another. More than three years had elapsed since he had launched the Fifth and Sixth in December 1808. Since then he had entered into the twilight of his great middle period, producing a series of imposing works that bore the stamp of a fully seasoned maturity. In 1809 he produced the heroic "Emperor" Concerto, the powerful and heartfelt "Lebewohl" sonata for Rudolph's departure and return; and the beautiful "Harp" Quartet, Op. 74—all in the key of E-flat major. There followed the astonishing F-minor Quartet, Op. 95, with its stringent compression of ideas and its idiosyncrasies; and the "Archduke" Trio, the grand summa of his lifetime work as composer of piano trios. Other new piano works included the sonatas Op. 78, in the rare key of F-sharp major, and its little counterpart, the sonatina Op. 79. Most striking of all his keyboard works of this time is the Fantasia Op. 77, in which he seeks to reproduce his manner of improvisation in a finished composition.

Beyond this, Beethoven also took on commissions to write incidental music for spoken dramas, the primary result being the *Egmont* music of 1809–10, composed for a Vienna production of Goethe's drama of political liberation. And as a sideline, but one that was to prove artistically interesting in leading him to the world of folksong, he took on a contract in 1809 with the publisher George Thomson to make settings of Scottish airs.

None of these buried his underlying wish for public exposure as a symphonic composer, although the surge that had led from the *Eroica* to the "Pastoral" was now behind him. In his main sketchbook of 1809 he entered some new ideas for symphonies, some of them very striking and original, but he did not flesh them out, then or later, into full-scale compositions nor lay out continuity drafts for single movements. Still, they represent clear evidence that his symphonic ambition was stirring, and he finally started work in the fall of 1811 on the A-major symphony that became the Seventh.

In 1812, turning forty-one, Beethoven was the most acclaimed composer in Europe, but he was finding each year a hard struggle. In February of that year he wrote to Nikolaus Zmeskall, a long-time confidant, expressing his deep resentment about his life in Vienna:

> Heaven, help me to bear it all; I am no Hercules who can help Atlas to carry the world, still less carry it for him—only yesterday I was told in detail about the nice things Baron Krufft said about me at Zizius's and how he judged me—well, let us forget about that, dear Zmeskall. It all won't last much longer, for I will not go on living here to be so insulted. The art of those who are persecuted finds asylum everywhere. Why, Daedalus when confined to the labyrinth invented the wings which lifted him upwards into the air. Oh I too shall find these wings.[1]

His personal afflictions were surely compounded by the troubled state of life in Austria. In 1811, the Habsburg regime, after years of war, had reached a stage of financial exhaustion and was forced to devalue its currency. That year was also marked by the bankruptcy of his steadfast patron Prince Joseph Franz Maximilian Lobkowitz, the dedicatee of the *Eroica*, the Fifth and Sixth Symphonies, and other works. In 1809, Lobkowitz had joined with Prince Kinsky and the Archduke Rudolph to guarantee Beethoven a lifetime annuity, but now, two years later, he was forced to end his payments. Meanwhile, Kinsky's contributions had been slow in coming, and they too stopped completely when he died suddenly in a riding accident in November 1812, forcing Beethoven to petition his widow for a settlement.[2] From now on Beethoven was more than ever dependent on the Archduke Rudolph, who remained his primary anchor of support for the rest of his life.[3]

Beneath the chaotic surface of Beethoven's life lay his perpetual dream of finding the ideal woman, his "distant beloved," who always remained an image and never a reality. His romantic involvements over the years had all failed, not only because of his irascible personality but because he must have known that no matter how he longed for such a relationship his total artistic commitment made it impossible to sustain. Years later we find him privately expressing his conflicted feelings about his early lover, Giulietta Guicciardi. Giulietta had been his piano pupil for a few years beginning in 1800, and she had been the dedicatee of the "Moonlight" sonata. She had married Count Robert Gallenberg, a theater administrator, in 1803, and they left for Italy. But in 1822 the couple returned to Vienna, and soon thereafter Beethoven wrote these remarks in one of his conversation books:

[Writing in French] I was beloved by her, and more than her husband ever was . . . She was already his wife before they moved to Italy, and she sought me out tearfully, but I scorned her . . . [and now continuing, in German] if I had wanted to devote my life's power to such a life, what would have remained for the nobler, the better things?[4]

After 1803, Beethoven had had several romantic attachments but none that he could sustain. But in the summer of 1812 the most serious love affair of his life reached a peak of intensity, as we know from his passionate letter to the unnamed "Immortal Beloved"— "my angel, my all, my very self"—in which he poured out his heart with intermingled passion and renunciation. Along with the Heiligenstadt Testament and his diary of 1812–18 it is the most revealing document by him that we possess.[5]

Yet again, all these troubles whether temporary or of long duration did not slow down his creative work any more than had the deafness crisis of 1802 or the suicidal thoughts he had confessed to Wegeler in 1810. As we contemplate his ongoing sense of desolation that was somehow balanced by immense productivity, we return to the problem of contemplating the intertwining of a great artist's life and work, which for an individual of such singularity remains veiled and obscure.[6] Some critics, among them Carl Dahlhaus, claim to dissolve the problem by regarding the events of Beethoven's life as essentially irrelevant to his works, but even Dahlhaus, while insisting on keeping biography apart from the main line of his interests, had to confess that "it is difficult to make plausible the idea that an oeuvre exists in itself, as a 'whole' independently of its author."[7]

NEW IDEAS FOR SYMPHONIES IN 1809

Productive as he was in the years from 1809 to 1812, Beethoven's strongest ambition was to return to the symphony, as we see from some thematic ideas, each marked "Sinfonia," that are documented in his sketchbooks. These are short concept sketches that remained unrealized, though some are of very high interest, and were superseded entirely by the new symphony in A major that became the Seventh, followed by the Eighth. The Eighth in turn had a curious beginning as a piano concerto but then became his main preoccupation in the summer and fall of 1812. The 1809 "Sinfonia" concept sketches include three entries that give us insight into his pool of current ideas for such works.

1. A musical idea labeled "first Allegro of a symphony" (*erstes Allegro einer Sinfonie*). It is a four-bar phrase in G major and 3/4 meter, a highly suggestive starter for an Allegro opening movement in a key he regarded as bright and spirited (see Example 8).

Example 8. Concept sketch for an opening theme of a symphony in G major from 1809, not developed

[First Allegro of a symphony] *

* erstes All[egr]o einer Sinfonie

Source: MS Landsberg 5, 55, st. 9.

2. Later in the same sketchbook, after drafts for the "Harp" Quartet and some other projects, he tried out another set of entries for two movements of a "Sinfonia" (see Example 9). Here we find a portentous and highly original introduction in G minor, followed by an Allegro in G major, both in 4/4. The introduction, no doubt intended to be in a slow tempo, has surprising features, above all its opening motif in longer note-values that continues with a short figure in sixteenth-notes that is set off by rests and is expressly marked "Viola" in m. 2. Then he repeats the same pair of dissimilar figures a half-step higher, beginning on A-flat. Thereafter an Allegro theme in G major brings rising scalar figures followed by a sturdy and square-cut theme.

Example 9. Concept sketch for two movements of a symphony in G minor/major from 1809, not developed

Source: MS Landsberg 5, p. 87, st. 3, mm. 1–4; "Allegro" on st. 5, then the G-major theme at st. 9–10.

3. Still later in the same sketchbook, we find the words "A moll Sinfonie" (Symphony in A minor) inscribed in large bold letters in the middle of the page (p. 104), but alas, with no musical notation. Still, the very idea of an "A-minor Symphony" stirs the mind. This key is rare for him, and later he wrote only one major work in it, the great Quartet Opus 132, composed in 1825. Two other sketches in this same 1809 sketchbook have been thought to be possible ideas for symphonies, but they are not labeled "Sinfonia" like the ones above.[8]

RHYTHM AND INTEGRATION

Every commentary on the Seventh Symphony stresses its essentially rhythmic character. Each movement is permeated by its own well-defined persistent rhythmic cell that shapes the musical substance. The only truly comparable case among the symphonies is the first movement of the Fifth—and in the Fifth the continuous repetitions of the opening motto are elaborated in other ways and belong to a different system of thematic organization. In the Seventh it is the visceral, bodily assertion of the rhythmic action, differently framed but clearly audible in every tempo and movement, that grips every listener. It lies behind Wagner's time-worn characterization of the work as "the apotheosis of the dance," and it is no surprise that this symphony became a favorite for choreographers. Yet the question remains: what may have been Beethoven's form-building purpose behind the idea of a symphony in which rhythm dominates so conspicuously, and what special consequences resulted from his decision to thrust rhythmic elements into the foreground?

Rhythm is a fundamental condition of music. It is the primordial element by which music shapes time and temporal experience. In music rhythm is always present, no matter what other factors are in evidence, and how it is used creates vital differences among works, styles, musical languages and dialects, of any period or any culture. As Beethoven came of age in the classical period, with its vast vocabulary of symmetrical rhythmic phrases and periods, he had shown his originality in using highly profiled rhythmic figures in a number of his early works. In some of them such figures achieved paramount roles. Tovey once pointed out how characteristic it is of Beethoven that his themes can often be identified from their rhythm alone, more easily than with Haydn or Mozart, though there are certainly exceptions. But no one before Beethoven had opened a movement so idiosyncratically as he does the Scherzo of his F-major Quartet, Op. 59, No. 1, with its four-bar phrase that is a fully intelligible and well-made musical sentence though it has only one pitch from beginning to end—the low B-flat on the cello.

But in the Seventh, rhythmic consistency governs even more pervasively than in most of his other works. Here the streaming flow of rhythmic events sometimes overshadows other elements that shape the work—melody, harmony, voice-leading, dynamics, the orchestral tone-palette. It animates the discourse at every level, and becomes a principal source of its organic unity. In effect, Beethoven found a new way of setting up a four-movement symphony that could match the Third and Fifth in power and excitement and serve to unify the whole.

Or, if it was not wholly new, certainly no one had conceived of it before in this way. In the Fifth he had integrated the four-movement cycle by means of a single rhythmic figure, the famous motto, that appears in every movement; the structural plan also entails the gradual emergence of the tonality of C major, which culminates in the explosive finale. In the "Pastoral," the five-movement cycle is integrated by means of a narrative program that takes us step by step through an experience of the world of nature in many of its most highly colored manifestations, ending with a hymn of thanksgiving for peace after the storm. In the Seventh there is neither an emerging tonal revelation nor a known program. So far as we know, Beethoven never said a word about this work except that he considered it one of his best. Nor does it have a single thematic or motivic idea that runs through all movements. Instead, and more than in any other work by him, even the Fourth Symphony, rhythmic action of many kinds and at varying speeds create the characteristic form of expression in the Seventh—exuberant in the first movement; slow and steady in the second; rapid, hurtling forward motion in the third; wild abandon in the finale.

One striking theory about the symphony, advanced by Maynard Solomon, is that its rhythmic formulas might have sprung from an interest on Beethoven's part in evoking the meters of ancient Greek poetry, some of which correspond to the metrical figures that dominate each movement.[9] This idea was first proposed by Beethoven's pupil Carl Czerny, who adopted it from a treatise by Anton Reicha. Czerny observes that the first movement Allegro uses "a wide range of dactylic figures," that the slow movement "is formed from weighty dactyls and spondees;" and that there is a comparable meter in the finale. The proposal is speculative, as we have no evidence for it beyond the general fact that the Homeric epics and some classical books were among Beethoven's favored reading and the even more general proposition that he was well acquainted with the contemporary tendency to associate political imagery, art, architecture, dress, and theater, with the forms and figures of Greek and Roman antiquity. His early *Prometheus* ballet contains a "dance of Bacchus" and in 1818, while thinking about new symphonies, he imagined a choral symphony that would include this sequence of movements: "in the text of the Adagio Greek myth, *Cantique Ecclesiastique*—in the Allegro, a celebration of Bacchus."[10] At best, however, the case for associating the rhythms of the Seventh with classical meters, as a matter of artistic intention, remains uncertain.

THE MOVEMENT-PLAN; TEMPI; OTHER WORKS IN A MAJOR

The scheme of the Seventh is as follows:

	Movement	Key	Meter	Measures
1.	Poco Sostenuto	A major	4/4	62
	Vivace	A major	6/8	388
2.	Allegretto	A minor	2/4	278
3.	Presto	F major	3/4	653
	Trio	D major	3/4	
4.	Allegro vivace	A major	2/4	465

The richly developed slow introduction is much longer than those he had written for the Second and Fourth. Its tempo, "Poco sostenuto," is a tempo marking that he liked to use in movements or works between about 1808 and 1815, all of them serious and foreboding—the introduction to the Piano Trio Op. 70 No. 2; the melodrama movement of the Egmont music; his song "An die Hoffnung," Op. 94; one of the *Equali* for four trombones, composed while he was finishing this symphony; and the "calm sea" section of his choral setting of Goethe's poem, "Meerestille und Gluckliche Fahrt" (Calm sea and prosperous voyage), Op. 112, of 1814–15.[11]

The true analogies for the slow introduction of the Seventh are those of the Quartets Op. 59 No. 3 and Op. 74, and the mysterious F-minor prologue to Florestan's dungeon scene in *Leonore*. In the Fifth and Sixth his slow movement tempi had been "Andante," but in the Seventh he prefers "Allegretto," and so this introduction not only establishes the emotional tone of the whole symphony but it is, in effect, its slow movement.

Other new elements in the layout and character of the whole symphony are these:

1. His use of "Vivace" and 6/8 meter for the first movement, for him a very unusual combination for the first movement of a three- or four-movement work;

2. The key-scheme of the middle movements, with the slow movement in A minor, the tonic minor, and the Scherzo in F major;

3. His use of "Presto" for the Scherzo, with the slower indication "Assai meno Presto" for the Trio.

Beethoven's choice of basic key, A major, is telling. Symphonies in this key had not been common. Haydn had used it four times before 1765 in early symphonies (Nos. 5, 14, 21, and 28) and twice more in the 1770s (Nos. 64 and 65), but later only in his No. 87 of 1785. Mozart wrote only three symphonies in A major: K. 114 (1771), K. 134 (1772), and K. 201 (1774), the last a work of special beauty. If Beethoven knew any of them is uncertain. Haydn had composed a few string quartets in A, including his Op. 55, No. 1 of 1789–90, but none among his great quartets of the 1790s. On the other hand, Beethoven admired Mozart's chamber works in this key, above all his Quartet K. 464, about which Czerny reports that Beethoven said, "That's a work! That was Mozart saying to the world, 'see what I can do, if only you were ready for it!'" Beethoven would also have known Mozart's Clarinet Quintet and the Concerto, both late works.

Beethoven was often innovative in A major. His Quartet Op. 18, No. 5, is modeled in its movement-plan on Mozart's K. 464, but it is wholly Beethoven's in thematic content and character. Of Beethoven's two A-major piano sonatas, one is early, Op. 2, No. 2 (1794–95); the other is the masterly Op. 101 of 1816. He also wrote four accompanied sonata in A major—the Violin Sonatas Op. 12, No. 2 (1797); Op. 30 No. 1 (1801), and the "Kreutzer" sonata (1802–3). Closest in time to the Seventh Symphony is the cello sonata Op. 69 (1808); there are also a few vocal works, including Clärchen's song in *Egmont*, "Freudvoll und leidvoll," in A.

THE INDIVIDUAL MOVEMENTS

We turn now to some of the salient features of the symphony. The slow introduction is one of the noblest statements in all of Beethoven's works, perhaps in all music. Its sectional plan is A^1–B–A^2–Coda. The opening measures proceed in solemn half-notes that only slowly give way to rhythmic animation, distantly recalling the opening of the Fourth Symphony—now not groping and strange but magisterial in character. Below the initial woodwind figures the first segment is underpinned by the basses, which move downward through half-steps from the tonic A to the dominant E. This outlines the descending chromatic interval of the fourth, a long familiar bass progression which Beethoven had also used elsewhere, as in his *Thirty-two Variations* for piano, WoO 80, of 1806.[12] Listeners who attend to the bass line of the first ten bars will have no trouble hearing this descent, and the interval from A down to E can also be heard as mirroring the opening two-note melodic motion of the oboe. This is the kind of relationship of detail to larger phrase that can only occur in music of the masters.

Further salient moments in the introduction are these:

1. In the A section, the running upward scale-figures in sixteenth-notes that occupy the second part of this section;

2. In the B section, the new melody, again in the oboe and now in C major, in *piano dolce*, with its distinctive two-note rhythmic figures in the second bar. All that follows in this introduction is now formed from the figures of sections A and B, and it eventually leads to the Coda in which the note E, the dominant, becomes the sole element of the last six bars, alternating in dialogue between winds and strings as the whole introduction prepares the Vivace.

THE FIRST MOVEMENT

The verve and energy of the first movement grows by gradual steps from the Introduction, then whips forward in 6/8 Vivace, announcing the three-note dactylic figure (twice in each 6/8 measure) that dominates the movement. Significantly, it is first given on the single pitch "E" in a high register in the winds, so it is first heard as a purely rhythmic motif before it emerges as part of a melodic phrase or is even harmonized. After a few measures, the A-major tonic chord is formed as more instruments join, and then the first theme proper appears in the solo flute (see Web Example M).

Opening a first movement with the main theme in high-register woodwinds is new in Beethoven's symphonic practice, just as the theme itself is of a new character. Beethoven's earlier uses of 6/8 meter, apart from slow movements, run along two different paths. One is the long-familiar pattern of 6/8 for Rondo finales, inherited from Haydn and Mozart.[13] Beethoven followed this model in some early chamber works, and in several of his concerto finales. In all of them he still used the label "Rondo," abandoning it in later works. The other path was his use of 6/8 in the first movements of the Quartets Op. 18, No. 5 and Op. 59, No. 2.[14] But none of them come close to the Seventh in the use of obsessive rhythmic formulas throughout.

While the first movement preserves the basic sectional features of a large sonata-form movement, it shows a number of idiosyncrasies. In choosing to give this movement its decisive rhythmic stamp, Beethoven had to diminish the degree of melodic contrast that in earlier symphonies had distinguished his second group themes from his opening themes. If we think about the contrasting shapes of Beethoven's first and second themes in the expositions of his earlier symphonies, we are struck by their differences in character, phrase-formation, and orchestration. Not so in the Seventh. Here he finds other ways to gain thematic contrast in every section of the movement. It must spin forward in its Vivace 6/8 meter, brilliantly varied in its smaller units but with nothing like the drastic contrasts in the exposition of the Fifth Symphony and to some degree in all the others.

One of those ways is through unusual harmonic shifts. In the introduction, Beethoven extended the harmonic range by moving from the tonic A major to the distant C major, and in the Vivace there are other sudden and surprising harmonic deviations, plus equally abrupt changes in dynamics and register. His subtlety of planning in the phrase-structure of this movement is fully apparent in the surviving sketches and in his autograph manuscript. About the latter we find a curious and revealing statement by the publisher Johann André, who visited Beethoven while he was writing out the autograph. According to Ferdinand Hiller

> André reported that he had seen the score of the A-major Symphony in which there were blank pages, so that what was written before the blank had no connection at all with what was written after the blank. Beethoven said that the connecting material would certainly be supplied.[15]

George Grove noted long ago that the autograph actually contains four blank pages in the Introduction and first movement, along with smaller blanks within the Vivace, "as if for filling up afterwards."

And in the finished version of the first movement there are significant moments of silence, as at the beginning of the development and the corresponding place at the beginning of the coda; we are reminded of Samuel Beckett's hearing "huge black pauses" in this movement.[16]

The coda is one of his strongest. It gathers up all the preceding energy of the movement and brings it home, using some of Beethoven's best and most characteristic techniques. It is laid out as follows, and the attentive listener will have no trouble in following its basic sequence of events:

1. As the recapitulation ends in the normal tonic key of A major, two silent measures give way to a surprising isolated A♭ (= G♯, the leading tone of the home key). This note then becomes the springboard for the next phrase, in which the basses, in *pianissimo,* move down stepwise from A♭ to E♭, steadily repeating the dactylic rhythm of the movement as they move down from the initial A♭ major to the home key, A major, at the end of this mysterious passage. Above them the winds join in with the dactylic figure but also sustain long-held chords, while the violins bring the original first measure figure of the opening theme.

2. This segment of twenty-two bars, more than twice the length of the preceding, is notorious above all because of the remark, evidently falsely attributed to Carl Maria von Weber by Schindler, that this passage showed that Beethoven was "ripe for the madhouse."[17] It is the passage in which the lower strings repeat the two-measure figure on the notes D–C♯–B♯–B♯–C♯ (a chromatic turning figure) eleven times while the winds and strings (later joined by trumpets and tympani) build a crescendo that leads to a climactic new section in which the dactylic figure now fully rules in the whole orchestra.

3. Now in *fortissimo,* recalling the triumphant descending arpeggio theme that had been prominent in the development, the

coda unleashes it again in full force. The winds and strings exchange a rapid dialogue using short fragments of the basic rhythm, and rush towards the final culmination.

4. The final measures reaffirm the arrival at the tonic A major, as we should expect, but as they do so, the whole wind section, with high-register horns adding a triumphant tone-color, drive the movement to its tremendous conclusion.

THE ALLEGRETTO

The earliest trace of the basic theme of this movement goes back to 1806, where amid sketches for Op. 59, No. 3 we find a sketch for the opening theme, instantly recognizable from its tone-repetitions and persistent rhythmic figures made up of dactyl and spondee. It looks as if Beethoven had been thinking of using this theme for the slow movement of this C-major quartet but then preferred the 6/8 A-minor Andante that became his final choice, which may have some inflections of Russian folksong.

Of all his symphonic slow movements, as memorable as they are, this one has held a special place in the modern imagination since its premiere in December 1813 in the great hall of the University in Vienna. Three years later a reviewer wrote,

> The second movement . . . which since its first performance in Vienna has been a favorite of all connoisseurs and amateurs, is a movement that speaks inwardly even to those who have no training in music; by means of its naïveté and a certain secret magic it irresistibly overcomes them—and it is still demanded to be repeated at every performance.[18]

How and why? We can begin with the movement's highly individual qualities of key, character, and mood. There is a consensus that it has a particular *Stimmung*, which literally means "pitch" and "tuning," but also refers to its emotional atmosphere. Another reason for its lasting impact is the gradual growth within the movement from quiet contemplation to an exalted state of profound emotional involvement. How this is accomplished calls for consideration.

The basic form of the movement can be described in several different ways, depending on the viewpoint and the analyst. But the primary choices are to hear it as either a freely developing set of variations (though it doesn't follow the traditional sectional plan of the older variation-type); or to hear it as a freely handled rondo that has some affinities with the form of the *Eroica* Funeral March. Its large-scale exposition (in this Allegretto it is 100 bars long, more than a third of the whole movement) is symmetrically divided into four twenty-four-bar segments, preceded by the bleak held chord at the beginning and ending with a little codetta phrase.

Then comes the beautiful and consoling A-major interlude, described by some as "dream-like." It offers release from the bleakness of the first section and yet has the original first-bar dactylic rhythm of the primary motif murmuring in the basses.

Thereafter, a succession of highly varied segments are built out of the previously established content. These are, in turn, the returns of the A-minor primary material in several different forms, followed by the reappearance of the lyrical A-major interlude. They appear in this order:

1. the return of both the primary theme and its counter-melody;
2. a fugue-like treatment of the primary motive, first for strings, then adding winds;
3. a climactic full orchestral statement of the eight-bar opening theme, again in the relentlessly present A-minor tonic;
4. an abbreviated restatement of the A-major lyrical interlude, and a short codetta that brings back the primary motive;
5. the coda of the whole movement. To close the movement

Beethoven once more brings the winds and strings in dialogue, now in close exchanges phrase by phrase; and the movement ends as it had begun.

As we have seen, Beethoven was aware of the traditional associations of particular keys with affects. But keys were also associated with the genre and performing forces for which he was writing, and his ideas could well be colored by his awareness of certain sonorities and registers in which particular instruments would sound well and would produce the effects he was seeking—e.g., the resonant open strings of the violin, viola, and cello, and the most effective registers of the flute, oboe, clarinet, bassoon, and horn.

For early listeners the opening of this movement, with its famous two-measure motive of dactyl and spondee, might have conjured up reminiscences of the slow march tempo that Beethoven had used to such powerful effect in the Funeral March in the *Eroica*. We do not have any clear basis for this association from sources of the time, but in 1811–12, Viennese concert audiences had lived through two decades of war, and, before that, the 1809 French invasion. Vienna was by necessity a garrison city in which Imperial army battalions were a constant presence, and the citizens were used to the sight and sound of military marches. Beethoven was in demand as a composer of new works for the military bands of the Austrian army, and he complied by writing several such marches between 1809 and 1816. His familiarity with the genre is shown on the autograph manuscript of one of them, where he writes "Allegro in the tempo that is now common for Marches."

That this Allegretto might evoke the genre of the march is suggested by the obsessive repetition of the opening two-measure motif, similar to the first movement though obviously in a different sphere. Its basic first theme has nothing in common with the lyrical melodies he had used for the slow movements of the Second, Fourth, and

Fifth Symphonies, or, in its special way, the "Scene by the Brook" in the "Pastoral" Symphony.

After the full presentation of the dactyl-spondee theme, Beethoven presents its counter-melody in the violas and cellos, an elegiac utterance that is notable for its small melodic span, its slight inflection of an A-major element within the prevailing A minor, and the sense of even greater bleakness that it adds to the first segment that is repeated along with it. The whole first large part of the movement is scored for strings alone except the very last measures, and each segment repeats and intensifies the same original material while gradually rising in octave-register and intensity. The crescendo from *piano* to *fortissimo* over this span must be one of the longest in any of his works. And the climactic effect of the final segment with its poignant decrescendo at the ending, is beyond words. This method of building a long section that rises gradually in register and gains in volume and power will later be a vital tool in the Ninth Symphony.

The later sections of the Allegretto are as well formed as the first one, but are now abbreviated. The beautiful A-major interludes that twice alternate with the basic A-minor variations cast rays of light into the prevailing shadow. In the coda, again in *pianissimo*, Beethoven gives pairs of instruments the two-measure phrases that have been heard from the very beginning, now in descending registers with new tone-colors in each statement. In the very last measures, the winds conclude this astonishing movement with a tonic chord using the same orchestration and in the same unusual sonority as at the beginning. It is a final chord Beethoven never used to end any other piece or section, and with it, this movement leaves through the same portal through which it had entered, as if in a dream.

THE SCHERZO

George Grove wrote about this symphony that, "There is no doubt that the mental image raised by No. 7 is larger than that of any of

its predecessors."[19] What Grove meant by "mental image" still resonates, and in our time, two centuries after its first performance,
there is a consensus that the Seventh is one of the most fully satis-
fying of all Beethoven's works, one in which everything that is in it
contributes equally to the quality of the whole.

This Scherzo-Trio is a five-part movement, like those of the Fourth
and Sixth. It is the biggest of all his symphonic scherzi to date, and
its proportions foreshadow those of the Scherzo of the Ninth Symphony, by far the longest such movement he was ever to write.

Despite their obvious differences in key, meter, and form, it
appears that the first movement and the Scherzo had a common
ancestor at the early sketch stage. At the very beginning of
Beethoven's main sketchbook for this symphony, he jotted down
a set of musical ideas that anticipates the opening theme of the
Scherzo but is written in 6/8 and in A major. At this stage it looks
like an early concept sketch for the first movement, and we can't be
sure if he might have thought that it might function equally well in
either movement, only later deciding to move it to the Scherzo (see
Web Example N).[20]

One of the many beauties of the Scherzo is the ingenuity with
which Beethoven maintains the obsessive repetition of a two-note
figure moving down one step (a half-note tied to a quarter-note) for
long stretches in *pianissimo*. His way of deploying it is to state it in
three four-bar phrases in succession on different pitches—first in
the winds, then in the high strings, then in the bassoons and basses,
and then to break the spell with a *fortissimo* explosion. This sequence
occurs twice in this form as the movement makes its full repeat of
the binary form of the Scherzo. Later, after the first statement of the
Trio, the Scherzo returns in full with the same sequence of four-bar
phrases but now the expected *fortissimo* crash is replaced with a soft
pianissimo arrival. It is a moment every listener learns to savor, the
more so when the full Scherzo comes back for the third time at the
end of the movement, and the *fortissimo* crash returns as well.

The Trio, thought by some to be a borrowed hymn-tune or a variant of one, is laid out first as a serenade for clarinets and horns, with the violins holding a long sustained A (the dominant of the Trio's D major). Only later, as the horns explore their lowest register with the persistent two-note chromatic figure that opened the Trio, does the full orchestra bring the Trio main theme as its culmination, in *fortissimo* with the tympani rolling, always a dramatic sign in Beethoven's orchestral language. And in the coda Beethoven brings back the soft Trio theme in two short phrases, one in major, one in minor, before whipping up the final Presto cadence.

THE FINALE

The two thundering gestures that open the 2/4 Allegro con brio finale, each followed by a full measure of silence, make clear that there will be no letup, that the last movement will if anything expand the use of driving rhythms that has dominated the work so far. In each initial four-note figure the strings slash a *fortissimo* chord that is answered at once by the rest of the orchestra, and since both figures project the dominant harmony of A major they set up an expected resolution to the tonic that will not occur until the twelfth bar. By this time the exuberant first theme has swung into action in the first violins over strong off-beat accents in the other instruments (see Web Example P).

From there the movement unfolds as a large-scale sonata-form structure, in which the exposition's second group contains strongly contrasting rhythmic features in its second group as the harmony moves not to the dominant key of E major, which would be the text-book norm, but to C-sharp minor, the key of the mediant, an unusual move even for Beethoven. The development section moves still farther afield, now to C major and F major (thus recalling the harmonic adventures of the long-past slow introduction to the first movement), and then it works its way still further along to the remote key of B-flat major just before exploding back into the tonic A major at the recapitulation. In the coda, as the great movement nears its end, the cellos and basses indicate that the finale will match the first movement and the Scherzo in that it will have its own obsessive repeated figure in the lowest regions of the sound-palette, repeating a two-note chromatic figure on the notes E and D-sharp for twenty consecutive measures and then for four more, undergirding a massive build-up of orchestral resources in the last climactic outbursts that end the movement. A mark of Beethoven's tremendous expectations for the force of the ending is his use of the marking "*fff*," (*fortississimo*), a dynamic he had not yet used in any other symphony.

Tovey called this movement "a triumph of Bacchic fury," and among Beethoven's many 2/4 finales it is, *par excellence*, the one in which the listener feels most fully caught up in a whirlwind of rhythmically driven events from start to finish. Some of Beethoven's other 2/4 finales of large middle-period works use highly profiled opening motives and themes, and many also culminate in rapid codas of great power—e.g. the Third and Fourth Symphonies, the quartet Op. 59, No. 1, the piano trios Op. 70, No. 2 and Op. 97 (the "Archduke"). But none of them, for all their own virtues, so completely overwhelm the listener with incessant forward momentum. It is all the more striking, then, to find that at an early stage, perhaps before he fully foresaw that the whole symphony would be so powerfully rhythmic in character, Beethoven imagined a different finale. We find it on an early page of his main sketchbook, where this theme appears, marked "Finale" (see Web Example Q).

As naive and square-cut as it is, this theme might have been perfectly serviceable for a work of lighter character, with its two eight-measure periods. But its melodic shape, its dynamic marking (*fp*) at the beginning of each two-bar unit, its *p* at bar 5 and the whole character of the theme, all these elements imply a softer, lighter tone than could ever have been adequate to end this symphony. It looks as if Beethoven plucked a sample from his memory bank of 2/4 finale thematic ideas, and tried it out on a sketch page to see if it might work. But we are not surprised to find, a few pages later, an early version of the finale's true opening theme (see Web Example R). With this sketch, the basic rhythmic form of the opening is firmly in place, and from here Beethoven could elaborate his ideas, refine the opening theme into its proper form, and work out the larger shape of the whole movement.

THE SEVENTH SYMPHONY AND "RUSTIC SIMPLICITY"

In the early nineteenth century the opening Vivace theme and the whole first movement were at times associated with what some critics labeled "rustic simplicity," as we learn from Berlioz:

> I have heard this subject [the initial theme of the Vivace first movement] ridiculed on account of its rustic simplicity. Probably the reproach of lack of nobleness would never have been applied had the author, as in the *Pastoral* Symphony, placed at the head of his allegro in plain letters the inscription "Ronde de Paysans" [Peasants' Round-dance].[21]

While Berlioz will not accept that the symphony is anything but a "masterpiece—alike of technical ability, taste, fantasy, knowledge, and inspiration"—he seems to agree that the first movement has an affinity to folk music. And the epithet "folkish," which continued to be used by some writers, is worth a moment's consideration. Perhaps this pure A-major 6/8 theme, with its highly unusual accented downbeats, using grace-notes on the first beat in two measures and a "Scotch snap" to start its fourth measure, reminded listeners of the melodic style of Scottish and Irish folksong. It is possible that Beethoven may have associated some aspects of this symphony with the Scottish, Irish, and Welsh folk-song traditions with which he had now been working for some years.[22] By 1812, he had made many arrangements of melodies from these repertoires that were sent to him by George Thomson in Edinburgh. He was still writing them in 1811–12 while this symphony was germinating, and he continued to do so until 1820. By then he had made as many as 179 of these arrangements, most for solo voice with piano and often with violin and cello parts. Beethoven took this task very seriously, as we see from his special interest in mastering their modal features, and from his comments in his letters to Thomson, in which he "repeatedly demanded the texts . . . arguing that he could not compose proper arrangements without them."[23]

These folksongs suggest that Beethoven could have associated 6/8 meter in moderate and rapid tempi with the many 6/8 settings that we find among his arrangements, where they occur much more often, proportionately speaking, than in his larger instrumental compositions. In his three Irish sets totaling fifty-seven pieces, eighteen are in 6/8, as are three of his twelve Scottish songs. A connection between the Seventh Symphony and his folk-song settings is not just a matter of metrical identity, but is also shown by a direct melodic correspondence between the postlude to one of his Irish songs and the main theme of the finale of the Seventh. It occurs in his setting of Thomson's Irish melody "Save me from the grave and wise" (WoO 154/8), based on the traditional tune known as *Nora Creina*. In Beethoven's postlude, while the violin and cello mark time with repeated notes, the piano plays the finale theme, fully recognizable even though it is in 6/8 and not the 2/4 meter of the symphony version. In addition, the four last measures of the setting make a clear allusion to a passage in the first movement of the symphony (see Web Example S).

Beethoven may have had this melody in hand as early as 1810, well before he began the symphony in the later part of 1811. This connection strengthens our understanding of the symphony's potential appeal to audiences at every level in Beethoven's time, including listeners steeped in the world of folksong. It's possible that Beethoven himself could have felt this affinity, that for him this small link between such disparate genres might have reinforced his belief that he could bridge the world of everyday popular music with the world of his grandest symphonic style. As an 1816 reviewer wrote, on the occasion of the first publication of this symphony in score and parts:

> we have the pleasant task of acquainting the reader of these pages, at least in outline and as much as space permits, with the strikingly beautiful elements of this wonderful work. The most beautiful of these, the spirit of the whole, cannot be captured here in words. Soon all of Germany, France, and England will share our opinion, and may even complain that we have brought out far too few of its good qualities and not said enough about them.[24]

Two centuries later, in the vastly transformed world of our time, we can agree.

8

THE EIGHTH SYMPHONY

"THAT'S BECAUSE IT'S SO MUCH BETTER"

The Eighth is singular. Usually described as a creature of wit and charm, somewhat in the manner of Haydn, its surface appropriation of classical-period dimensions masks its subtleties and forward-looking features. Its diminutive inner movements make it the shortest of all Beethoven's symphonies, as he acknowledged when he called it a "smaller Symphony" in comparison to the Seventh.[1] It also differs by having no true slow movement, not even a slow introduction comparable to the opening portal of the Seventh.

Its four movements are laid out as follows:

Movement	Meter	Key	Measures	Form
1. Allegro vivace e con brio	3/4	F major	373	Sonata form
2. Allegretto scherzando	2/4	B♭ major	81	Two-part form plus coda
3. Tempo di Menuetto	3/4	F major	122	Three-part Minuet–Trio–Minuet da capo
4. Allegro vivace	2/2	F major	502	Modified sonata form

Beethoven ca. 1815, painting by Willibrord Josef Mähler
(Gesellschaft der Musikfreunde, Vienna / Mondadori Portfolio / Bridgeman Images)

If its return to late eighteenth-century symphonic proportions is a defining feature, so is the idiosyncratic character of each movement, in which surprise and paradox stand out more sharply than in any other Beethoven symphony. While the Seventh swept away its listeners in Beethoven's time (and still does), the Eighth puzzled them. Yet Czerny reports that when some listeners compared it unfavorably to the Seventh, Beethoven remarked, "That's because it's so much better."[2] About which, Tovey wrote,

> This is neither a matter-of-fact judgment nor wholly ironical; what it expresses is the unique sense of power which fires a man when he finds himself fit for a delicate task just as he has triumphed in a colossal one.[3]

Yet if the task was delicate it was also guided by a strong sense of purpose. We can linger for a moment over the question why Beethoven moved forward in this odd new direction and what the Eighth implies about his artistic situation at this time. Like any prolific artist, Beethoven was sensitive to the place of each new large work within its genre, and what it might seem to add to all that he had done before. If this was true for his piano sonatas and string quartets, it was surely true for the symphony as the most public sector of instrumental music. Defiantly writing symphonies in Vienna in these years, when the genre, despite its traditional prestige, was difficult to get performed, he aimed to make each one worthy of his ambition to write "great works," as he put it in a late letter. The concentration we see in the laborious sketch-process that led to each finished work reflects his inner drive to create a new symphonic world.

Accordingly, his re-animation of the classical manner in the Eighth should be seen not as a regression, but as a further widening of artistic space, an expression of his sense of freedom. It reflects his command of a wide range of stylistic directions, and its internal features display curious and subtle play with form and expectations about continuity that foreshadow aspects of the late style. In effect, in this work, Beethoven tells his contemporaries that he can wield the rapier as well as the hammer, that he can return to the world of the high classical symphony but use its conventions in his own way. We can believe that this turn to smaller dimensions, unusual harmonic moves, and subtle inter-movement relationships was all the more appealing as he confronted an aesthetic project completely different from the breadth and energy of the Seventh and one that was at least as difficult to master.

ORIGINS

Work on the Eighth followed on the Seventh by about half a year. The autograph of the Seventh is dated "13 April 1812," probably the date he started it, about two months before his journey to Teplitz. On the autograph of the Eighth he wrote "Linz in the month of October 1812." His extensive sketches for both works are found in the so-called Petter Sketchbook, which he used from about September 1811 until December 1812.[4]

The sketches for the Eighth are ample and revealing, though up to now only a small proportion of them have been made available, even to specialists.[5] What we have so far for the first movement, however, brings a major surprise. The sketches show that in its initial stages, Beethoven conceived these musical ideas not for a symphony but for a piano concerto.[6] An extended early draft of what looks exactly like the exposition of the first movement of the Eighth Symphony (in F major, 3/4) shows its first theme and continuations that clearly foreshadow its later themes. This draft extends to almost 70 bars, then closes on a fermata on the dominant, whereupon Beethoven writes out what is clearly a sketch for an elaborate solo cadenza for a piano soloist, extending over seven measures (see Web Example T).

Beethoven followed this draft with a few more sketches that

unmistakably point to a piano concerto, marking some passages "solo" and others "tutti." In the light of his background as a public performer, the idea of a new concerto in 1812 would have been daring and courageous. He had played his first four concertos in public in the earlier years, but as his deafness grew, he did not perform the "Emperor" Concerto, written in 1809. He could still play and improvise for audiences, but his damaged hearing would now have made the interplay of soloist and orchestra in concerto performance a high personal risk.

Still, he conceived new ideas for other piano concertos in 1812 and even a few years later. Concept sketches for a concerto in G major appear in this same sketchbook of 1812 on nearby pages.[7] In 1815, he came back again to try out ideas for still another piano concerto, in D major, for which he wrote out not merely an array of sketches but a long draft of the autograph manuscript of the first movement. But that plan failed as well, and the 1815 concerto materials were buried alive among his posthumous papers.[8] In 1812, in any case, the F major concerto idea soon became transformed into the emergent Eighth symphony. A little further along we see that he was even thinking about a third symphony at this time, this one in D minor—but then the third symphony idea was set aside for another day.[9] There is no other Beethoven symphony for which we can find evidence that Beethoven definitely considered using its material for a concerto or for any other genre at the sketch stage.

From the same period, that of the Seventh and Eighth Symphonies, plans for still two more unfinished symphonies have recently been located on sketch leaves, and they can be briefly mentioned here. One is for a symphony in E minor, with a first movement in 4/4 time in E minor and a sketch for an apparent second movement in C major. They appear on a sketch leaf that became detached from his main sketchbook of 1812.[10] Still another idea for a symphony surfaced at this time, in E-flat major, for which Beethoven jotted down ideas for all four movements and marked it "sinfonia

3," meaning that he thought of it as a possible third symphony to go with the Seventh and Eighth. Like the E-minor movement-plan that evidently preceded it, this idea remained unrealized, but it shows Beethoven exploring a wide range of ideas for symphonies at this important turning point in his career.[11]

THE FIRST MOVEMENT

Exposition

The first movement opens with a memorable first figure that maintains its importance throughout. It is especially striking that this opening six-note motif, with its firm landing on the tonic on the downbeat of its second bar, can ultimately serve as the closing figure of the whole movement. Looking ahead, the idea of ending a symphonic first movement with its initial short phrase reappears in the first movement of the Ninth Symphony, a work as different in character as we can imagine. We saw that in the Seventh's first movement, the pervasive dactylic rhythm governs all of its themes, however different they are in other respects. In the Eighth, Beethoven pursues the opposite tack, that of linking together a chain of highly diverse thematic segments, some of them lyrical, some decisively rhythmic, some moving in stepwise melodic patterns, some in arpeggiated harmonies. The type of thematic process that Beethoven had forged in the first movement of the Seventh is one that expands similarities, while in the Eighth he is engaged in integrating dissimilarities. To show this we only need to look at the six basic thematic segments of the Eighth symphony first movement's exposition:

1. Three four-bar phrases: a b b[1]. It is important to note that the first and third phrases are in *forte* with the full orchestra, while the second phrase is in *piano* and in mid-register with the winds alone; also that b[1] lands decisively on the tonic (this will be important at the recapitulation).[12]

2. A new declamatory phrase in the first violins is underpinned by tremolo motions in the lower strings. A second phrase of thirteen bars eventually peters out and pauses on an unstable harmony that brings a new harmonic move towards the key of D (unusual for an F-major exposition, which would normally move to C major, its dominant key).[13]

3. After a strange one-bar pause, the strings and then a solo bassoon introduce the lyrical second group theme in D major, which then by sleight of hand wends it way to C major where the winds can take over the theme.[14]

4. A harmonic cloud in *pianissimo* opens this fourth segment and eventually proceeds in the halting rhythm that had introduced the second subject; then a long crescendo from *pp* to *ff* builds to a climax in *fortissimo.*[15]

5. Now two new elements enter the discourse. First, a strongly defined syncopated dotted rhythm of three bars. Second, following at once, a new seven-bar lyrical flowing theme in the winds. Then the whole large pair of phrases is repeated but the lyrical portion is now led by the violas, cellos, and bassoon, the other winds joining in.[16]

6. The final segment of the exposition opens with another new rhythmic figure and then emphatic C major arpeggios prepare the firm close of the exposition, with a four-note jumping octave-figure on the note C to end the whole.

The Development[17]

The jumping octave-figure from the end of the exposition leads us directly into the development. Now fully detached, the opening six-note figure appears once in each of the four woodwinds in rising registers (bassoon, clarinet, oboe, flute) in *piano dolce;* then the full orchestra answers with a four-bar *fortissimo* blast in which the strings restate the rising and falling arpeggios that had first been heard at the end of the exposition. This way of starting the development—

with the first and last figures of the exposition—brings together themes that had been widely spaced apart in their original presentation. It is a further indication of the unusual way of thinking that governs this entire movement.

After two more large statements of this same thematic juxtaposition, which move through other keys, the development incessantly repeats the opening figure of the movement through a long passage of growing intensity in sustained *fortissimo*. It passes through a new series of keys and textures and gradually builds to a tremendous climax on the dominant of the home key to prepare for the recapitulation.

Recapitulation[18]

The recapitulation calls for special comment. In classical sonata-form movements by master composers, the recapitulation is much more than a structural return to the opening theme and the tonic key, often called a "double return." It is a home-coming, a return to harmonic stability after the wanderings of the development section through subordinate keys. It is the moment at which the opening theme and its subordinate themes from the exposition re-emerge in their original form and original order after the thematic fragmentation of the development section. It is against this background that Beethoven's innovative treatment of this vital moment in his sonata-form movements must be seen.

As he grew in maturity, Beethoven gave his most careful attention to this place in his sonata-form narratives, dramatizing it in several different ways. In the *Eroica*, where everything is on the largest time-scale, he intensifies the listener's sense of expectation by extending the dominant harmony over an enormous expanse of time, then raises the tension another notch by having a solo horn enter two bars too soon with the long-awaited opening tonic motif against the sustained dominant harmony—whereupon the whole orchestra, first in forte then *fortissimo*, sets matters straight with two bars of the full dominant harmony and moves swiftly to the long-awaited tonic recapitulation. In the Fourth, instead of using the dominant harmony, Beethoven holds the long period of suspenseful preparation steady by prolonging the tonic harmony itself but in its least stable configuration (the six-four tonic chord, with its fifth in the bass). To increase the suspense, he lets the timpani roll for many measures in *pianissimo* while fragments of the opening theme gradually emerge in a slow crescendo—then he whips up the material into a frenzy until the recapitulation arrives in full *fortissimo* with the real tonic in root position.

These and other alternatives abound in his early and middle-period works. But in the Eighth's first movement recapitulation, he has another card to play. Here we see that we are looking at a magician's trick of high subtlety, and one that has spurred controversy as to exactly where the recapitulation actually begins. Here the development ends with its repetitions of the dominant harmony, already *fortissimo* for many measures but with Beethoven calling for *più forte* in the last two measures, and then the full orchestra blazes forth with the tonic harmony, the long-awaited F major, in the extreme dynamic *fff*. At this moment, as expected, the opening theme returns as well, but with a difference. Instead of being in the upper voices (the first violins or high winds) the theme is now in bass register (bassoon, cellos, basses). Because these bass instruments are at risk of being overwhelmed by the rest of the orchestra (what Tovey calls the "noontide glare" of this moment), some conductors have actually altered Beethoven's scoring by inserting decrescendo markings into the upper orchestral parts.[19] Beethoven's way of scoring the return of the first theme suggested to them that perhaps his deafness had gotten the better of him.[20]

But a close look at the score reveals that there is more to the story, although views can differ as to what Beethoven is up to. One view is that, although this *fff* passage has all the earmarks of a thematic recapitulation, it is not in fact the real one but is an illusion, a passage that presents the elements of a recapitulation but undercuts it at the same time. Supporting this view is the assignment of the theme to the bass instruments, which struggle to be heard against the rest of the orchestra in *fff*. It is true that the movement has now reached the tonic, F major, but in fact it is the tonic harmony in a functionally less than stable version—its six-four inversion, with the note C in the bass. This note is both the first note of the theme itself, in low register, and is also the note literally pounded out by the timpani on the downbeat of the recapitulation—and since the timpanist's customary two drums are tuned to play F (tonic) and C (dominant), this means that Beethoven deliberately avoided using the tonic when he could easily have done so. Moreover, the timpani continues with C for the full eight measures of the theme until it resolves to F at the end of the phrase. The opposing view, that this strong return in *fff* is the real recapitulation, after all, despite its peculiar features, also has its proponents. For them the full orchestral sound, the return of the first theme and the climactic impact of these measures carry the day.

To which we can offer these observations:

1. the first theme does reappear in *fff* but in an abbreviated form that brings the original segment a (four bars in length) followed not by b but by the closing segment b¹;
2. immediately following this abbreviated form Beethoven presents the same first theme all over again, now in its full original twelve-bar form, but with new orchestration—as if confirming that the *fff* version had been an illusory recapitulation and that now we have the real one.

Still another way of looking at this paradox is prompted by other situations in which Beethoven sets up a large musical narrative in which the sonata-form recapitulation is in some way less than complete. In such circumstances, the final definitive return of the structural tonic is deferred until the coda or until the very end of the movement. An example occurs in the String Quartet Op. 59, No. 1, the first "Razumovsky" quartet.[21] In the first movement, Beethoven opens the work with the theme in the cello in low register with notes that imply the tonic harmony in its 6/4 inversion. At the beginning of the development he comes back to the same first theme in the same unstable harmonic position; and at the recapitulation, besides re-ordering the thematic units, he brings the same low-register version still again, now for the third time. Not until the coda, near the very end of this gigantic movement, does the tonic in root position truly arrive, and now the theme is in the highest voice, the first violin, and the dynamic is *ff.*

It seems clear that in the Eighth Symphony's first movement, Beethoven is aiming once again to maximize the dramatic effect of arrival at the recapitulation, maintaining the conditions of the larger form while adjusting them to suit his subtler purposes. We can hear the recapitulation in *fortissimo* as a hybrid moment that satisfies some of the normal expectations of first-movement form while also telling the keen listener that the true tonic arrival will occur later. As in fact it will, in the coda.

Coda

Of all Beethoven's formal innovations, his extended codas are among the most prominent. He often made the coda a counterpart to the development, thus fashioning a four-part sonata form rather than a three-part form with at most a short extension at the end. In Haydn and Mozart, for the most part, either there is no coda at all, or the tail of the movement is a brief closing segment. Beethoven has several ways of making his codas new.[22] One of them is prominently on display in this movement, and it is interesting to see that he put the final version of the coda through several variants before he was satisfied with it.[23]

Beginning exactly like the development section, his coda in final form gradually progresses through another crescendo to a firm and clear statement of the first theme in all its glory, in the tonic, *fortis-*

simo, closing on a powerful fermata on the dominant chord. From here a resumption of lyrical elements from section 5 of the exposition again rises to a tremendous climax on an unstable harmony (for which again he writes the rare dynamic *fff*) which in turn sets up the final closing paragraph.

The ending brings the biggest surprise of all. The last sixteen bars begin with a progressive softening of the volume and a gradual slowing of the rhythmic action. First, three-note figures sound in the full orchestra, each followed by a measure-long rest. Then more three-note figures alternate between plucked strings and winds, now in *piano*. The three-note figures then give way to two-note figures. At last, to our astonishment, the whole movement ends in *pianissimo* with its original opening figure in the strings. Somewhat like the famous Andante of the Seventh Symphony, but in a different world, the first movement goes out the way it had come in.

SECOND MOVEMENT: ALLEGRETTO SCHERZANDO

Berlioz wrote that this movement seemed to have "fallen from heaven and to have immediately entered the composer's mind."[24] Even if it did nothing of the kind, as Beethoven's sketches show, the spirit of his remark remains valid. This buoyant 2/4 masterpiece is the capstone of a small group of movements that Beethoven conceived of as "scherzando," that is, having a playful character, all of them showing a lightness of touch and delicacy of articulation that are scarcely to be found in his lyrical Adagios, let alone those symphonic situations in which he needs a grand array of orchestral forces for the display of power.[25] Movements like this one partake of the older meaning of the word "Scherzo" (literally, joke) which Beethoven had swept away from his third movements when he transformed the classical Menuetto into his muscular Scherzos, not just in the symphonies but in every genre. Although the Menuetto had already been transformed by Haydn and Mozart in many late works, Beethoven's radical treatment had given it a new strength and stature equal to that of the other movements of his four-movement cycles.

The opening woodwind chords, with their steadily repeated staccato sixteenths, evoke the opening of the Andante of Haydn's "Clock" Symphony, as listeners have noted time out of mind and which Beethoven probably knew better than anyone.[26] Like Haydn's opening sixteenth-notes, Beethoven's clock-ticks establish the metrical framework for the whole movement and set up the arrival of the main melody; unlike Haydn's, Beethoven's do not alternate notes of the tonic chord but continue repeating the same pitches. As the insouciant upper-line theme then appears, the harmony finds its way to a firm tonic, a moment marked by the first note in the cellos and basses, which enter with the tonic B-flat.

This Allegretto is the shortest of Beethoven's symphonic slow movements. He had written pithy and compact Adagio and Andante movements in early chamber works, but in the symphony he needed more space to allow for the expansion of ideas that came with the varied tone-colors of the orchestra. In the scherzando movement of the string quartet Opus 18, No. 4, in 3/8 meter, he needed 261 measures compared to only 81 for the Eighth Symphony Allegretto. The form of our movement is as follows:

Section	Measures	Thematic Material
A	1–39	a–b–c
A1	40–73	a^1–b^1–c^1
Coda	74–81	Closing figures

Within these smaller dimensions, Beethoven finds room for striking details and contrasts, the latter by means of repartee between strings and winds, as well as sudden shifts in dynamics and lightning-quick changes in mood. The last seven measures of the movement offer one of the most charming and clever moments in all the symphonic literature. At the very end, *ff* outbursts alternate with laconic *pp* replies in the strings, then the whole orchestra moves from *pp* to *ff* again within three short measures and the movement romps to its close with a full bar of rapid repeated notes, all on the tonic B-flat—the very repeated notes that have been its trademark from the beginning.

THIRD MOVEMENT: TEMPO DI MENUETTO

As if to give assurance that this movement is nothing like his dynamic Scherzos, whether in traditional three-part form or his extended five-part scheme, Beethoven calls it "Tempo di Menuetto." It is a tempo marking he had used earlier in other ways, and not only for third movements; for example, the intricate first movement of his piano sonata Op. 54, the companion to the "Appassionata," is marked this way. Beethoven knew his way around in the literature of popular dance-genres that were familiar in Viennese ballrooms. In the 1790s he had written sets of "Minuets" (redolent of the older aristocratic world, but long since appropriated and extended by master composers); "Waltzes" (sometimes called "Deutsche" or "Deutsche Tanz"); and "Ländler" or peasant dances. Some of these short dances, for orchestra or for piano, showed considerable charm and craftsmanship, among them the "Minuet in G" of 1795, which became a recital encore.

His portfolio of dance compositions serves as the backdrop to the Eighth Symphony's "Tempo di Menuetto," a movement that is not so much an imitation of Haydn and Mozart as a modernistic reflection upon the masterly third movements that abound in their symphonies and string quartets. In length and layout, this movement is a compact example of the form:

Tempo di Menuetto	‖: a:‖: b–a¹–Codetta:‖
Trio	‖: c–d–c¹:‖
Menuetto da capo	‖: a:‖: b–a¹–Codetta:‖

Opening with heavily marked *sforzando* accents on each beat in the lower strings and then a loud third beat in the trumpets and drums, the initial accompanying figures give way to two graceful and parallel melodic strains in the violins. This opening creates the hybrid effect of waltz and Ländler styles from the outset. In the "b" section of the Menuetto, the first motif of the waltz-like tune alternates in upper and lower strings, with loud sudden attacks on the second beats (instead of the third). Winds and violins then alternate in the melodic motion that ends in diminuendo (somewhat reminiscent of the first movement's way of preparing for its second subject)—and finally the "c" section has a solo bassoon with the melody, but in the subdominant, B-flat major, giving way at last to the tonic. In the last bars there is a close interplay of three elements: *fortissimo* arpeggios in the horns and trumpets; a three-note cadential figure in the strings; and a striking figure in the winds with an offbeat accent.

The Trio, virtually a chamber-music episode within the symphony, recalls instrumental solos in some of Haydn's symphonies. With flutes and oboes *tacet,* two solo horns form a melodic duet over a running accompaniment in triplets, presumably to be played by one cellist.[27] After this section, a solo clarinet takes on a major role in the further unfolding of the Trio's material, forming a woodwind ensemble with the two horns. The entire Trio resides within a dynamic level that is essentially *piano dolce* throughout, rising just once to a modest crescendo and ending softly to prepare the return to the vigorous opening of the Tempo di Menuetto. The whole movement exemplifies simplicity that conceals art.

FINALE: ALLEGRO VIVACE

One baffled early reviewer called it *musica stravagante*. Another, perhaps Antonio Diabelli, said it was "abounding in exuberance, new turns of phrase, surprises, a highly original, curious structure that cannot be compared with any other."[28] This extraordinary finale, which combines features of rondo and modified sonata form, is laid out as follows:

Section	Measures	Description
A	1–90	Exposition: F major–A♭ major; C major
B	91–160	First Development
A	161–266	First Recapitulation: F major–D♭ major; F major
C	267–354	Second Development
A	355–437	Second Recapitulation: F major
Coda	438–502	

As more than one commentator has said, the dramatic use of half-step motions is crucial for the whole course and character of the movement. The first occurs as early as m. 17, when, after the first theme and continuation have started the action in *pianissimo*, a *fortissimo* C-sharp suddenly erupts in the full orchestra. This intrusion of the unexpected C-sharp into the prevailing F major seems at first not to have large-scale consequences, since directly afterwards F major resumes its course. But the C-sharp will obstinately return later in the movement. In the first recapitulation, this same isolated C-sharp comes round again in *fortissimo* at the comparable passage, but again it gives way to F major as it did before. At last, with its third appearance in the second recapitulation, it takes command—now it appears three times in quick succession, at first spelled D-flat, then twice as C-sharp, each time with a slightly different continuation. Then it suddenly wrenches the harmony on to the distant key of F-sharp minor (a half-step above the tonic F major).[29] After this, within a few more measures, the harmony finds it way back to F major where it remains.

For early listeners, such moves were truly *musica stravagante*, as they tried to fathom the sleight of hand by which Beethoven prepares the ear for an expected goal, then deviates at the last minute to a new one. It is true that by our time the harmonic language of Western music has undergone a vast evolution, through the chromaticism of the Romantic period, through extended tonality and through myriad outgrowths broadly grouped under the heading "atonality" in the twentieth century. Such developments might seem to render Beethoven's tonal maneuvers comparatively innocuous to the modern ear, but it remains that his command of form, proportions, thematic content, and dynamics, is still fully capable of seizing modern listeners, arousing their full and devoted attention, and carrying them along to the end.

The story of the intrusive C-sharp and its influence on the movement has been told many times, and there are some observers for whom it is not a master-stroke but a trick in questionable taste. To quote a recent comment:

> There is [a] question whether the C-sharp is to be taken seriously, but there is no question that it disrupts, then warps, then shapes the movement. It is too defiant, however, to be the typical good-humor of Haydn. It is comedy bordering on rage. It is rough, it is crude, it is calculating of the lowest sort. It suggests that the Classical finale *as part of the symphony* [the writer's italics] remained an enigma to Beethoven.[30]

This claim raises more questions than it answers. Anyone who knows something about Beethoven's life knows that he could engage in rough banter that could well be described as "comedy bordering on rage . . . crude [and at times] calculating."[31] His brand of humor was often boorish and extreme, not only with his intimates but with acquaintances as well, and it was symptomatic of a deeply human being who was isolated by deafness, trapped in misery, and completely dedicated to creating his works, whether or not they were understood by the outer world. In the private "Tagebuch," or diary, that he began to keep precisely at the time of writing the Eighth Symphony (1812) and used until 1818, we find such entries as this:

> Submission, deepest submission to your fate, only this can give you the sacrifices— . . . Oh hard struggle!—Do everything that still has to be done to arrange what is necessary for the long journey . . .
>
> You must not be a human being, not for yourself, but only for others; for you there is no longer any happiness except within yourself, in your art.[32]

We sense that the loud, boisterous, and harmonically subversive C-sharps in the finale of the Eighth Symphony have a latent connection to his personality style, a style that emerged not only in his daily dealings with all around him but also in his life in music, in his perpetual improvising at the piano, which linked directly to his sketching and thus to his works.[33]

As for the efficacy of the finale as the completion of this symphony, its quirks and surprises form the culmination of those of the earlier movements. The first movement had its share of unexpected and adventurous moments. The two inner movements, like rare delicacies, convey ironies within their pseudo-retrospective style features. And the finale, in its length, assertive power, and unusual formal structure, as in its eccentric details, resolves all the earlier conundrums while presenting its own.

9

THE NINTH SYMPHONY

LATE BEETHOVEN

By the time Beethoven completed the Ninth Symphony in 1824, he had passed through another phase of transformation, longer and more difficult than his earlier one—in Maynard Solomon's term, a "sea-change." After the public success of *Fidelio* in 1814 and his renewed recognition by the aristocracy of Europe at the Congress of Vienna, Beethoven entered into a comparatively fallow period that lasted until about 1818. He brought out some important individual works during this time, but with nothing like the steady productivity of his middle years. This was a period of deep introspection as he readied himself to move in new directions as a composer. His *Tagebuch* shows him attempting to gain new strength after the Immortal Beloved crisis of 1812, resolving to accept his isolation and endure his emotional difficulties, whatever they might be. In his artistic life he was seeking new paths once again, now looking far back to older models, above all his beloved Bach. After 1818, new forms of mastery were to result in some of his greatest and most profound works, many of them utterly baffling to his contemporaries, technically challenging even to the best performers of his time, and only

Sketches for the "Ode to Joy" melody used in the finale of the Ninth Symphony
(Private collection / Bridgeman Images)

gradually accepted as monumental achievements. Fugue and counterpoint, which he had always used to deepen the complexity of his dynamic works, now became central techniques for entire movements, especially as finales of multi-movement instrumental compositions. The capstone of his fugal imagination is the *Grosse Fuge*, originally intended as the finale of his Quartet Op. 130, but later separated from the quartet to become an independent composition, published as his Op. 133. At its first performance a reviewer said it was "incomprehensible, like Chinese."[1] In the twentieth century Igor Stravinsky declared that

> at eighty I have found new joy in Beethoven, and the Great Fugue now seems to me—it was not always so—a perfect miracle . . . it must stand by itself, this absolutely contemporary piece of music that will be contemporary forever.[2]

The complexities of late Beethoven can never be adequately intuited, let alone understood, without the repeated experience of hearing and pondering the characteristic features of his earlier works in the genres that meant the most to him—the piano sonata, the string quartet, and the symphony. Despite much modern criticism aimed at separating the "late style" decisively from his earlier achievements—partly, it seems, in order to link the innovations of late Beethoven with those of the twentieth-century avant-garde—the many progressive features in his late works really need to be seen as the outcome of a lifetime of desire to move forward, of relentless self-criticism of whatever it was he had just accomplished, of a restless struggle to achieve works that would reflect the "freedom and progress" to which he aspired.

Still, generations of listeners have felt that many of the late works, especially the quartets, belong to a more rarefied sphere than even his best achievements of the earlier years—and I will argue that this is equally true of the Ninth Symphony. Though much recent criticism, following Adorno, has taken the position that the Ninth Symphony lies outside the aesthetic of "the late style"—in Adorno's words, it is "not a late work"—this view is based on much too narrow an understanding of the scope of that style and of the breadth of Beethoven's final phase.[3] The last piano sonatas, the "Diabelli" Variations, and the late quartets show him entering into a domain beyond the range of his earlier accomplishments. Nevertheless, there are pathways below the surface, many of them still to be explored, that show the ways in which his middle-period achievements anticipate aspects of the late style. It is clear from such remarks as the one he made to a violinist about the Op. 59 Quartets—"they are not for you, they are for a later age"—that Beethoven was already thinking of the future in the middle years.

Both the *Missa Solemnis* and the Ninth Symphony assimilate features that arise from his profound engagement with Bachian counterpoint—but both were also predicated on his belief that his role as an artist was to speak as a modern composer, to maintain the importance of high artistic expression in his own time. Beethoven's letter to Rudolph of 1821, for whose installation the *Missa Solemnis* had been intended and to whom he inscribed it with the words, "from the heart, may it go to the heart," tells as much:

> There is nothing higher than to approach the Godhead more nearly than other mortals and by means of that contact to spread the rays of the Godhead through the human race.[4]

In the Ninth Symphony, when seen not merely as the vehicle for the "Ode to Joy" but as his largest symphonic project, he does not merely set to music Schiller's tremendous gesture of love for humanity— "Oh ye millions I embrace you, Here's a kiss to the whole world!"— but joins with Schiller to express his Utopian faith in mankind and in the power of art to redeem the world. No matter how far he had come from the early years, we remember that in a heartfelt letter of 1812, written to a young girl whom we only know as "Emily M.," Beethoven had urged her to "persevere, do not only practice your art . . . for only art and science can raise men to the level of gods."[5]

Another clue to Beethoven's outlook in these years is found in an earlier letter to Rudolph from July 1819. He was then in the thick of work on the "Diabelli" Variations, which had been commissioned a few months earlier, and had also begun composing the *Missa Solemnis*. Just before writing this letter Beethoven had been visiting the Archduke's music library, looking at older music, evidently of the 17th and early 18th centuries. Reflecting on past and present, he writes:

> the older masters do us double service, since there is generally real artistic value in their works (among them only the German Handel and Sebastian Bach had genius). But in the world of art, as in the whole of creation, freedom and progress are the main objectives.
>
> If we moderns have not the same solidity as our ancestors, still the refinement of our manners has in many ways enlarged our sphere of action.[6]

Though the names of Bach and Handel appear only once in the *Tagebuch,* along with Gluck, Haydn, and Mozart as deeply admired predecessors, there is no doubt that Bach, and to some degree Handel, had become Beethoven's guiding stars.[7] He had known the *Well-Tempered Clavier* from early childhood, had repeatedly acquired Bach's music as more of it became available during his lifetime—and now in the full tide of his late maturity he was coming to grips with Bach's mastery in integrating contrapuntal complexity with expressivity, albeit in a range of older compositional styles that Beethoven now felt he could master but also bring into modernity.

TOWARD THE NINTH SYMPHONY

In 1817, in ill health and dealing with the problematic guardianship of his nephew Karl, Beethoven expressed a desperate wish to escape from Vienna. He nourished the hope of traveling to London, from where had come an invitation to write two symphonies. He writes in the *Tagebuch*,

> There is no other way to save yourself except to leave here; only through this can you again lift yourself to the heights of your art, whereas here you are submerged in vulgarity. Only a symphony— and then away, away, away.[8]

London beckoned as a European capital where his works were being well received and where honors awaited him. His English admirers included the conductor Sir George Smart, the pianist Charles Neate, and his former pupil Ferdinand Ries, who had been in England since 1813 and was now a director of the Philharmonic Society. It was Ries who had written to Beethoven on 9 June 1817, formally inviting him to come to London "next winter" [i.e., the winter of 1817–18], offering a substantial fee for "two grand symphonies for the Philharmonic Society." Ries also assured him that "friends will receive you with open arms."[9] Beethoven replied enthusiastically on 9 July 1817, accepting the proposal to write "two grand symphonies, completely newly composed"—even though he must have known he could hardly expect to fulfill it.[10]

In the event, matters took a different turn as other opportunities arose. He made a few sketches for the Ninth Symphony in 1818 but abandoned all thoughts of a journey to London. Instead, as the guardianship struggle continued, he began work on the "Hammerklavier" sonata, originally meant to celebrate Rudolph's name-day. With this sonata the great achievements of his last years effectively began.

In 1819, publisher Anton Diabelli requested that Beethoven write a single variation on Diabelli's own waltz theme, along with similar variations by "the leading composers and virtuosi" of Austria. Beethoven's characteristic response was not to write a single short piece like all the others, but to embark on a lengthy and pathbreaking set of variations.[11] But the Diabelli project was then cut off in midstream by a still more demanding task—to compose a Mass for the Archduke's installation as Archbishop of Olmütz in Moravia. Begun in 1819 and intended for the ceremony in March 1820, the *Missa Solemnis* was not finished until two years later. By then still other projects had come along, above all the three piano sonatas Opp. 109, 110, and 111 (in 1820–21), after which the "Diabelli" Variations were finally completed in 1823.

It was only in that year, then, that Beethoven was finally ready to resume work on the D minor symphony that had been in his mind for two decades. Despite all obstacles—nephew troubles, illnesses, and perpetual dreams of still other works that he might perhaps undertake—including operas—he now settled down to work on the Ninth. As Beethoven conceived it in the largest terms, this symphony would combine two long-held ambitions—to write a symphony in D minor, and to make a setting of Schiller's ode *An die Freude*. These notions had lain dormant for many years, but now might be merged in one large work that would further revolutionize the symphonic genre.

SKETCHES: AN OVERVIEW

Up to now, it has been generally accepted that Beethoven first sketched ideas for a D minor symphony (thus named) in 1811–12, along with his work on the Seventh and Eighth. But a much earlier entry from the early spring of 1804 survives in the *Eroica* Sketchbook, although it has only recently surfaced in the Beethoven literature.[12] It is a short entry marked "Sinfonia in D moll," in 6/8 meter on two staves, with a bass D in the first measure and a rising arpeggiated D-minor theme in the upper line. This entry of early 1804 looks at first like a passing thought but it holds the seeds of later growth (see Example 6, page 103).

This fragmentary sketch for a "D minor symphony" emerged only a few months after Beethoven had completed all his early drafts for the *Eroica* symphony and the "Waldstein" Sonata, and shortly after he wrote down his first ideas for the Fifth Symphony, as well as those that later developed into the Sixth. Thereafter, the next clear-cut idea for a D minor symphony came in 1812, when it would have been a pendant to the Seventh and Eighth. The few sketches he made then are interesting but do not yet clearly anticipate the thematic material he would eventually use in the Ninth. Still, the proximity of this imagined symphony to his work on the Eighth, with its mixture of traditional and progressive features, is suggestive.

In 1815–16, a year of experimentation, Beethoven was sketching ideas that were actually to find their way into the Ninth. The most striking is a short D minor phrase, marked "Fuge" (Fugue), which clearly prefigures the main theme of the Scherzo of the Ninth, though it ends, curiously, with the remark, "Ende langsam" (end slowly).[13] On the verbal side, in the same sketchbook, we find him musing over a symphony that will begin in a special way. He writes:

> A symphony that can begin at first with only four voices—2 Violins, Violas, and Basses—and in among them *forte* [entries] with other voices, and if possible each of the other instruments entering one after the other.[14]

This entry shows that his way of opening the Ninth, with its long-held open fifths and gradual accumulation of instruments, was in his mind before he developed the musical material by which he would realize it.[15] Though much remains to be done to elucidate the sketches that survive for the Ninth, it looks as if he began to formulate ideas for the first movement in 1816, kept on developing them in 1817, and by 1818 had the basic thematic material for the first movement clearly in hand.[16] Then came the interruptions of 1819–22, above all the Diabelli project and the *Missa Solemnis*, which delayed his return to the symphony but probably infused it with new ideas. He eventually completed the Ninth in February 1824, about three months before its famous premiere on 7 May 1824 in the Kärntnerthor Theater in Vienna. This was the occasion on which at the end of the performance, with the crowd cheering, the deaf composer had to be turned around by one of the singers because he could not hear the applause.

A PROJECTED SECOND SYMPHONY?

A lingering question about the Ninth concerns a projected second symphony to accompany it and how firmly Beethoven may have nurtured such an idea. The primary pieces of evidence are these:

1. a verbal description that Beethoven wrote down in 1818 on a leaf containing sketches for the "Hammerklavier" sonata;[17]
2. sketchbook entries of 1822–23 that seem to embody another, quite different, idea for a second symphony.[18]

Let us consider these two items separately.

The 1818 verbal description of a symphony in the "ancient modes"
The entry reads as follows:

> Adagio Cantique—Pious song in a symphony in the ancient Modes—Lord God we praise thee—alleluia—either by itself alone or as introduction to a fugue. Perhaps the whole second Symphony might be characterized in this way, whereby the vocal parts would enter in the last movement or already in the Adagio. The orchestral

violins etc. are to be increased tenfold in the last movement. Or the Adagio would be repeated in a certain way in the last movement, whereby the singing voices would enter one by one—in the Adagio a text from Greek myth, a *Cantique Ecclesiastique*—in the Allegro a celebration of Bacchus.

Beethoven explicitly refers here to a "second symphony." Clearly he thinks of it as a radically new kind of work, with its "pious song in a symphony in the ancient modes;" with its vocal parts in the finale "or already in the Adagio;" with his fantastic notion of a "tenfold increase in the orchestral violins etc." in the last movement; and with the idea that the singing voices would come in one by one.

The idea of having the voices come in one after another harks back to his sketchbook entry of 1815–16, in which he had broached the idea of the instruments entering in this way. Of these ideas from 1818, only two eventually remained, one of them being the concept of a choral finale (but now with Schiller's Ode, not a text from Greek myth or "a celebration of Bacchus"). The other, of a "pious song in the ancient modes," resurfaced later in the A-minor Quartet Opus 132 with its "Holy Song of Thanksgiving by a Convalescent in the Lydian Mode." There is no evidence that this colorful description of a modal symphony ever advanced any further but the possibility of a different second symphony lingered for a while longer.[19]

The 1822 Concept Sketches; for a Second Symphony?

In 1822, Beethoven apparently returned to the idea of a second symphony, this time not with a verbal description but with a series of musical concept sketches. His plan now was to open with a slow introduction in E-flat major and in 2/4 meter, followed by a "rapid" (Beethoven writes "*geschwind*") Allegro in C minor in 6/8.

This slow introduction, which underwent some further changes, has some melodic affinity to the first theme of the Adagio of the

Ninth in finished form, and in further sketches Beethoven revised it and added more ideas for other movements, including one that resembles the Scherzo theme of the Ninth.[20] These sketches from 1822 also contain a brief reference to Schiller's Ode when Beethoven mentions an "*alla marcia introduzion[e]*" and then writes the words "perhaps also the chorus [singing] Freude schöne [Götterfunken]" (but here without any music).[21] A real surprise is that this material, some of which found its way into the Ninth, was to end with the Andante moderato theme in D major that became the contrasting theme in the eventual slow movement.

How important are these sketches of 1822 for Beethoven's conception of the Ninth in final form? The answer, here as elsewhere, depends on our interest in deepening understanding of the final artistic product through knowledge of how Beethoven conceived his ideas and elaborated them, some sense of what the range of his vision was at the early stages of the process and how it changed as the work grew in his hands. Although much remains to be known about the background of the Ninth, we can agree with Nicholas Marston's conclusion about the eventual slow movement themes, that

> the compositional origins of the Adagio molto theme [the first theme of the slow movement] lie in the first movement of an unfinished symphony from autumn 1822, and that even when Beethoven had taken this material over into the Ninth he did not intend to combine it with the eventual Andante moderato [theme].[22]

Looking ahead, we can see that, in the final flowering of the Adagio of the Ninth, Beethoven was determined to have the contrasting qualities of these two themes as a basic formal condition—that is, the first theme in very slow tempo in B-flat major in 4/4, and the other theme in Andante moderato, D major, 3/4—and that he then combined variations on the first theme with the beautiful second theme stated twice as a Rondo-like episode.

A CHORAL OR INSTRUMENTAL FINALE?

Although it remains speculative we have no reason to believe that the idea of setting Schiller's Ode ever truly left Beethoven's mind. This is probably true even if at a late stage he wrote out some sketches for a "*Finale instromentale.*" As has been pointed out, it is sometimes hard to tell whether his ideas for an instrumental finale are meant as a new movement altogether, are entirely provisional, or are thoughts jotted down about the instrumental introduction preceding the arrival of the vocal forces.[23]

At all events, the theme he considered for an instrumental finale, and wrote out three times, later emerged in the finale of the Quartet Op. 132.[24] As these sketches cannot be dated closely, we cannot be sure that Beethoven was seriously considering abandoning the idea of the choral finale at a very late stage; in the absence of evidence this is possible but far from certain.

My own impression, based on my reading of all the available musical and biographical evidence, is that the notion of a choral finale using Schiller's text remained his fundamental aim, and that as the whole symphony became fleshed out, it must have become clear that this movement would be a monumental completion of the earlier movements and a culmination of his life-work as a composer of symphonies. In its final form, it became an artistic expression of mankind's desire to reach a Utopian plane of brotherhood under a benign God. It has affinities to the inscription he had recently attached to the "Dona nobis pacem" at the end of the *Missa Solemnis*, a "Prayer for inner and outer peace." But in the Ninth Symphony finale, Beethoven is not setting the language of the liturgy but that of the secular poet he most admired, writing in the vernacular and in a classic poetic form brought down to modern times. He joins Schiller in expressing the hope that "all men shall become brothers"—a message of belief in the ideal of human equality that had reverberated through the revolutionary writings of the late eighteenth century, including the American Declaration of Independence in 1776 and the French Declaration of the Rights of Man in 1789. It had become an important part of Beethoven's vision that these values might be restored to human consciousness through art.

BEETHOVEN AND SCHILLER'S ODE

Friedrich Schiller's "An die Freude" had been an early poem, originally written in 1785, when the poet was twenty-five, published in 1786 and revised in 1803. Ostensibly an imitation of the classical ode, with stanzas and choruses, it celebrates "Joy" as the personified "daughter of Elysium" whose magic can unite both individuals and peoples who are thrust apart by societal conventions, and, implicitly, by differences of every kind. Broadening his vision, the poet in the first Chorus of the "Ode" ecstatically proclaims, "Be embraced, oh you millions—here's a kiss to the entire world," and brings his image of human brotherhood under the all-embracing wing of a benevolent God ("Brothers—above the starry canopy, A loving Father must dwell").

The "Ode" is richly sprinkled with Enlightenment sentiments, and radicals in the 1780s could read it as a veiled endorsement of political upheaval. It would have been especially timely in 1789, when the French revolutionaries shook the world by overthrowing the monarchy in the name of liberty, equality, and fraternity. In 1785, Schiller's original seventh line had been "Beggars shall become brothers of Princes" (*Bettler werden Fürstenbrüder*) but in 1803 he changed it to the benign, "All men shall become brothers" (*Alle Menschen werden Brüder*). This was a safer sentiment in the period after the bloody Reign of Terror and amidst the long wars between France and the European coalition powers. Still, some of his contemporaries, including Beethoven, remembered that line. Schiller also dropped a final verse that hailed "Salvation from the chains of tyrants" and also cut out a vision of the dead awakening and the forgiveness of sins.[25]

Beethoven revered Schiller and knew his works well, including his dramas. He might have been aware that Schiller's initial support of the French Revolution had fallen off sharply in 1793, after the execution of Louis XVI, as reflected in his aesthetic writings. Among these was the essay *On the Aesthetic Education of Man* (1794), in which Schiller shifted towards his famous dictum that "Beauty is nothing else than freedom in appearance." In effect he was rejecting the idea of the violent overthrow of regimes, seemed to regard the French Revolution as a failure, and had shifted his gaze towards a Utopian future.[26] It is not difficult to find parallels for this viewpoint in Beethoven's letters and aesthetic statements, in which a vision of Elysium remains unmistakably present as he ponders the world around him, feels the miseries that perpetually beset him despite his great career, and senses the disillusionment of having lived through the years of the French Revolution followed by the Terror, then the Napoleonic hegemony, and finally the repressive Austrian regime under Metternich, which took power after 1815.

When Schiller wrote the "Ode" in 1785, Beethoven was the young prodigy of Bonn's musical life, already ambitious for a great career. By 1787, he had gained further ground through his journey to Vienna to visit Mozart, increasing his visibility—witness the two cantatas of 1790, one for the funeral of Joseph II and the other for the accession of Leopold II. The breadth of his early creative activity is evident both in finished works and in his sketch portfolio, both of which included songs, and it was in character for him to plan a setting of Schiller's Ode, of which more than forty settings were made by various composers.[27] In a letter from 1793, a Schiller disciple in Bonn, Bartholomaeus Fischenich, wrote to Schiller's wife, Charlotte, sending along another early Beethoven song. He noted that the composer proposes also to set Schiller's "Freude" and indeed strophe by strophe. I expect something perfect, for as far as I know him he is wholly devoted to the great and the sublime.[28]

This message served to introduce a brilliant young composer to Schiller's circle and it could have implied that, if he is to set it "strophe by strophe," he is in sympathy with the revolutionary cast of the "Ode" as it was then known and published.[29] Five years later, Beethoven's sketches show fragmentary settings of a single line from the "Ode," "Muss ein lieber Vater wohnen." We then have to wait until 1811–12 for evidence of his continued interest in setting the poem, which is then expressed in more developed ways. The prose entry among his ideas for what became the *Namensfeier* Overture (for the reigning Emperor Franz I) contains this remark:

"Freude schöner Götterfunken Tochter / Overture ausarbeiten"
(Joy, sweet spark of the Gods, to be worked out as an overture)

and, significantly, with an inversion of the words "beggars" and "princes:"

abgerissene Sätze wie Fürsten sind Bettler u.s.w. nicht das Ganze"
(disconnected lines like "princes are beggars," etc., not the whole thing)

Accordingly, it was at the time of the Seventh and Eighth Symphonies that Beethoven was thinking about incorporating Schiller's verses into an instrumental work, and from here on the idea of returning to Schiller's poem (now in its toned-down version of 1803) seems to begin to merge with his thoughts about a new symphony.

MASS AND SYMPHONY

In March 1819, hearing of Rudolph's election as Archbishop, Beethoven wrote to him to remark on "what an enlarged sphere of activity is going thereby to be opened to you and to your fine and noble qualities [and to] add my congratulations to the many others that Your Imperial Highness must have received."[30] In the same letter, Beethoven, as Rudolph's severe teacher, criticizes a set of variations that Rudolph had written on a theme Beethoven had given him earlier. Then Beethoven offers to continue to be Rudolph's composition teacher "as . . . time permits." Now comes the larger point:

> Your Imperial Highness can thus create in two ways, both for the happiness and welfare of very many people and also for yourself. For in the present world of monarchs creators of music and benefactors of humanity have hitherto been lacking.

The manner and style are revealing. Rudolph is a member of the imperial house of Austria and has just been raised to a high ecclesiastical post, but Beethoven is telling him that he should not abandon his creative gifts when he becomes Archbishop, because his artistic work is as valuable as his impending career as a church magnate. Soon thereafter, Beethoven writes that "the Austrians are now aware that the spirit of Apollo has come to life again in the Imperial dynasty."[31] The sense of these messages is that art, not social or political power, is the high road to immortality, and that he, Beethoven, can guide Rudolph on that tortuous path.

This image helps us to understand the spirit behind the *Missa Solemnis*, and, by extension, those portions of the Ninth Symphony finale that refer to God and to mankind's search for salvation. Having agreed to write a Mass for this special occasion, Beethoven wants to create a setting on the highest imaginative level, a work of universal importance that will ennoble the genre and in some way form a modern counterpart to Bach's B Minor Mass. All of this came at a time when much church music was under criticism for its adoption of theatrical, that is, operatic, styles, a view declared by E. T. A. Hoffmann in a famous 1814 article.[32] Unlike his earlier Mass in C of 1807, this new Mass offered Beethoven fertile ground in which to employ his increasingly strong interest in older music. The *Missa Solemnis* contains much musical symbolism, using time-honored rhetorical devices in its text-setting of key words and phrases that go back to the Renaissance and the Baroque.[33] And certain symbols, above all that of the Deity, appear both in the Mass and in the Ninth finale.[34]

Behind the Mass are many layers of intention, but Beethoven made two of them explicit. In 1821, he wrote to Rudolph (in the letter quoted earlier) expressing his aim "to spread the rays of the Godhead through the human race." In 1824, he wrote to his friend Johann Andreas Streicher that "my chief aim, when I was composing this grand Mass was to awaken and permanently instill religious feelings not only into the singers but also into the listeners."[35] As Maynard Solomon put it,

> the resulting work [the *Missa Solemnis*] is an amalgam of archaic and modern styles, more deeply rooted in older traditions than any other work of Beethoven's but retaining the grandeur and dynamic thrust of a symphonism growing out of the sonata style.[36]

Beethoven's religious faith finds its highest expression in this Mass. In composing the Ninth Symphony, the roots of which were in his mind while he was so deeply engaged with the Mass over more than four years, he comes to a parallel vision. It is obviously informed by the secular ideals of human brotherhood expressed in Schiller's "Ode" and in the very notion of communal song—but Beethoven's choice of verses from the "Ode," and his treatment of these verses, make clear his belief that the human race can achieve its ideal state, its Elysium, as it recognizes the still higher presence of God. In the most solemn passage of the Ninth finale, for chorus only with no solo voices, he sets this portion of the "Ode to Joy":

> Do you prostrate yourselves, oh you millions?
> Do you sense the Creator, world?
> Seek him beyond the tent of Heaven,
> Above the stars he must surely dwell!

It is not accidental that when Beethoven sets these lines in his finale, he moves from the preceding "Andante maestoso" (beginning "Be embraced, oh you millions/Here's a kiss for the entire world!" etc.) to the slower tempo of "Adagio ma non troppo ma divoto" (Adagio, not too slow, but devout). So far as I know this is the only use of the term "*divoto*" in all his tempo markings. Throughout this section, modal harmonies intermingle with the familiar tonal language of the rest of the finale, and strange juxtapositions of *pianissimo* and *fortissimo* thrust certain words into the foreground, as when the whole chorus suddenly shouts "*Welt*" (world), with rests before and after.[37] And the whole extraordinary passage ends with the choral voices seeking God "above the stars" as they and the whole orchestra, in *pianissimo* and in primarily high registers, sustain a long-held dominant seventh harmony as they declaim the presence of God on high with the words, "He must dwell above the stars" (*Über Sternen muss er wohnen*).[38]

THE NINTH: AN OVERVIEW

The layout of the Ninth Symphony is as follows:

Movement	Key	Meter	Measures
1. Allegro ma non troppo e un poco maestoso	D minor	2/4	547

Movement	Key	Meter	Measures
2. Molto vivace – Presto	D minor	3/4; 2/2	954
3. Adagio molto e cantabile –	B♭ major	4/4; 3/4;	157
Andante moderato		12/8	
4. Finale: Presto –	D minor	Varied	940
Allegro assai –	D major		
Allegro assai vivace –			
Andante maestoso –			
Adagio ma non troppo			
ma divoto –			
Allegro energico e			
sempre ben marcato –			
Allegro ma non tanto –			
Presto –			
Maestoso –			
Prestissimo			

The larger form of the Ninth is obviously still that of the traditional four-movement cycle as Beethoven had inherited it. But any serious approach to this immense work has to reckon with the world-wide appropriation of its "Ode to Joy" melody, which in modern times has attained a life of its own to such an extent that for some people its origins in a symphony written nearly two hundred years ago may come as a merely curious historical fact. Over the past century the Ode has become a popular melody sung at large-scale political and social events, not only as the official anthem of the European Union, but also in its wide use in other countries, including China and Japan. Written and visual media in our time celebrate the uses of the melody in diverse contexts, and some of them, whether spoken or written, often identify their subject not as the "Ode to Joy" but as the "Ninth Symphony" itself, at times making little if any reference to the earlier movements or the symphony as a whole.[39] For present purposes, then, it seems more important than ever to offer a brief overview of the work as a whole, along with a brief look at the Ninth as a realization of Beethoven's aesthetic outlook and as his final statement in this genre.

THE FIRST MOVEMENT

The Introduction and Its Returns

The symphony begins in mystery. A skein of sound emerges out of silence, at first with open fifths that are indeterminate as to key, though suggesting A minor, created by two horns with low-register violins and cellos, all in *pianissimo*. The movement is marked 2/4, "Allegro ma non troppo e un poco maestoso" but only gradually does any sense of form and shape come into being as fragmentary descending two-note figures begin to dimly outline four-bar units.[40] A growing body of orchestral sound emerges, moving from *pianissimo* to *fortissimo,* adding instruments in successively higher registers, until at the last moment the bassoons move to a low D that signals D minor just before the great theme breaks out in all its force. It feels something like the process of composition itself, from premonition to embodiment.

Although the pre-thematic opening of the symphony is indeed an introduction, opinions differ as to whether it should be heard as a prologue or if, as Tovey said, it "plunges us into the middle of things."[41] In a sense it is both, and it is enlightening to find that in Beethoven's earlier drafts, he began not with the descending main theme itself but with the short fragments that precede its first full statement, showing that the idea of building up the theme from its particles and having the instruments enter one by one was fixed in his mind from very early on.[42] Furthermore, the larger dramatic shape of the first movement is established from the beginning by the gradual growth that connects the "introduction" (bars 1–16) to the gigantic principal theme, with its descent through the elements of a D minor triad plus the powerful closing figure that ends the theme with the descending fifth that lands on the tonic D (see Web Example U).

What happens next is revolutionary in Beethoven's exposition procedures. Instead of restating the main theme after its first appearance, as in the *Eroica* first movement, or proceeding at once to a transition that will prepare for the second thematic group, Beethoven soon returns to the open fifths of the Introduction, again in *pianissimo* but now on D and A, the open fifth of the tonic chord. Once more he builds up the sound-structure from a low to a higher register, bringing in the instruments incrementally. Again he creates an enormous crescendo from *pianissimo* to an immense *fortissimo,* whereupon the main theme returns in full force, but now in the key of B-flat major.

And so the larger shape of the first movement springs from this initial contrast of two large statements—the first, which starts with a strangely ambiguous passage of indeterminate character and culminates in the main theme in D minor; the second, which restates the passage on a different tonal level and again arrives at the main theme, but now in a major key. The juxtaposition of these two keys, D minor and B-flat major, will play out over the drama of the first movement. To these is added an eventual promise of D major that is ultimately fulfilled, long afterwards, as the key of the "Ode to Joy."[43]

From here on, the movement unfolds in complex ways, leading through new transitional figures to its main array of contrasting subjects, some of which incorporate rhythmic references to the introduction and the main theme, and some that do not. The individual thematic ideas are often highly complex in their contour, articulation, stress patterns, and open-endedness, more like themes from chamber music than like those in most symphonies. Firm, clear cadences are not found except at the moments of strongest structural definition.

The freedom of Beethoven's approach to form is nowhere clearer than at the end of the exposition, where for the first time in all his symphonic first movements we find no double bar and no repeat of the exposition.[44] Instead, he opens the development section by returning once again to the murmuring introduction, again on A and E, which momentarily suggests that he might, in fact, be observing the traditional exposition repeat. But now the harmonic path deviates towards the key of G minor, from which the full development section begins.[45]

And so the vast unfolding of the first movement emerges from the contrast of the mysterious introduction and the main theme that follows—a theme that seems to be carved in granite—and then from the repetition of this same contrasting pair, with a change of key. The development opens with still another return of the introduction, now modified as it continues, and leading in a new direction. All of this prepares the thoughtful listener for what will happen at the recapitulation, after the development section has run its course. This course includes a fugal episode and a build-up of energy as Beethoven prepares the arrival of the introduction at the recapitulation, where once it returns in a completely transformed state.

"Transformed state" is putting it mildly. The recapitulation begins with the tonic chord of D major, *fortissimo* in the full orchestra with the tympani thundering—yet it is not a rooted D major chord, but is in its first inversion, with F-sharp in the bass, the lowest strings striding up and down through three octaves, and the winds and brass sustaining their chord tones with all their might. It is a passage unparalleled in fury and power in the whole history of orchestral music up to this time. We remember Ries's remark in 1803 when Beethoven played the *Eroica* for him at the piano—"heaven and earth will tremble when it is performed."

This tremendous passage at the recapitulation has aroused vivid metaphors. Beethoven's early critic A. B. Marx likened it to a "horrifying phantom;" Tovey saw it as a "catastrophic return" in which we see the "heavens on fire."[46] In recent times, as politics and ideology have come to dominate much commentary about music, as in the "new musicology," some have taken this passage to represent the power and violence that they associate with Beethoven's work in the large, accepting the premise that all art, and its aesthetic and analytical interpretation, is intrinsically a matter of ideology, whether its practitioners know it or not.[47]

About this famous recapitulation Leo Treitler eloquently refers to "the shock of being now pulled into the opening with great force, instead of having it wash over us." And David Levy writes that "never before had a composer destabilized this critical formal juncture [the recapitulation] as does Beethoven with his first-inversion D-major triad . . . never before had a major chord sounded so apocalyptic!"[48]

If we hear this remarkable recapitulation not as an isolated event but within the movement as a whole, we gain further insight. The main point here is that this *fortissimo* version of the introduction is the fourth and last appearance of the opening passage. The first two statements of the bare fifths, at the beginning of the movement, had begun in *pianissimo* and culminated in *fortissimo* with the main theme (each time in a different key). The third statement opens the development section, again beginning softly and remaining at a soft dynamic level for a very long time, including the return of the main theme in G minor. But now, at this gigantic return at the recapitulation, the passage is as different in force, dynamic level, harmony, orchestration, and character as Beethoven can make it. And so it can and should be heard as the immense culmination of the three earlier statements—that what was once a mystery is now an immense uproar. When the main theme now returns, it continues in *fortissimo*, but is also undergirded in the bass by a rising version of its intervals in contrary motion, a counter-statement which moves upward as the theme moves downward.[49] To sum up, the introductions form a series of related statements that are spread out over the whole movement, each beginning a principal section. It will turn out that the same is true of the symphony as a whole—that each of its four movements opens with an introduction, something like the four acts of a drama—but also that each introduction is integrated into the movement as a whole.

We can hardly help associating the immense outpouring of the first movement recapitulation with what we know of Beethoven's turbulent inner world, so strongly evident in his erratic life as well as in his letters and in the *Tagebuch*, in which for so long he had expressed his anguish over his deafness and his recurrent thoughts of suicide. Consider this passage from the *Tagebuch*:

> He who is afflicted with a malady which he not only cannot change, but which little by little brings him closer to death and without which his life would have lasted longer, should consider that he could have perished even more quickly through assassination or other causes. O happy, who only for— [left incomplete].[50]

And in this passage from the letter to the "Immortal Beloved," in which he mourns her absence and writes:

> My heart is full of so many things to say to you—ah—there are moments when I feel that speech amounts to nothing at all—[51]

Second Movement: *Molto vivace*

Especially striking in Beethoven's late style is the breadth of imagination he brings to his Scherzi, the movements most constrained by tradition in their larger form, meter, and regularity of rhythm and phrase-structure. Though by now Beethoven had largely abandoned the term "Scherzo," he kept to the basic lineaments of the genre and for the most part kept it in its traditional place between the slow movement and the finale. That it stands as the second movement in the Ninth, with the Adagio to follow, is new in his symphonies, although he had done it in the Quartet Opus 59, No. 1, the "Archduke" Trio, Opus 97; and the two recent piano sonatas Opp. 106 and 110. In each of these, the re-positioning of the slow movement allows him to forge an expressive bridge to the finale as the slow movement ends.[52]

His late Scherzi are typically in very rapid tempo, can vary from minuscule (e.g., the Quartet Op. 130) to enormous (the present movement), and are either in traditional three-part or in five-part form.[53] That the Ninth Symphony Scherzo is in three-part form does not prevent it from being the longest such movement that he had ever written or was ever to write, more than double the length of the Scherzo of the Seventh Symphony if all its repeats are observed. His marking here, "Molto vivace," signals a tempo perhaps a little faster than the "Vivace" of the Scherzo of the Quartet Opus 135, perhaps not quite as fast as the "Presto" of the quartets Opp. 130 and 131.

Its scope is not merely a matter of length, but of concentration of means extended over a long time-span. It is as if Beethoven wants to give this Scherzo much the same stature as the first movement, even if it cannot have its complexity of discourse. One way he achieves this is by adopting a sonata-form plan with a C-major second group, then contrasting it with a much shorter D-major Trio (2/2, Presto) of a completely different character. He follows custom by repeating the Scherzo in full, but replaces its original coda with a new one. At the end, he makes a dramatic stroke in which he feints a return of the Trio, then cuts it off abruptly in mid-phrase, inserts a bar of rest, and ends with three *ff* cadential bars—the same ones with which he had started the Trio when it first appeared. The attentive listener will readily hear that these cadential bars use the same two descending notes, A and D, that started the Scherzo and that hark back still further, to the opening of the whole symphony.[54]

Another way in which Beethoven deepens the substance is to open the exposition of the Scherzo with a five-voice fugue on the opening four-bar theme. Fugal writing had been a special technique as used in the classical period, but in the world of late Beethoven it takes on importance, not only in his fugal finales but in many other works. We cannot forget that behind this symphony stand the immense contra-puntal textures of the Gloria and Credo of the *Missa Solemnis*.[55]

As every movement of this symphony must have an introduction, that of the Scherzo sets the stage in its famous eight-bar opening ges-ture, in which the pitches of the D minor triad appear in descending order with a four-note dactylic figure but with unprecedented rhyth-mic discontinuity.[56] The first two statements are interrupted by rests; the third, with F, is placed in unexpectedly low register in the tim-pani; and the final figure on D is enunciated by virtually the whole orchestra, followed by two more bars of rest.

The timpani's role in the introduction signals its later importance, especially in the development section, where Beethoven constructs a long section headed "Ritmo di tre battute" (rhythm of three-bar units) in which the timpani has a leading role, and its presence con-tinues to be felt as the phrase-structure reverts to four-bar units. Beyond all else, the listener is caught up in the headlong motion of the Scherzo from start to finish, which pounds out its dactylic rhythms throughout except when it gives way to the more measured duple meter of the Trio, after which it resumes its manic forward motion in the Scherzo da capo until at the very end, the final inter-ruption slams the door shut.

Third Movement: Adagio molto e cantabile

After the deeply tragic first movement and the dynamic Scherzo, we enter a domain of deep melodic beauty, slow time, and all that

Beethoven meant by the word *cantabile*.[57] The choice of key, B-flat major, is an island of repose from the tonal storms, mainly in minor, that dominated up to this point. The contrasting tonal motions in this third movement, as they expand through modulation, are to other major keys—first D major and, later, G major for the "second theme" in Andante; then E-flat major and the distant C-flat major for the excursion late in the movement. The avoidance of minor-mode elements is dimly reminiscent of the "Pastoral" Symphony, prior to its storm, but the atmosphere in this Adagio is that of a cosmos of musical thought and feeling in which melodic utterance is of the essence all the way through. Beethoven is too little appreciated as a melodic composer because of the powerful developmental character of so much of his music, but in fact, as he wrote in a letter of 1825, his basic feeling was that "melody must always be given priority above all else."[58]

Views differ as to the form of this movement. To Schenker it is a "variation movement, albeit one of special structure;" to Tovey it is a "Theme with Alternative and Variations;" to Levy it is a "Sonata-rondo with varied reprises;" and to Nicholas Cook it is a special kind of "double variation."[59] I see it as a free adaptation of the alternating variations scheme that Haydn had employed in some of his late works, notably the "Drum-roll" Symphony No. 103. Earlier, Beethoven had used the alternation of two primary themes in masterly ways in the Fifth Symphony Andante and in his E-flat-major Piano Trio Opus 70, No. 2; later, he would give it his most personal imprint in the A-minor Quartet, Opus 132, in the "Holy Song of Thanksgiving," where the main theme twice alternates with a D-major theme marked "Feeling new strength."

From what is presently known of the genesis of this movement, it appears that Beethoven worked intensively on the Adagio in 1823, after his preliminary work on the Scherzo. He had to develop the first theme through several stages, while the beautiful alternative theme, always in 3/4 and Andante, was fully formed from the start. The further elaborations of the main theme, when it returns at later points in the home tonic, are beautifully crafted figural variations. They form another embodiment of Beethoven's deep love of writing slow-movement variations in late works, among them the piano sonata Op. 111, the slow-tempo variations in the "Diabelli" Variations, and the inner movements of the quartets Opus 127, 131, and 135.

The great surprise here is the long passage that stands between the second presentation of the "alternative" theme (in G major) and the last variation on the main theme. This section, beginning in E-flat major, wanders into the remote key of C-flat major before finding its way back to the home tonic of B-flat major for the next section. Its orchestral sound is like no other. It starts with the opening of the main theme in a solo clarinet supported by lower winds and then the leading voice becomes a single horn (for some reason, the fourth horn player). This passage is unprecedented in Beethoven's orchestral works—as Levy writes of it, "its otherworldly beauty seems to shield the listener from all possible harm."[60]

Berlioz wrote that, as great and comprehensible as Beethoven might be in his fast-tempo movements, his Adagios (and he meant those in the piano sonatas and chamber music as well) are like "extra-human meditations."[61] Alongside this one, Berlioz might well have been thinking of the slow movements of the Fourth Symphony; the "Emperor" Concerto; the Quartet in E-flat, Opus 74; the Violin Sonata in G, Opus 96; and the Piano Trio in B-flat Major, Opus 97 ("Archduke")—all of which evoke what Wordsworth called "thoughts that do often lie too deep for tears."

The Choral Finale

Though it may be the most thoroughly discussed movement in Beethoven's symphonies, not only by virtue of the "Ode to Joy" melody, the choral finale remains ever open to new insights. The movement stems from multiple strands which converge here in an unprecedented way. To build the finale, Beethoven had to reconcile its role as structural completion with its unusual form and content as an instrumental-vocal hybrid. He had to find a way to construct a dramatic narrative by which he could justify the introduction of voices, place the "Freude" theme in its proper poetic context and develop its variations as well as provide the main contrasting theme for the religious choruses ("Seid umschlungen Millionen!"). And he had to frame the whole effectively by combining these two primary themes in a climactic closing section of great length and eloquence.

These are only the broadest issues that Beethoven confronted, and he labored hard and long over the macro-structure of the finale and over every one of its components, including the melodic form of the Ode to Joy theme itself. Some of these efforts have been elucidated by earlier commentators but even now the vast bulk of the sketch material for the finale has yet to be fully collected, transcribed, and made known. Still, we can paint a broad picture, even if many details remain to be filled in.

A PRELIMINARY PLAN FOR THE INTRODUCTION AND WHAT IT TELLS US

Beethoven's primary work on the finale took place in the summer of 1823.[62] His sketchbooks show him completing his earlier sketches for the melody of the Ode to Joy and working to find a convincing way of introducing the vocal parts into this symphonic finale. A remarkable early document of this process is a preliminary verbal and musical plan that Beethoven wrote down as he pondered the right way of bringing Schiller's text into this movement.[63] This musical-verbal outline is shown in Example 10.

Example 10. Early musical-verbal outline of the introduction to the Ninth Symphony Finale

Source: Berlin Landsberg 8/2, from N II, 190f.

To read this document intelligently—for it is clearly an early, raw, and naive effort to frame the introduction to the finale—we have to accept that, rather than scorn its direct and naive language, as Nottebohm pointed out when he first published it, these passages "were not written for us."[64] They represent Beethoven's first idea of how to open the movement, with a dialogue between the orchestra and the solo tenor voice. It begins with the "horror fanfare." Then the Tenor proclaims that "today is a solemn day" that should be celebrated with song. Then come a set of brief orchestral reminiscences of the earlier three movements, each of which is rejected by the tenor in turn, with words written by Beethoven. The tenor declares that the short first movement excerpt reminds us of our despair and that "something more pleasing is what I require." After the Scherzo excerpt the tenor sings, "Oh, no! Not this one either, it is not better but only somewhat more lively." And then after the Adagio excerpt, the tenor declines the slow movement theme, saying that "this too is too sweet, we need something more animated." And at last, when the "Ode" melody appears, the tenor exults—"This is it! Yes, now it has been found!" Thus each such rejection prepares the way for the "Ode" melody, and each short verbal phrase offers a moment of insight, however simple in expression, into Beethoven's way of characterizing the first three movements of the Ninth Symphony in relation to the finale, and his exultation on arriving at the melody that can carry Schiller's message.

The whole long sketch constitutes the basic model for what Beethoven later did when he decided to have a double introduction in the final version—the first introduction purely instrumental, the second with the solo tenor. In the first introduction, the cellos and basses, in effect, intone segments of recitative after each quotation from the earlier movements. These passages in the lower strings have the character of virtual speech. Then, after the "Ode" melody and its first variations have been launched by the orchestra, the Tenor voice dramatically steps on to the stage with his famous words, "Oh friends, not these sounds . . ." The rest of the finale then unfolds as a virtual cantata, with solo and choral voices working their way through the remaining variations of the "Ode" melody, introducing the "Seid umschlungen, Millionen" choral section, with its mysteries, then combining the two great melodies in a double fugue and ending with a gigantic peroration.

THE "ODE TO JOY" MELODY

The melody, Beethoven's most famous single tune, went through stages of gestation similar to so many of his thematic ideas in years past. In a fascinating study of its evolution, Robert Winter distinguished as many as nineteen stages in the "hammering out of this synthetic folk tune."[65] I offer an early version of the melody in Web Example V.

Some broad observations can be made from even these few examples. Beethoven's consistent aim is to construct a melody whose simplicity and strength make it memorable and easy to sing. It falls readily into four-bar phrases; the whole tune uses just the span of a single octave and moves essentially in stepwise motion through the scale-steps of D major. It maintains a steady quarter-note motion almost throughout, which allows for text-setting that brings one note per syllable, with only three tiny eighth-note pairs that are tucked in within the second part of the tune. There is only one lightly syncopated accented rhythmic shift in the whole melody, precisely on the first syllable of the all-important phrase, "Al-le Men-schen wer-den Brü-der" (for the sung melody in final form see Web Example W).

Some have associated the melody with the popular style of the high Classical period. Beethoven, like Haydn and Mozart, was well aware of popular music and music-making and had a close acquaintance with European folksong traditions as well as high-classical compositions that made use of simple and clear melodies. His settings of folksongs included not only arrangements of Scottish, Irish, and Welsh songs, but those of other lands and languages, from Spain to Russia.[66] He had included elements of popular style within more than a few of his higher-level works, not only in quasi-programmatic moments like the peasant dance material in the Scherzo of the "Pastoral" Symphony, but in his occasional use of other dance idioms, as in the contradance that he used in the finale of the *Eroica* and the waltz in the Scherzo of the "Archduke" Trio.

In style and purpose the "Freude" melody has a kinship with the national anthems of the late 18th and early 19th centuries. National anthems were coming into being at this period as communal musical expressions of collective political identity. In the aftermath of the French Revolution, outdoor musical performances by massed performers became familiar as composers such as Gossec and Méhul composed hymns that celebrated the revolutionary spirit of the times.[67] Partly overlapping with music for civic and national celebrations were the military marching songs that were written or adapted for use by European armies, along with the military marches played by bands that accompanied troops to the battlefields.

The British "God Save the King," the first known national anthem, had been popular since the 1740s, though the tune may be older than that. The melody was actually used by some other countries in the nineteenth century as well—and Beethoven knew it well, as witnessed by his early piano variations on it.[68] Everyone knew *La Marseillaise*, the most famous marching song ever written, composed by Rouget de Lisle in 1792 and soon employed as the "Chant de guerre pour l'armée du Rhin." To compete with it and to arouse Austrian fervor for war with France, in 1797 Haydn had written his patriotic hymn to the words "Gott erhalte Franz den Kaiser," which Beethoven also quoted in an 1815 song for bass and chorus that he wrote for Treitschke's drama *Die Ehrenpforten*, a play that honored Europe's (and especially Austria's) triumph over Napoleon.[69] In 1809, the year of the French occupation of Vienna, he sketched a hymn-like military melody to words by the poet Heinrich von Collin, entitled "Österreich Über alles" (Austria above all others).[70]

It seems likely that in formulating the "Ode" melody, Beethoven was reflecting on his experience of music written for communal singing in political and national contexts, and that the formation of the theme reflects his ambition to create a kind of supranational anthem that could express the universal brotherhood of man, rather than the chauvinistic feelings of nationhood. The later spread of his melody into all the broader contexts in which it is now known and sung, not only in the Western world but globally, is a rare example of music's power to embrace the wider world and to enter into the consciousness of millions—just as Schiller might have dreamed.

EPILOGUE

It is not my purpose here to review the vast "reception history" of the Beethoven symphonies, which would need a five-foot shelf and more. But a brief overview of some aspects of this vast subject may be in order.

Within Beethoven's lifetime the first eight symphonies were on their way to becoming classics of the repertoire. Though it took longer for the Ninth, with its anomalous features, to reach the same acceptance by the general public, its tremendous acclaim by composers and performers brought it to the status of an established masterwork by the end of the nineteenth century. By around 1900, the same recognition had come to be accorded to all of the mature symphonies from the *Eroica* to the Ninth, and Beethoven's symphonic output as a whole had become the criterion against which later composers measured their own achievements. His influence continued to be felt by the major composers of symphonies—beginning in Beethoven's lifetime with Schubert and continuing with Mendelssohn, Schumann, Brahms, Bruckner, and Mahler—to whom we can add, among non-German symphonic composers, Dvořák, Franck, and many others. And the Beethoven image continued to loom large as well for the self-described revolutionaries who turned

away from the traditional formal patterns of instrumental music
and moved to program music and the symphonic poem—chiefly
Berlioz, Liszt, and later Richard Strauss.[1] Above all, Beethoven was
an immense influence on Wagner, whose transformation of opera
into "music-drama" was, as he put it, deeply indebted to his lifetime
study of Beethoven's instrumental music, especially the Ninth Symphony. Wagner grew up in the 1830s under Beethoven's spell, as he
openly confessed in his autobiography, as well as in his early novella,
A Pilgrimage to Beethoven, and in his 1870 essay *Beethoven,* along
with a host of other published writings.[2]

Through the nineteenth century, with its proliferation of orchestral concert halls and the standardization of the symphony orchestra,
typically led by its dominating leader, the conductor or "Maestro,"
who often surpassed composers in public idolatry (and in our time
continues to do so on a grand scale), the Beethoven symphonies
stood at the center of the canon of Western classical music. They
were the touchstones against which new works would be measured,
compared, and judged, the more so in the light of the gradual development of the musical language towards greater harmonic complexity and expanded orchestral tone-colors. Not only composers and
performers, but audiences, critics, and the general concert-going
public joined in the acclamation that led to the modern image of
Beethoven.

In the modern age, in which visual imagery seems to triumph so
easily over all verbal discourse, the mythic figure of Beethoven was
depicted many times over, unforgettably by Max Klinger in his monumental sculpted figure of the heroic Beethoven seated on a throne,
god-like, naked before the world. Created in 1902 for the Vienna
Secession building, Klinger's portrayal of the composer crowned the
late Romantic vision of Beethoven as the dominating musical figure
of the preceding century. As Alessandra Comini has pointed out in
a seminal study of the changing image of Beethoven, the creation of
this sculpture coincided with the broad acceptance of Beethoven's

music as possessing "revelatory dimensions," a process Comini describes as "still at work in the 1980s when we find public television presenting an international pilgrimage to Beethoven through the medium of a white-haired Leonard Bernstein conducting the Vienna Philharmonic."[3] To which we can add that if Comini's book had been published in 1989, rather than two years earlier, in 1987, she might have extended this portrait of Bernstein's "international pilgrimage" to include his famous and dramatic performance of the Ninth Symphony at the Berlin Wall in 1989, to celebrate the collapse of the Soviet Union and the end of the Cold War.[4]

It is worth remembering that the idea that Beethoven's music could possess "revelatory dimensions" had its roots in the composer's own belief that his greatest works, certainly the symphonies, were not merely products of high craftsmanship, but were the expressions of a moral vision, a deeply rooted belief that great music can move the world. It was a vision that also found expression in the other genres in which he composed, but publicly above all in the symphonies. And despite the cultural transformations that have taken place as the twentieth century has given way to the twenty-first, audiences and listeners both within and beyond the traditional domains of classical music performance continue to respond to what a modern philosopher has characterized as the "inspirational value" of great works of art, despite postmodern pessimism about every element of that characterization.[5]

* * *

I now turn to two exemplary historical situations that stand a century apart from one another and occurred in very different countries and circumstances—but in which deep public response to the Beethoven symphonies reflects the intrinsic human significance of these works The first is from nineteenth-century America; the second is from Poland under Nazi occupation during World War II.

As symphony orchestras were founded in the United States in

the mid-to-late decades of the nineteenth century, and concert halls were built to be their permanent homes, Beethoven remained the ruling deity for musicians, patrons, and audiences alike. His symphonies became the basic standard works that listeners expected to hear, and nowhere was this more true than in nineteenth-century Boston, a city whose wealthy patrons prided themselves on emulating European cultural trends. For twenty years after the Boston Symphony was founded in 1881, the orchestra performed in a music hall in which a large statue of Beethoven stood in the back of the stage, something like a tutelary god presiding over the concert hall.[6] When the Boston Symphony moved into its permanent home in the newly built Symphony Hall in 1900, the first work performed was Beethoven's *Missa Solemnis*, and one name was inscribed on a scroll above the proscenium arch where it is still visible—"Beethoven."

The patrons who helped found this orchestra and built its concert hall were the spiritual descendants of the Transcendentalists of the 1830s and '40s, members of a literary and philosophical movement that derived many of its tenets from Kant, Goethe, Schiller, and Hegel.[7] Its spiritual leader was Ralph Waldo Emerson, and its circle included John Sullivan Dwight, a pioneering music critic and later the founder of *Dwight's Journal of Music*.[8] In 1841, Dwight and other members of this group founded Brook Farm, the best-known if short-lived Utopian community of this period. For Dwight and his companions, the Beethoven symphonies were not cultural entertainment, they were embodiments of high moral values. A recent study states that Dwight "disseminated an idealistic vision of a universal Beethoven whose symphonic music he hoped would become emblematic of a new era marked by the amelioration of society."[9]

Margaret Fuller, the prolific American writer on women's rights and social issues, was also a vital figure in this scene. Fuller was a Beethoven devotee of such passion that she not only attended concerts of his works but also wrote with great emotion about what

these hearings meant to her. In 1841, she wrote a passionate letter
to Beethoven, then dead for fourteen years, professing her allegiance
to him, her "beloved master," and to his music.[10] There are affinities between these gentle idealists, dreaming of a better world in
which great music would flourish, and the eloquent abolitionists of
New England, who denounced the wrongs of slavery in the name of
human equality and of the rights of man in America, the promised
land.

* * *

My second example comes from between 1914 and the present, a century so deeply scarred by wars, catastrophes, and threats to human
existence unimaginable in Beethoven's age. The question here is
whether his moral vision, as he intended it and as it was understood
by his devotees in the nineteenth and early twentieth centuries, can
be sustained in our time. From innumerable examples from modern
history that might offer partial answers and modest insights, I want
to discuss one that may at first seem somewhat esoteric but which
will, on reflection, speak volumes about the modern condition.[11]

It comes from a chronicle written by an inhabitant of the Łódź
ghetto in Poland under Nazi occupation in the early 1940s. The
ghetto in this venerable city was the second largest in occupied
Poland, after that of Warsaw.[12] In 1941, the entire Jewish population of Łódź, including other Jews shipped in from elsewhere, nearly
164,000 people, were sealed inside a small district of the city surrounded by barbed wire, eking out a bare existence under a Jewish
administration headed by its notorious leader, Chaim Rumkowski,
the so-called King of the Jews.[13] Hanging on in desperate conditions
of squalor, deprivation, and disease, the ghetto inhabitants were
under perpetual threats of deportation to the death camps, which in
fact began to be carried out early in 1942 and continued until 1944,
when the Russian army took the city. No words are adequate to
describe such conditions, but we can get something of an idea from

a historian of the ghetto, Gordon Horwitz, describing conditions in May 1941 as reported by an eye-witness:

> Hunger was visible in the appearance of those who daily dragged themselves to work along the ghetto streets. At six o'clock each morning the army of slave laborers could be seen hurrying to work, undernourished and ill dressed, the worst off without shoes and basic attire, comparable to "homeless dogs," one diarist remarked. By the thousands they waited at the gates across the main road-ways, impatient to cross, knowing that if they were only a minute late, they would forfeit even their meager ration of bread.

Horwitz continues:

> As of May 22 there had been no new food distributions for two weeks. Suicides, aggravated by hunger, were on the rise.[14]

Somehow, despite such conditions, by force of will some of the best Jewish musicians managed to assemble a symphony orchestra and to put on concerts for the ghetto public. Chronicler Oskar Rosenfeld, who arrived from Prague in 1941 and kept a set of diaries until he was sent to his death in Auschwitz in 1944, documented these events.[15] Rosenfeld had originally been a journalist in Vienna, writing mainly on theater. In his diary for May and June 1942 we find the following report:

> The Ghetto Symphony Orchestra has performed Beethoven three times in succession, namely on May 26, June 2, and June 7. The three full houses testify to the ghetto dwellers' need for uplifting classical music. This is not to be made little of. What intellectual and mental appetite remains after these last two years of privation is not to be thoughtlessly given up. These concerts, therefore, had to be fashioned with the greatest care.[16]

The first movement of the Fifth Symphony was the main piece. The demonic blows with which Fate batters on our doors are common knowledge. Here was a momentous theme that became more gripping the more deeply one became absorbed in it . . . The small orchestra (almost exclusively strings) performed brilliantly. The saying that Jews have a special talent for the fiddle was confirmed. Theodore Ryder conducted with devotion. The yellow Star of David on his right shoulder quivered in sympathy when Ryder swayed emotionally to the music. The audience—mostly Łódź natives—were magnetized.

Then Rosenfeld comes to the concert of July 1, 1942:

The individual movements of the Fifth Symphony heard during the concerts of June 2nd were now performed in their entirety for the first time. The effect on the audience was, of course, even more profound and impressive than before. The emotional impact here in the ghetto was greater than was ever felt in the concert halls of any European major city. Even the fugue-like passage in the third movement, which presents the highest challenges to musical understanding, was greatly appreciated.

The deliverance motif thundered majestically throughout the hall, and conductor Ryder seemed to be carried away in this finale. In that instant, one felt, almost bodily, the experience of future salvation.[17]

Rosenfeld's language calls for careful consideration. He understands what these concerts meant to the ghetto inhabitants, including the orchestra members, who arrive in the hall "in dark street suits, serious, silent, as is fitting for this type . . . most of them work during the day in some officially assigned job, like making straw shoes or sorting stinking rags or gluing soles or serving some such magic."[18] We have to imagine what it took for these players to maintain their instruments, find strings, bows, everything needed for an orchestral performance including orchestra parts, music stands, lights, chairs.

Rosenfeld's account is that of a knowledgeable listener. He knows that the celebrated opening motto of the Fifth had long been compared to "Fate knocking on the door," a remark that takes on new meaning in this context, and he feels the force with which this "momentous theme" grips its listeners. The conductor's yellow star quivers on his shoulder as he conducts, and the audience is "magnetized." A few weeks later, the whole Fifth Symphony resounds through the hall, and the audience is even more deeply moved. Remembering Vienna and Prague, Rosenfeld feels the spell of the Fifth in this degraded setting, "more than in the concert halls of any European major city." He is relieved to find that the "fugue-like" (*fugenartig*) passage in the Trio of the third movement was well received, since he feared it might be too complicated for the audience. And when the finale opens with its triumphal fanfare, he senses that a momentary vision of deliverance floods the minds of the listeners. That they chose the Fifth could not have been a coincidence. Rosenfeld writes that

> four hundred people each follow the playing on the stage. It doesn't bother them . . . that before them in a dimly lit hall, directly adjacent to one of the cruelest realities, through the movements of a gesticulating man with a yellow star on his back, Beethoven becomes audible; and exactly that Beethoven about whom so much had been pondered and written, and exactly that work which is seen as the most profound revelation—the Fifth Symphony.[19]

We sense the irony by which the Ghetto Jews were dedicating themselves to the humane values of the Fifth's composer while the Nazis who were holding them under a death sentence were destroying these values in the name of a ruthless ideology. We can hardly imagine a more vivid example of what great art can mean in conditions of extreme hardship and necessity. In this fleeting moment the Ghetto inhabitants could feel that their music-making released them from their death warrant and granted them an imagined spiritual victory. Thus Rosenfeld's reference to their almost feeling a "bodily experience of future salvation."

If there is a prophetic analogy elsewhere in Beethoven it would be in the "Prisoners' Chorus" in *Fidelio,* in which the ragged, starving prisoners, victims of obscure political forces, come out of their dungeons into the prison courtyard, half-blinded by the sunlight, singing of "Freiheit," dreaming of liberation.

I end on a personal note. In 1984, I made my first trip to Kraków to study some of the autograph manuscripts of Beethoven that had been displaced from the Berlin State Library and have been kept in Poland since the end of World War II. These manuscripts, including works by Bach, Mozart, Beethoven, Schumann, and other composers, are in safe-keeping in Kraków in the University Library. I found myself one day holding in my hands Beethoven's autograph manuscript of portions of his C-sharp Minor String Quartet, Opus 131, one of his most profound and tragic masterpieces. The next day, I went with my wife for the first time to visit Auschwitz, not far from Kraków. Whoever has set foot in Auschwitz knows that no words can describe the unfathomable evil and aura of death that pervades this place. It was and is impossible for me to measure the monstrous contradictions in German history and culture that I felt in those days and have felt since. It was an experience no doubt replicated by others over the years and shared by everyone who understands what the Holocaust meant and continues to mean in our time, for its survivors and their children and grandchildren, the keepers of memory, now distanced from these events by three generations.

In a sense, when we listen to Beethoven now, we are all descendants of the Łódź ghetto dwellers. On tragic occasions, after civic and national tragedies such as 9/11 or comparable events, we want to hear the *Eroica* and the Fifth Symphonies, and we want to gather together for the reassertion of human brotherhood that is brought home by performances of the Ninth. In his later years Beethoven wrote down an excerpt from Kant—"the moral law within us and the starry skies above us."[20] This pithy fragment sums up his belief that personal recognition of both the earthly and the transcendental enables the realization of the human potential. Beethoven's best works display something like these same properties, intertwining what is intensely human with the feeling that the listener is being carried to a higher plane. They stand as examples of what great music can still mean in our fragmented and pessimistic age.

SYMPHONIC CONCEPT SKETCHES AND MOVEMENT-PLANS: A PROVISIONAL LIST

This table shows all of the currently known instances in which Beethoven noted down brief concept sketches or movement-plans for symphonies in his sketchbooks. Almost all of them are marked "Sinfonia" or "Sinfonie" by him, and the majority were ideas that remained undeveloped, but a few are early ideas for symphonies that he did complete. These sketches and plans form a rich body of evidence that shows Beethoven returning to the idea of the symphony across the span of his career from early to late.

Dates	Sketchbook	Comments
1788–89	Kafka: 70r–v	C-minor draft of 1st movement: "Sinfonia"
1790	Kafka: 88v	C-major draft, 1st movement: "Sinfonia"
ca. 1790?	Kafka: 81v	E major, slow movement: "Sinfonia"
ca. 1795–96	Kafka, "Fischhof"	C-major 1st movement and Minuet: "Sinfonia" (See Buurman, 63ff.)
1800–1801	Landsberg 7: 110	Brief idea for a C-major Symphony: "Sinfonia"
1801–2	Kessler: 8v	Andante, G major: "Sinfonia"

Dates	Sketchbook	Comments
1802	Wielhorsky: 44f.	Movement-plan in E-flat major: not marked "Sinfonia" but clearly is drawn from Op. 35 and links to the Eroica sketches in Landsberg 6
1803	Landsberg 6: 70	Early plan for finale of the Eroica Symphony: "Var[iationen]"; shows instruments and sectional plan in brief form
Early 1804	Landsberg 6: 155–58	C minor [Scherzo] & 1st movement (Fifth Symphony) "Sinfonia" plus C-major Adagio and C-minor 6/8 finale ("could end with a March")
Early 1804	Landsberg 6: 64, 96	Ideas related to the "Pastoral" Symphony
Early 1804	Landsberg 6: 159	Idea for 1st mvt: "lustige Sinfonia"
Early 1804	Landsberg 6: 177	Idea for opening of D minor symphony, 1st movement: "Sinfonia"
1807	Landsberg 10; Landsberg 12; "Mass in C Sketchbook"	Early ideas for movements of the "Pastoral" Symphony (see Buurman, 134–41; re: "Mass in C Sketchbook," see JTW, 156–59)
1807–8	"Sketchbook of 1807–8"	Sketches for Fifth Symphony, 2nd, 3rd, and 4th movements (see JTW, 160–65)
1809	Landsberg 5: 55	Idea for "First Allegro of a symphony" [G major, 3/4]
1809	Landsberg 5: 87	Ideas for Introduction and first Allegro of a symphony in G minor
1809	Landsberg 5: 104	Verbal entry, "A moll Sinfonie" ["Symphony in A minor"], no music
1809	Landsberg 5: 50, 59	These pages contain ideas for multi-movement works that are not labeled "Sinfonia" or "Symphonie," but are proposed by Clemens Brenneis, editor of the Grasnick 5 Sketchbook, as being possibly intended for symphonies.
1812	Petter: 5r	Ideas for Seventh Symphony, movements 1, 2, and 4 (see Buurman, 158ff.; Knowles, "The Sketches," 67)

Dates	Sketchbook	Comments
1812	Petter: 44v	Ideas for Eighth Symphony (begun as a piano concerto), movements 1, 2, and 4 (see Buurman, 161ff.; Brandenburg "Ein Skizzenbuch," 135ff.; and chapter 8 of this book)
1812	Petter: 45r–50r	Ideas for a "3tes Sinfonie" [Third Symphony] in D minor (see Buurman, 163ff.; Cahn, "Beethoven's Entwürfe," 123–29; and Brandenburg, "Ein Skizzenbuch," 140)
1812	Petter: 42v	Brief idea for a "Sinfonie in C dur" ["Symphony in C major"] (see Brandenburg, "Ein Skizzenbuch," 148, n. 29)
1812	Petter: 42v	Brief idea for a "Sinfonie" in B-flat major (see Brandenburg, "Ein Skizzenbuch," 148, n. 29)
1812	Bonn, BH 119 (originally part of Petter): 1r	Ideas for a symphony in E minor (see Buurman, 158, 166–68)
1812	Bonn, Mh 86: 1r	Ideas for a symphony in E-flat major (see Buurman, 158, 169–71)
1814	Dessauer: 141	Ideas for movements for symphonies in E minor and D minor (see N II, 299; Buurman, 158, 174f.)
1815–16	Scheide: 33	Idea for a "Sinfonia" in D major (see N II, 347)
1815–16	Scheide: 51	Verbal description for a "Symphony beginning with just four voices . . ." (see N II, 329 and chapter 9 of this book)
1815–16	Scheide: 106	Brief idea for a "Sinfonie" in E-flat major (see N II, 348)
1815	Mendelssohn 1 pocket sketchbook	Idea for a "Symphony in B minor" ["Sinfoni[e] in h moll"] (see N II, 317)

Dates	Sketchbook	Comments
1817/18	Bonn, BSk 8/56	Verbal description of a "symphony in the old modes," including reference to the entrance of voices in the last movement, with the "orchestral violins to be increased tenfold in the last movement." (see N II, 163; Levy, *Beethoven: The Ninth Symphony*, 20–48, especially 30; Brandenburg, "Die Skizzen zur Neunten Symphonie," 99–103; and Buurman, 198f.)
1819–23	Sketches for the Ninth Symphony	The genesis of the Ninth Symphony has been traced through several sketchbooks of this period and is far too complex to be described here in summary form (for outlines of the basic material and valuable discussion of the sketch material see N II, 157–92; Levy, op. cit., 20–48; Brandenburg, "Die Skizzen zur Neunten Symphonie"; Cook, *Beethoven: Symphony No. 9*, 1–18; and Buurman, 207–13)
1822–25	Sketches for an unfinished Tenth Symphony	Historical and sketch evidence exists to indicate that before completing the Ninth and after its premiere, Beethoven was thinking about a Tenth Symphony and left a number of sketches for it. Views differ on the degree to which these sketches add up to a well-conceived composition, and the attempt at a realization of the Tenth by Barry Cooper has aroused controversy. One can say, however, in the context of Beethoven's many fleeting ideas for symphonies that were not realized (as documented in the above list), that he did make a large number of sketches for this project, and, according to his secretary Karl Holz, actually played it for Holz at the piano. Holz writes, "Beethoven played the Tenth Symphony in its entirety at the piano, he had sketched all of its movements, but no one but he could decipher them." (On this project see especially Winter, "Noch einmal;" Cooper, "Newly Identified Sketches;" Cooper, *Beethoven and the Creative Process*, 3, 13, 164; and Brandenburg, "Die Skizzen," 111–13. For later published comments, see Winter, "Of Realizations;" Cooper, "Beethoven's Tenth Symphony;" and Winter, [Response].)

NOTES

For bibliographic abbreviations, see page 263.

PREFACE

1 Douglas Johnson, Alan Tyson, and Robert Winter, *The Beethoven Sketchbooks: History, Reconstruction, Inventory* (Berkeley, 1985). See the important review by Richard Kramer in *Journal of the American Musicological Society* 40 (1987): 36–67.

2 Lewis Lockwood and Alan Gosman, eds., *Beethoven's "Eroica" Sketchbook: A Critical Edition.* 2 vols. Urbana, IL, 2013 (hereafter *ESk*).

3 Erica Buurman, "Beethoven's Compositional Approach to Multi-Movement Structures in His Instrumental Works" (Ph.D. diss., University of Manchester, 2013). I am grateful to Dr. Buurman for sending me a copy of her dissertation and for fruitful exchanges of ideas on this body of sketch material.

INTRODUCTION:
"THE TRIUMPH OF THIS ART"

1 Beethoven, *Konversationshefte*, edited by Karl-Heinz Köhler, Grita Herre, Dagmar Beck, and Günter Brosche (Leipzig, 1968–2001), vol. 8, p. 268, dated between January 16 and 22, 1826. This translation differs slightly from the one in *BML*, 350. An English translation of the Beethoven Conversation Books by Theodore Albrecht of Kent State University is now in preparation.

2 For an overview of the symphony across Europe in the eighteenth century, see *The Symphonic Repertoire*, vol. 1, "The Eighteenth-Century Symphony," ed. by Mary Sue Morrow and Bathia Churgin (Bloomington, 2012).

3 On the impact of the Haydn "London" symphonies on Beethoven in the 1790s see Douglas Johnson, "1794–1795: Decisive Years in Beethoven's Early Development," *Beethoven Studies 3*, ed. Alan Tyson (Cambridge, 1982), 1–28.

4 We know that Haydn's symphonies were collected in Bonn by a collector named Mastiaux, among others. We also know that Mozart was the favorite composer of the Elector Max Franz, who hoped at one time to bring Mozart to the Electoral Court as his principal composer. For the new evidence regarding Beethoven's journey to Vienna in 1787, see Dieter Haberl, "Beethovens Erste Reise nach Wien—Die Datierung seiner Schülerreise zu W. A. Mozart," *Neues Musikwissenschaftliches Jahrbuch*, 14 (2006): 215–55.

5 See *BML,* 56 and my "Beethoven before 1800: The Mozart Legacy," *BF* 3 (1992): 39–52.

6 See *BML*, 57–59. Beethoven's piano quartets' (WoO 36) dependence on Mozart's violin sonatas is well known. The C-minor sketch passage appears in the portfolio of early sketch leaves known as the "Kafka" collection, published by Joseph Kerman, ed., *Ludwig van Beethoven: Autograph Miscellany from circa 1786 to 1799: British Museum Additional Manuscript 29801, ff. 39–162* (London, 1970), vol. 1: fol. 88r; vol. 2: p. 228 and comment, 293.

7 See *ESk*. Later, while sketching ideas for his C-major Quartet Op. 59 No. 3, Beethoven writes an opening phrase that is an unmistakable parallel to a well-known theme from Mozart's Clarinet Quintet; see N II, 86.

8 *Briefe* No. 6, Anderson No. 6, a letter known only through Neefe's publication of part of it in the *Berlinische Musikalische Zeitung*, No. 39, dated October 26, 1793.

9 David Wyn Jones, *The Symphony in Beethoven's Vienna* (Cambridge, 2006), 168. Wyn Jones's study offers valuable insights into the state of the symphony as a genre in Vienna in these years, as cultivated not only by Beethoven but also his contemporaries, such as Eberl, Anton and Paul Wranitsky, and Gyrowetz.

10 Letter to the Archduke Rudolph of 29 July 1819; *Briefe* No. 1318.

11 Feruccio Busoni, *Von der Einheit der Musik, Verstreute Aufzeichnungen* (Berlin, 1922, 290.

12 *The Letters of Samuel Beckett 1929–1940,* 514, from a letter of 9 July 1937 to the editor Axel Kaun.

13 Amadeus Wendt, "Über den Zustand der Musik in Deutschland," originally published in *Allgemeine Musikalische Zeitung, mit besonderer Rucksicht auf den Österreichischen Kaiserstaat*, Jg. 6 (1822), col. 761; quoted in Stefan Kunze, ed., *Ludwig van Beethoven: Die Werke im Spiegel seiner Zeit* (Laaber, 1987), 629.

14 Anonymous writer in the *Musikalisches Taschenbuch*. I (Penig, 1803), 78–81. For the original text see Kunze, op. cit., 626f. The translation given here is modified from that in Wayne M. Senner, ed., *The Critical Reception of Beethoven's Compositions by His German Contemporaries*, vol. 1 (Lincoln, NE, 1999), 29–31.

15 For an overview of the rise of the concept of music as an autonomous domain of expression see John Neubauer, *The Emancipation of Music from Language: The Departure from Mimesis in Eighteenth-Century Aesthetics* (New Haven, CT, 1986).

16 Hoffmann's review, frequently cited, is best read in the original and is readily found in Kunze, op. cit., 100–112.

17 *The World as Will and Representation*. Trans. E. F. Payne (New York, 1969), vol. II, 450. Partially quoted in *BML*, 16.

18 Buurman, op. cit.

19 Richard Will, *The Characteristic Symphony in the Age of Haydn and Beethoven* (Cambridge, 2002).

20 On 18 March 1827, only nine days before his death, Beethoven wrote to Mosche-

les in London to thank the Philharmonic Society for their generosity to him, and claimed that he had sketches for "a new symphony" in his desk. Other historical evidence and surviving sketches have persuaded some scholars that Beethoven had at least the idea of a Tenth Symphony in hand before he died, and Holz reported that he actually played it for him (see Appendix). In 1988 Barry Cooper brought together various sketch elements in an attempted "realization" of a Tenth Symphony first movement, and it was recorded by MCA Classics, MCAD-6269, with a recorded lecture by Cooper. The result remains controversial, as it has not been accepted by some scholars, notably Robert Winter in his article, "Of Realizations, Completions, Restorations, and Reconstructions: From Bach's *The Art of Fugue* to Beethoven's 'Tenth Symphony,'" *Journal of the Royal Musical Association* 116 (1991): 96–126. Cooper replied to Winter in his "Beethoven's Tenth Symphony," *Journal of the Royal Musical Association* 117 (1992): 324–29, to which Winter responded in the same issue, 329–30.

THE FIRST SYMPHONY

1 Franz's son, Ferdinand Ries (1784–1838), later became Beethoven's student around 1801, and had a notable career as composer and pianist. He tried his luck in Paris in 1807–8, was again in Vienna in 1808–9, and, after other stops, arrived in England in 1813, where he found success. His memoirs of Beethoven, written with his fellow Bonner, Franz Wegeler, and published in 1838, remains an important source. Ferdinand Ries's piano works reveal him as a highly capable composer, and are currently being recorded by Susan Kagan.

2 On Reicha at Oettingen-Wallerstein see Sterling Murray, "The Symphony in South Germany," in Mary Sue Morrow and Bathia Churgin, eds., *The Eighteenth-Century Symphony*, 318f., 322f.

3 The orchestra in 1784 had 27 players, smaller than that of Mannheim but sizeable for a modest-sized court like Bonn; in 1791 it had 39. On orchestra sizes across Europe in the late eighteenth century see Neal Zaslaw and John Spitzer, *The Birth of the Orchestra: History of an Institution, 1650–1815* (New York, 2004), Appendix; for a convenient table for the years 1754–96, Morrow and Churgin, eds., *The Eighteenth-Century Symphony*, 76.

4 For a vivid portrait of Bonn as a musical center in Beethoven's early years see TF, chapters 4 and 5; on Beethoven as violist see TF, 95. Still the most comprehensive portrait is that of Ludwig Schiedermair, *Der Junge Beethoven* (Leipzig, 1925).

5 See my remarks in *BML*, 30f.

6 For a conspectus of Neefe's career see Peter Clive, *Beethoven and His World* (Oxford, 2001), 247.

7 *BML*, 36, quoted from Leslie Sharpe, *Friedrich Schiller: Drama, Thought and Politics* (Cambridge, 1991), 29.

8 See Maynard Solomon, "Beethoven and Schiller," in Robert Winter and Bruce Carr, eds. *Beethoven, Performers, and Critics: The International Beethoven Congress Detroit 1977* (Detroit, 1977), 163. This essay was later reprinted in revised form in Solomon's *Beethoven Essays* (Cambridge, 1988), 205–15. A valuable recent contribution on Neefe's relationship to the Grossmann theater company is Ian Woodfield, "Christian Gottlob Neefe and the Bonn National Theatre, with New Light on the Beethoven Family," *Music and Letters* 93/3 (2012): 289–315.

9   For example, the quotations from Schiller plays entered into Beethoven's farewell album on his departure from Bonn in November 1792, his own quote from *Don Carlos* in another album of 1793, and his later references to Schiller plays, always fresh in his mind, in later letters, e.g., his letter to the Archduke Rudolph in 1819 when Rudolph had just been confirmed as Archbishop of Olmütz (*Briefe*, No. 1292, of early March 1819).

10 The recipient of the 1793 entry was Theodora Vocke; see Joseph Schmidt-Görg, "Ein Schiller-Zitat Beethovens in Neuer Sicht," in *Musik, Edition, Interpretation, Gedenkschrift Günter Henle* (Munich, 1980), 423–26.

11 See my "Beethoven as Sir Davison," in *Bonner Beethoven-Studien* 11 (2014): 133–40.

12 See Solomon, "Beethoven and Schiller," in his *Beethoven Essays*, 211 and 347 n. 25.

13 Carl Schachter, "Mozart's Last and Beethoven's First: Echoes of K. 551 in the First Movement of Opus 21," *Mozart Studies*, ed. Cliff Eisen (Oxford, 1991), 227–52.

14 The closest counterpart to the symphony's Andante is the C-major 3/8 slow movement of the string quartet Opus 18, No. 4, marked "Andante scherzoso, quasi allegretto," which similarly opens with a fugato exposition and has much the same delicate character as this 3/8 Andante in the First symphony—but the quartet movement is a much stronger achievement overall.

15 Also, years later, by his 1817 metronome marking, half-note = 108.

16 For the C-minor Sinfonia draft in the Kafka papers see Joseph Kerman, *Beethoven: Autograph Miscellany from circa 1786 to 1700* (London: Trustees of the British Museum, 1970), vol. I, fols. 70r–v; II, 175f. It had been published as early as 1912 by Fritz Stein in SIMG, xiii (1912): 131–32. It was briefly commented upon by Cooper, *Beethoven*, 23f. and by Wyn Jones, *The Symphony in Beethoven's Vienna*, 155f., who notes that the draft "reveals the composer's acquaintance with the nervously energetic *Sturm und Drang* idiom."

17 Including the Piano Trio Op. 1, No. 3, the String Trio Op. 9, No. 3, and the piano sonata Op. 10, No. 3.

18 Kerman, *Beethoven: Autograph Miscellany* II, 228 (folio 88r of the miscellany); see Lockwood, *BML*, 57f.

19 I am thinking of such movements as the Andante cantabile of the C-minor Trio Opus 1, No. 3, or the parallel movement of his Quintet for Piano and Winds, Opus 16, which he sketched on the verso of this same leaf.

20 As proposed by Kerman, op. cit., II, 291. Kerman supposes that the following sketches on the same leaf, marked "Zum andante" and in F major, are further ideas for this movement as transposed into F major.

21 Kerman, op. cit., first movement sketches on fols. 71v; 56f; 127f; 158f; Minuet sketches on fols. 59r, 128v; 159r. On the Fischhof Miscellany, see Douglas Johnson, *Beethoven's Early Sketches in the "Fischhof" Miscellany, Berlin Autograph 28*, 2 vols. (Ann Arbor, 1980).

22 Johnson, vol. 1, 466f.

23 For an extended and insightful discussion of these sketches for a C-major symphony see Johnson, *Beethoven's Early Sketches,* vol. I, 461–69 and for the music examples in full, vol. 2, 163–76.

24 *AMZ* 3 (October 15, 1800): 49, as translated in Wayne Senner, ed., *The Critical Reception of Beethoven's Compositions by His German Contemporaries* (Lincoln, NE, 1999), vol. 1, 162f.

25 H. C. Robbins Landon in *Haydn: Chronicle and Works* (London, 1976–80), vol. 4, p. 545, suggests either the "Prague," K. 504, or the G-Minor Symphony, K. 550. Johnson, "Beethoven's Early Sketches in the 'Fischhof' Miscellany," 975, suggests the "Linz," K. 425. But although the question cannot be settled now, for lack of hard evidence, I note that in the first editions of the Mozart symphonies No. 39–41, issued in the 1790s by André, only No. 39 was dubbed "grosse Sinfonie" in the edition (1797), as in Beethoven's program, whereas No. 40 (published 1794) and 41 (1793) had been given no special title other than "Sinfonie." See Köchel-Verzeichniss, K. 543, 550, 551 for details of the editions.

26 Harry Goldschmidt, "Beethoven in neuen Brunsvik-Briefen," *Neues Beethoven Jahrbuch* 9 (1973–77): 109, shows that the Septet had already been performed privately in December 1799 by an ensemble led by Schuppanzigh. His decision to program the Septet with excerpts from *The Creation* may help explain the ironic, half-deprecating remark that Dolezalek later attributed to Beethoven about the Septet—"That is my *Creation*."

27 The reference is to Paul Wranitsky (1758–1808), a Czech composer, brother of Anton Wranitsky (1761–1820), an equally prominent Viennese musician. On the Wranitsky brothers and their symphonies, see Wyn Jones, *The Symphony in Beethoven's Vienna*, chapter 4.

28 Review in the *AMZ* 3 (25 October 1800).

29 See Nottebohm, *Beethovens Studien*. For an illuminating study of Beethoven's studies with Haydn, Albrechtsberger, and Salieri, see Julia Ronge, *Beethovens Lehrzeit* (Bonn, 2011). Most recently, Ronge has published Beethoven's study materials with his teachers for the first time in complete form in *Beethoven Werke,* ser. XIII, vol. I.

30 See N II, 566, and Ronge, op. cit., 55f.

31 See, e.g, the commentary of 1806 in Senner, ed., op. cit., I, 164.

32 *Beethoven by Berlioz: a Critical Appreciation of Beethoven's Nine Symphonies*, compiled and translated by Ralph De Sola (Boston, 1975), 14; the original essays had been contained in Berlioz's *A travers chants* (Paris, 1862).

33 For an extended discussion of the ways in which the Adagio slow introduction foreshadows the primary structural moments of the first movement Allegro see my "Beethoven's First Symphony: A Farewell to the Eighteenth Century?" in *Essays in Musicology: A Tribute to Alvin Johnson*, ed. by Lewis Lockwood and Edward Roesner (Philadelphia, 1990), 235–46.

THE SECOND SYMPHONY

1 Roger Kamien, "The Slow Introduction of Mozart's Symphony No. 38 in D, K. 504. ("Prague"); A Possible Model for the Slow Introduction of Beethoven's Symphony No. 2 in D, Op. 36," *Israel Studies in Musicology*, V (1990), 113–30.

2 Measures 102–7.

3 Measures 73–88.

4 For example, the slow movements of his first two piano trios, the famous slow movement of the "Pathétique" Sonata; and in the string quartets, the Andante of Op. 18 No. 6.

5 See Kunze, *Ludwig van Beethoven: Die Werke im Spiegel seiner Zeit* (Laaber, 1987), 36. It is indicative of reactions in 1805 that the First Symphony was regarded by the same reviewer as "a favorite of the present-day concert public."

6 Kunze, op. cit., 37, quoting an anonymous review from the *AMZ* of 1812, col. 124.

7 That it begins on the dominant seventh, not the tonic, is only the most obvious of its anomalies, certainly calculated to amaze his listeners. No earlier symphonic finale by Haydn or Mozart opens with such a surprising gesture.

8 The larger shape of the finale is as follows:

Section	Measures	Tonality
A	1–25	I
B	26–51	V
C	52–107	V
A + free development	108–184	I modulating
A	185–209	I
B	210–225	I
C	236–293	I
Coda	294–442	

9 As Kerman puts it in a study of Beethoven's codas, a general principle in early codas seems to be that there is "some kind of instability, discontinuity, or thrust in the first theme which is removed in the coda." See his "Notes on Beethoven's Codas," in Alan Tyson, ed., *Beethoven Studies 3* (Cambridge, 1982), 149.

10 Schubert's first symphonic fragment of 1811 (D. 2b) consists of a sketch for an Adagio and an Allegro, both in D major, both exhibiting direct influences from Beethoven's Second, as does (much later) the slow movement of Schubert's justly celebrated "Grand Duo" for piano four-hands (D. 812, of 1824), which shows unmistakable recollections of the slow movement of this Beethoven symphony.

11 See my "Reshaping the Genre: Beethoven's Piano Sonatas from Op. 22 to Op. 28 (1799–1801)," *Israel Studies in Musicology* 6 (1996): 1–16, which deals with the sonatas up to Op. 28 but not the three of Op. 31.

12 See Daniel Coren, "Structural Relations Between Op. 28 and Op. 36," in *Beethoven Studies 2*. ed. by Alan Tyson (Oxford, 1977), 66–83. Coren shows that the four movements of the sonata are related through thematic affinities and other structural features, and that a number of these features also appear in the Second Symphony. Coren's discussion strengthens the view that for Beethoven, the genre of the piano sonata was a laboratory for experimentation with ideas and procedures that he could also utilize in other works, especially his symphonies.

13 For the original text of the Heiligenstadt Testament, written in two parts dated October 6 and 10, 1802, see *Briefe*, No. 106. For a sensitive discussion of his deafness, the letters, and this famous document see Solomon, 2nd ed., 145–62. As Brandenburg points out in *Briefe*, I, 124, n. 6, Beethoven was also suffering from abdominal difficulties at the same time, as we know from his own testimony and that of close observers.

14 From *Briefe* No. 65, to Wegeler, of 29 June 1801, modifying Anderson's translation.

15 The translation here is by Solomon, *Beethoven*, 152.

16 Letter of 16 November 1801 to Wegeler (*Briefe* No. 70, Anderson No. 54).

17 Richard Ellman, *Golden Codgers: Biographical Speculations* (New York, 1973), p. ix. See my "Reappraising Beethoven Biography," *Yearbook of Comparative and General Literature* 53 (2007): 83–99.

18 For a firm statement of this credo in artistic biography, see the remarks of Frederick R. Karl, a recent biographer of Joseph Conrad and Franz Kafka, in his contribution to Jeffrey Meyers, ed., *The Craft of Literary Biography* (New York, 1985), 69–88. Karl writes, "The biographer of a literary subject must relate the latter's life and work to each other meaningfully and profoundly. If he cannot achieve that end, the biography, whatever its other illuminations, fails" (69). Not surprisingly, it turns out that the methods pursued by Karl and other similar biographers rely primarily on interrelated psychological readings of both life and works. At a later stage of this essay, Karl notes that since Freud's treatment of Leonardo "psychoanalysts have found difficulty in relating life and art," and cites Jung's view that the artist is "nothing but his work, and not a human being." Taking up Jung's position, somewhat extreme for a biographer, Karl suggests that for Conrad "words would have become the reality . . . and he would lie exposed wherever language and memory took him . . . just as Conrad was transforming pastness and memory into present creation, so he was himself undergoing a transformation from a conscious, acting person to a man who was 'receiving' messages from the unconscious which he could not ignore. Retrieval meant transformation" (83–84). This last formulation is suggestive for artists of Beethoven's type, who seem to be able to shut down their awareness of pain and anxiety at the conscious level when they immerse themselves in the fiercely concentrated domain of their creative work. In that world, Beethoven's problems, however difficult and omnipresent, were apparently capable of solution if he worked hard enough and long enough.

19 J. W. N. Sullivan, *Beethoven: His Spiritual Development* (London, 1927).

20 Sullivan, 86–87.

21 Reviews of 9 May 1804 and of 15 August 1804, both in the *AMZ*, as translated by Wayne Senner in *The Critical Reception of Beethoven's Compositions by His German Contemporaries*. vol. 1 (Lincoln, NE, 1995), 196f.

22 The quotation is from his letter of October 1802 to Breitkopf and Härtel offering both works for publication. On these variations and the tradition to which they belong see the excellent study by Elaine Sisman, *Haydn and the Classical Variation* (Cambridge, 1993).

23 This "Sinfonia" idea is found in the sketchbook Landsberg 7, published by Karl Lothar Mikulicz as *Ein Notierungsbuch von Beethoven* (Leipzig, 1927), <u>110</u> (underlined) = 100, st. 5. See appendix.

24 Michael Broyles, *Beethoven: the Emergence and Evolution of Beethoven's Heroic Style* (New York, 1987), 119–26. Broyles provides a useful chart (120f.) showing which works by Beethoven have been compared by contemporary and later writers to works by French composers. Not surprisingly, the strongest claims for close relationships made by writers contemporary with Beethoven refer to *Leonore*, the *Coriolanus* overture, the *Leonore* overtures and the music for *Egmont*—all of these being theater works on explicit themes of political heroism or tragedy. The claims for connections with the Beethoven symphonies (the First, Fourth, Fifth, and Seventh finale) were all made in the twentieth century by Arnold Schmitz (*Das Romantische Beethovensbild*, 1927), and only one of these goes

back to the nineteenth century, Schumann's comparison of the Fifth, first movement, to Méhul's G-minor Symphony (Schumann, *Gesammelte Schriften über
Musik und Musiker* [Leipzig, 1889], II, 169). For a convenient short summary
on the claims of French influence, see Solomon, *Beethoven*, 138. Doubts about
Schmitz's claims of direct thematic connection have been voiced by Broyles, 121.
See also Alexander Ringer, "A French Symphonist at the Time of Beethoven: Etienne Nicolas Méhul," *The Musical Quarterly* 37 (1951): 543–65.

25 See Boris Schwarz, "Beethoven and the French Violin School," *The Musical
Quarterly* 44 (1958), 431–47; also his Ph.D. dissertation, "French Instrumental
Music between the Revolutions, 1789–1830" (Columbia University, 1950).

26 See Mary Sue Morrow, *Concert Life in Vienna, 1780–1810* (Stuyvesant, NY,
1989), Appendices 1–2 (Calendars of Public and Private concerts with programs).

27 See Broyles, op. cit., 121ff.

28 Alfred Einstein, "The Military Element in Beethoven," *Monthly Musical Record*,
69 (November 1939): 270–74; cited by Broyles, 123.

29 See Karl Josef Mayr, *Wien im Zeitalter Napoleons* (Vienna, 1940), especially
222ff. on military garrisons in Vienna. Mayr (222) reports that the imperial
regime used the military forces to keep order at times when the citizenry showed
signs of unrest and even political resistance, as in July 1805.

30 Examples are his three "Marches for Piano Four Hands," Op. 45, in 1803, and
other keyboard marches found in the *Eroica* Sketchbook, exactly at the time
that he is composing the *Marcia funebre* as the slow movement of the Third
Symphony. This is an instance of Beethoven's "high" and "popular" uses of a
genre at the same time. The "Marches" Op. 45 are a type of "relaxed version"
of the genre worked out while he is attempting the most powerful orchestral
funeral march he or anyone else had yet written. Admittedly, Claude Palisca has
shown more convincing connections between the slow movement of the *Eroica*
and French revolutionary examples of funeral marches, including Gossec's
Marche lugubre, a much-performed piece in the 1790s which Beethoven might
possibly have known while still at Bonn before November 1792. Palisca seems
to be on the right track in suggesting not that Beethoven necessarily borrowed
directly from French models for the thematic material of his *Marcia funebre* or
other related works, but that Beethoven, sensitive to the current French orchestral style, "assimilated it so thoroughly that the characteristic phrases and cli-
chés poured forth effortlessly." Claude Palisca, "French Revolutionary Models
for Beethoven's *Eroica* Funeral March," in Anne Dhu Shapiro, ed., *Music and
Context: Essays for John Ward* (Cambridge, MA, 1985), 198–209; the quotation
is from 209.

31 The primary sketchbook for Opus 36 is the MS Landsberg 7 of the Berlin State
Library. Beethoven used this sketchbook between the summer or fall of 1800
and about March 1801. For a preliminary study of these sketches for the Second
Symphony see Kurt Westphal, *Vom Einfall zur Symphonie* (Berlin, 1965), 47–75.

32 As did Nottebohm in his study, *Ein Skizzenbuch von Beethoven* (Leipzig, 1865),
11. Earlier sketches for the Larghetto are in the miscellany Landsberg 12, 59–63.
An argument that this G-major concept sketch is independent of Beethoven's
work on the Second Symphony was made by Sieghard Brandenburg in his edition of the Kessler sketchbook, *Ludwig van Beethoven, Kesslersches Skizzenbuch*
(Bonn, 1978), transcription volume, 32f.

33 See Sieghard Brandenburg, *Ludwig van Beethoven: Kesslersches Skizzenbuch*, vol. I (Bonn, 1978), 46f., and also Richard Kramer, "An Unfinished Concertante by Beethoven," in Alan Tyson, ed., *Beethoven Studies 2* (Oxford, 1977), 33–65.

34 Its presentation of triad-members in sequence (1–3–1–5–1–3–1) is nearly identical to the interval sequence that Beethoven eventually uses for the first theme of the *Eroica*.

35 Wegeler and Ries, *Biographische Notizen über Ludwig van Beethoven* (Koblenz, 1838), 77; published in English as *Beethoven Remembered* (Arlington, 1987), 66f.

36 Anonymous review in the AMZ, 2 January 1805, translated in Senner, *The Critical Reception of Beethoven's Compositions by His German Contemporaries*, I (Lincoln, NE, 1999), 209.

THE *EROICA* SYMPHONY

1 Ries to Simrock, October 22, 1803; *Briefe* No. 165; Theodore Albrecht, ed., *Letters to Beethoven and Other Correspondence* (Lincoln, NE, 1996), No. 71.

2 TF, 337. In 1804, Mähler painted his famous portrait of Beethoven, frequently reproduced. See Comini, *The Changing Image of Beethoven*, 33–36. Although Comini refers to the year as 1804 and to Beethoven's having played and improvised upon the first movement, Thayer specifically identified it as the finale. In view of the close relationship of the *Eroica* finale to the Piano Variations Op. 35, we can speculate on the possibility that Beethoven improvised a version of the finale that might have incorporated some elements of Op. 35 along with newly invented ones. In any case, Mähler was immensely impressed by the quality and originality of Beethoven's playing, as Thayer reports he told him when he described this visit. Mähler gave Thayer this information sometime before 1860, the year in which Mähler died at age 82.

3 *Beethoven Hero*, xvif.

4 Franz Wegeler and Ferdinand Ries, *Biographische Notizen*, 77f.; Schindler, *Beethoven As I Knew Him*, 115f.

5 *Briefe*, No. 84, letter to Hoffmeister of 8 April 1802.

6 *Briefe* No. 188, letter to Breitkopf and Härtel; "die Simphonie ist eigentlich betitelt Ponaparte."

7 See my "Beethoven, Florestan, and the Varieties of Heroism," in Scott Burnham and Michael P. Steinberg, editors, *Beethoven and His World* (Princeton, 2000), 27–47.

8 *Briefe* No. 64, letter to Hoffmeister January 15, 1801 (Anderson No. 44). On this letter see Solomon, "Beethoven's '*Magazin der Kunst*,'" in *19th-Century Music* 7 (1984): 199–208.

9 *Briefe* No. 747, letter to Kanka, undated but assigned by Anderson and Brandenburg to Autumn 1814;. Beethoven's expression is "*das geistige reich*" which could also be translated as "the empire of the soul."

10 The basic study of Beethoven and the "Archduke" is Kagan, *Archduke Rudolph: Beethoven's Patron, Pupil, and Friend* (Stuyvesant, NY, 1988). She has also published Rudolph's *Forty Variations on a Theme by Beethoven* and his F-minor Sonata for Violin and Piano, in *Recent Researches in the Music of the Nineteenth and Twentieth Centuries*, vol. 21 (Madison, 1992). See also my brief account in "Beethoven and His Royal Disciple," *Bulletin of the American Academy of Arts and Sciences* 57/3 (Spring 2004): 2–7.

11 *Briefe* No. 2003, of about 6 July 1825.

12 For the first critical edition of the sketchbook, with a complete facsimile, full transcription, and commentary, see *ESk.*

13 *Briefe*, No. 51 of 29 June 1801.

14 *Briefe* No. 123, Anderson No. 67, letter to Breitkopf of about 18 December 1802. See also Hans-Werner Küthen, "Beethovens 'wirklich ganz neue Manier'—Eine Persiflage," in *Beiträge zu Beethovens Kammermusik, Symposion Bonn 1984,* ed. by Sieghard Brandenburg and Helmut Loos (Munich, 1987), 216–24. He was clearly concerned that the public would notice that the Op. 35 Variations were based on the same theme he had used in the finale of the ballet, and some months later he wrote again to Breitkopf to complain that on the title page of the Opus 35 *Variations* they had forgotten to say that the theme "was taken from the allegorical ballet *Prometheus*" which "should have been stated on the title page." He added, "beg you to do this [include the *Prometheus* reference on the title page] if it is still possible, that is to say, if the work has not yet appeared. If the title page has to be altered, well, let it be done at my expense."

15 See JTW, 130–36. Complete edition edited by Nathan Fishman, *Kniga eskizov Beethovena za 1802–1803,* 3 vols (Moscow, 1962). It is to Fishman that we owe the first identification of the "Ur-*Eroica*" sketches as being intended for Beethoven's Third Symphony.

16 We find it later only as the title of his quartet Opus 95 ("Quartetto serioso") and later for one variation in the "Diabelli" Variations, Opus 120 ("Allegro ma non troppo e serioso").

17 The expression "more the expression of feelings than tone-painting" was included in the program for the first performance of the Sixth Symphony in December 1808; see Kinsky-Halm, 161; and Nottebohm in N II, 378 reports its appearance in an early violin part.

18 On Beethoven's studies with Salieri see, most recently, Ronge, *Beethovens Lehrzeit* (Bonn, 2011), 141–70.

19 Reinhold Brinkmann, in his important essay, "In the Time of the *Eroica*," in S. Burnham and Michael Steinberg, eds., *Beethoven and His World* (Princeton, 2000), 1–26 and especially 20.

20 In 1801, Beethoven and Paer had appeared on the same concert, when Beethoven performed his Horn Sonata with Giovanni Punto, and Paer conducted an orchestra in vocal works. In August of that year, Paer was present at one of Beethoven's musical entertainments. See Peter Clive, op. cit., 255.

21 Unsigned review in *Der Freymüthige* 3 (17 April 1805): 332, translation in *The Critical Reception of Beethoven's Compositions by His German Contemporaries,* ed. by Wayne M. Senner, Robin Wallace, and William Meredith (Lincoln, NE, 2001), vol. 2, 15f. The reference to a "Quintet in D Major" is a blatant error, as there was no such Beethoven work at the time; the reviewer may have been thinking of the Quintet in C Major Op. 29.

22 Robin Wallace, "Beethoven's Critics: An Appreciation," in *The Critical Reception of Beethoven's Compositions by His Germanic Contemporaries,* vol. 2, p. 6.

23 *Allgemeine musikalische Zeitung* 12 (1810): 632-330.

24 A. B. Marx, *Beethoven,* originally published 1859 (Leipzig, 1902), 203 See Scott Burnham, *Beethoven Hero* for an extended discussion of Marx and other critics; also Robin Wallace, *Beethoven's Critics.*

25 Quoted by Burnham in *Beethoven Hero*, xv.

26 I am borrowing this anecdote from my essay, "*Eroica* Perspectives: Strategy and Design in the First Movement," originally published in *Beethoven Studies*, ed. Alan Tyson (New York, 1973), 97–122; reprinted in my *Beethoven: Studies in the Creative Process*, 118–33, especially 120f. Its source was Erich Roeder, *Felix Draeseke, Der Lebens-und Leidensweg eines deutschen Meisters*, vol. 1 (Dresden, 1932), 106, quoting from Draeseke's own account in an essay published in *Signale*, 65 (1907): 1–12.

27 Wagner, "Ueber die Anwendung der Musik auf das Drama," in Richard Wagner, *Gesammelte Schriften*, ed. Julius Kapp, vol. 13, 290f. Cited earlier in my *Beethoven: Studies in the Creative Process*, 121.

28 For a recent overview of this tradition with regard to the symphony, see Mark Evan Bonds, *After Beethoven* (Cambridge, MA, 1996).

29 Kinsky-Halm, 129f., quoting the original edition of October 1806.

30 There are many published analytical commentaries on the dense motivic and thematic connections in the symphony, but I will point out just two here. The first is that of David Epstein his book *Beyond Orpheus* (Cambridge MA, 1979), especially 111–38; the second is the discussion of the relationship of the first movement to the Op. 35 Variations in *ESk*, vol. 2.

31 See Roger Sessions, *The Musical Experience* (Princeton, 1949).

32 This procedure could sometimes change at late stages, as when in a few cases he substituted an entirely new movement, as with the "Kreutzer" Sonata finale, originally intended for an earlier sonata, or his replacement of the Andante favori of the "Waldstein" Sonata with the mysterious and dramatic *Introduzione*. Samples of these outlines of "movement-plans" are found in the sketchbooks from early to late, from the early work on the Opus 26 Piano Sonata to the late string quartets. For a larger view of his procedures, beginning with an "image," see my "From Conceptual Image to Realization: Some Thoughts on Beethoven's Sketches," in William Kinderman and Joseph E. Jones, eds., *Genetic Criticism and the Creative Process* (Rochester, 2009), 108–22. A recent study of his movement-plans for multi-movement works is Buurman, "Beethoven's Compositional Approach."

33 On Beethoven's writing of Masonic symbols in the margins of a pair of pages in the *Eroica* Sketchbook, see *ESk*, vol. 2, 20–23.

34 For example mm. 88, 478, and, most tellingly, in the coda at mm. 605–11.

35 See mm. 29–35, which falls between the second and third statements of the main theme; here Beethoven had originally thought of having a restatement of the main theme itself, in the dominant key, a redundancy that he had trouble getting rid of in the sketches; but his solution, here, is to write a powerful passage in syncopated chords in the full orchestra, while the first violin rises through the pitches of the dominant harmony itself, in the order 1–3–1–5–1 (in the dominant key) thus literally anticipating the first theme itself that is about to reappear. I discuss this passage as it appears in the sketches in my "From Conceptual Image" (n. 31).

36 *Beethoven by Berlioz*, compiled and translated by Ralph de Sola (Boston, 1975), 17.

37 I am indebted here to Alan Gosman, my collaborator on the critical edition of the *Eroica* Sketchbook.

38 *Beethoven by Berlioz*, 18. It is noteworthy that Beethoven uses the same disintegration of an opening C-minor theme at the end of his overture *Coriolanus*, a work of great power that stands between the *Eroica* Funeral March and the Fifth Symphony, both eminent expressions of what has been called Beethoven's "C-minor mood." See Michael Tusa, "Beethoven's 'C-Minor Mood': Some Thoughts on the Structural Implications of Key Choice," *BF* 2 (1993): 1–19.

39 Grove, *Beethoven and His Nine Symphonies*, 76f.

40 *Beethoven's "Eroica" Sketchbook,* 10. Nottebohm proposed the reading "St" (= "Stimme" = Voice), which makes conceptual sense. But the symbol is clearly a capital "M" for "Menuetto," still Beethoven's term for third movements. There was not enough room to fill out the sentence because he had already written the "M" in the middle of the upper margin.

41 C. Floros, *Beethovens Eroica und Prometheus-Musik* (Wilhelmshaven, 1978).

42 See P. Mies, "Quasi una fantasia," S. Kross and H. Schmidt, eds., *Colloquium Amicorum . . .* (Bonn, 1967), 239–49.

43 See my "The Compositional Genesis of the *Eroica* Finale," originally published in *Beethoven's Compositional Process,* ed. William Kinderman (Lincoln, NE, 1991), 82–101, reprinted in my *Beethoven: Studies in the Creative Process,* 151–66.

44 Burnham, 60.

45 First discussed by Nottebohm, N II, 180f.

46 Thus most recently, Burnham writes "taken as a whole, this finale cannot be said to resolve the rest of the work unequivocally" (60). As early as 1807, a critic in the AMZ had written, "The finale pleased less, and it seemed to me that here the artist often wanted only to play games with the audience without taking its enjoyment into account." For this and other early reviews see Wayne M. Senner and Robin Wallace, editors, *The Critical Reception of Beethoven's Compositions by His German Contemporaries*, vol. 2 (Lincoln, NE, 2001), 15–42; the above quotation is from a review in the *AMZ* of 1807.

47 TF, 673f.

48 *Briefe* No. 65, dated 29 June [1801]; see n. 1 on the date.

THE FOURTH SYMPHONY

1 Schumann, *On Music and Musicians*, ed. K. Wolff (New York, 1948), 99.

2 Cosima Wagner offered Richard Wagner the opinion that the Fourth "followed naturally from the Second Symphony," as it seemed so distant to her from the great power of the *Eroica*; see *Cosima Wagner's Diaries*, II, 942.

3 *ESk,* 4–92.

4 *ESk,* 155–58; see Commentary, 80–83.

5 *ESk,* 64, staves 1 and 5; p. 96, the "Murmeln der Bäche" (Murmurs of the brooks); and on p. 159 the entry marked "*lustige* Sinfonia." The sketches in the *Eroica* Sketchbook that do relate at least partially to the Sixth Symphony are not developed with anything like the same clarity of purpose as those in C minor that prefigure the Fifth. But several of them are close enough to themes and figures in the Pastoral Symphony to permit us to see them as harbingers of the later finished work.

6 See Tyson in JTW, 160–65, and especially 161, on a presumably lost large-scale

sketchbook that Beethoven would have used in 1806, which would in all likeli-hood have contained sketches for the Violin Concerto, Op. 51, the Fourth Piano Concerto, Op. 58, the Fourth Symphony, and the *Coriolanus* Overture. JTW does discuss in detail the scattered leaves of a large sketchbook that Beethoven used from the fall of 1807 to about February 1808, which contain sketches for the Overture *Leonore* No. 1; for portions of the Fifth Symphony, for the Cello Sonata Op. 69; and for his settings of Goethe's "Sehnsucht" (WoO 134).

7 For a list of the few known sketches for the Fourth Symphony see Bathia Chur-gin, ed., *Beethoven Werke, Symphonien II* (Munich, 2013), 228 and 238. She writes (238, in my translation), "The Fourth Symphony was evidently composed for the most part in 1806." Churgin's critical edition, extensive commentary, and years of scholarship on the Fourth Symphony are of very high value.

8 This encounter apparently took place in October of 1806. For more details see Clive, *Beethoven and His World*, 204.

9 On Beethoven's relationship to Lichnowsky in general, and on this supposed letter, see Jurgen May, "Beethoven and Prince Karl Lichnowsky *BF* 3 (1994): 29–38.

10 *Briefe* No. 302 and Anderson III, 1444–46. In his petition, however, he attached conditions that he may have known he was never likely to fulfill. These included writing "at least one grand opera every year" and also "a little operetta or diver-tissement, choruses, and incidental pieces." In any event, his petition was turned down in December of that year. The authorities probably knew better than to believe he would really become a full-time opera composer.

11 Text in *Die Neun Sinfonien Beethovens* (essay by Wolf-Dieter Seiffert on the Fourth), "Dokumente," 140; translation in Anderson, III, 1426.

12 *Briefe* No. 256.

13 *Briefe* No. 260.

14 *Briefe* No. 325, "March 1808."

15 *Briefe* No. 340; Anderson No. 178.

16 Clive, *Beethoven and His World*, 253.

17 Anderson No. 763, surmises that the "musical friend from Silesia" to whom Beethoven refers in a letter of 1817 could be Oppersdorff. But the claim is denied by Brandenburg in his notes to this letter (see *Briefe* No. 1092 of 23 February 1817 to Haslinger, and n. 4). Brandenburg proposes that he is referring to Joseph Ignaz Schnabel, a church musician in Breslau who saw to the performance of many Beethoven works.

18 See Tyson, "The 'Razumovsky' Quartets: Some Aspects of the Sources," *BS* III, p. 134, on a page apparently from 1807 on which Beethoven wrote down drafts for the title pages of seven works that include the names of their current dedica-tees and some possible changes in these dedicatees. The Fourth Symphony's dedi-cation is listed as Count Oppersdorff, without any indication of change.

19 In what follows I take note of a valuable unpublished essay on the Fourth by Cecil Isaac for my 1981 NEH Seminar for College Teachers, given at Harvard University.

20 *Briefe*, No. 54. These remarks were meant in part to explain to Hoffmeister why he was asking the same price, 20 gulden, for the piano sonata as for his Septet arranged for piano and for his First Symphony, even though, as he says in his letter of January 1801, Beethoven foresaw that Hoffmeister might think that

a sonata should be cheaper than a symphony. Tovey suggests that an idiomatic translation of these words would be "this sonata takes the cake," or "that's the way to do it;" see his *Companion to Beethoven's Pianoforte Sonatas* (London, 1931), 82.

21 Except for differences in octave placement, the succession of triad members in the opening phrase in the Fourth first movement Allegro is, curiously, exactly the same as that of the *Eroica* opening, despite the gigantic differences in character and expression. This suggests a deeper level of Beethoven's conceptual thinking about melodic writing and thematic formation than has usually been considered. An early attempt to deal with such relationships was Ernest Newman, *The Unconscious Beethoven* (New York, 1927).

22 Pointed out by Ludwig Misch in his *Neue Beethoven-Studien und andere Themen* (Bonn, 1957), 56–58.

23 See John Daverio, *Robert Schumann: Herald of a "New Poetic Age"* (New York, 1997), 227; and Reinhold Dusella, "Symphonisches in den Skizzenbüchern Schumanns," in *Probleme der Symphonische Tradition*, ed. Siegfried Kross (Tutzing, 1990), 204.

24 Beethoven used the two terms interchangeably in earlier published works but "Scherzo" displaced "Menuetto" after 1803–4. The term "Tempo di Menuetto," referring to a longer movement in Menuetto meter and style, became a contrasting movement-genre, as in his Piano Sonata Op. 54 and the Eighth Symphony. He sometimes wrote third movements called "Menuetto" well after "Scherzo" had become his preferred term (as in Opus 59, No. 3) but then in later works does not use even the term "Scherzo" for movements that clearly belong to this category.

25 *Studien zu Beethovens Personalstil* (Leipzig, 1921).

THE FIFTH SYMPHONY

1 *Beethoven As I Knew Him*, 147; also in Elliot Forbes, ed., *Beethoven; Fifth Symphony* (New York, 1960), 5.

2 Holz's remark was made known by Wilhelm von Lenz, *Beethoven: Eine Kunst-Studie* (Kassel, 1855–60), 1: 216f., based on written testimony from Holz that he had given to von Lenz in 1857.

3 As we read this letter, written from the depths of extremity, we can wonder if Beethoven might have felt an affinity between his personal situation and that of the characters in Schiller's plays who railed against their fate—their "Schicksal"—and vowed to overcome it. See among other discussions of Schiller's plays, P. A. Claasen, *The Fate-Question in the Dramas and Dramatical Concepts of Friedrich Schiller* (Leipzig, 1910).

4 See Douglas Johnson, "1794–95: Decisive Years in Beethoven's Early Development," *BS* 3 (1982): 18f.

5 Churgin, "Beethoven and Mozart's Requiem," *Journal of Musicology* 5 (1987): 476. N II, 531 points out the proximity of Mozart G-minor symphony excerpt to sketches for the Fifth Symphony Scherzo. The sketchbook miscellany in which it occurs is Berlin, Landsberg 12; see Schmidt, *Verzeichnis der Skizzen Beethovens,* No. 66.

6 TF, 802.

7 For his comments to Rochlitz (not the most reliable of witnesses, as Maynard Solomon has shown) see TF, 800–804. The B-minor entry with comment is in the Scheide Sketchbook (Princeton), and was first cited by Nottebohm in N II, 326.

8 For a thorough and highly informative study of the subject see Michael Tusa, "Beethoven's 'C-Minor Mood': Some Thoughts on the Structural Implications of Key Choice," *Beethoven Forum* 2 (Lincoln, NE, 1993), 1–29.

9 See Senner and Wallace, *The Critical Reception of Beethoven's Compositions*, vol. 2, 95–112.

10 Schenker's central preoccupation with Beethoven runs through his entire life and works, from his monograph on the Ninth Symphony (1912) to *Der Freie Satz* (1925). His published analysis of the Fifth Symphony appeared in *Der Tonwille* (1921–24) and as a monograph in 1925; the English translation is in *Der Tonwille* by William Drabkin (Oxford, 2004). For a critique of Schenker's analysis of the Fifth see Scott Burnham, *Beethoven Hero*, 89–102.

11 See *ESk*.

12 These sketches appear on 155–58 of the sketchbook, and after Beethoven's first composite sketch of the first movement's basic themes, the next pages show fragmentary and non-continuous jottings that show his first ideas breaking down as he thinks about various possible later points in the first movement at which they might be used. The movement plans for the third and first movements are comparatively clean and unblemished, suggesting he is copying them from other sketch pages that we do not have; beyond that we cannot say more for now. Equally incomplete and fragmentary are the sketches in Aut. 19E, the collateral source.

13 Brandenburg, ed., *Kesslersches Skizzenbuch* (Bonn, 1978), fol. 8v., st. 1, marked "Andante sinfonia."

14 Berlin, Aut 19E, fols. 32v–33r.

15 Originally published in N I, 10–15, along with the accompanying sketches for the Fourth Piano Concerto. See also William Meredith, "Forming the New From the Old: Beethoven's Use of Variation in the Fifth Symphony," in William Kinderman, ed., *Beethoven's Compositional Process* (Lincoln, NE, 1991), 107–9 (Meredith gives all the sketches for the Fifth from Aut. 19E in new transcriptions).

16 *Eroica* Sketchbook, 158, st. 8–11.

17 This is the type of figure I call a "folded arpeggio."

18 In a recent book by Matthew Guerrieri, *The First Four Notes: Beethoven's Fifth and the Human Imagination* (New York, 2012), a broad range of uses of, and references to, the opening four-note motto are reviewed, but Guerrieri rejects Schenker's view that the opening should be heard as a pair of four-note figures that form a complex.

19 The one writer after Schenker who does point it out is Walter Riezler, *Beethoven*, 8th ed. (Zurich, 1951), 145; English translation (New York, 1972), 142.

20 Measures 59–62.

21 Measures 65–93.

22 A diagram may be seen in *BML*, 222.

23 On the very important metrical shift and its consequences see Andrew Imbrie, "'Extra' Measures and Metrical Ambiguity in Beethoven," *BS* 1, 45–66, especially 55ff.

24 In the finale of Op. 18, No. 6, I, mm. 12–16 and Op. 59, No. 1, I, mm. 33–38,

146–51, and 332–37; on the latter my comments in *Inside Beethoven's Quartets*, 119.

25 Martin Geck, "V Symphonie in C moll, Op. 67," in Renate Ulm, ed., *Die Neun Symphonien Beethovens* (Kassel, 1994), 158.

26 Earlier works in minor that have similar slow movements in the major key of the flat sixth include, in C minor, the piano sonatas Op. 10, No. 1 and Op. 13 ("Pathetique"), and the violin sonata Op. 30, No. 2. In other minor keys we find the piano sonata in D minor Op. 31, No. 2, and, much later, the Ninth Symphony, Op. 125 and the A-minor Quartet Op. 132.

27 Jonathan Del Mar, ed., *Beethoven: Symphony No. 5 in C Minor, Critical Edition* (Kassel, 1999), Critical Commentary, 55–59; and his "Beethoven's Five-Part Scherzos: Appearance and Reality," *Early Music* 11/2 (2012): 297–305, esp. 299–300 on the Fifth Symphony Scherzo problem.

28 Beethoven, *Konversationshefte*, ed. K-H. Köhler et al., II (Leipzig, 1968–), 53.

29 I am indebted here to Jonathan Del Mar's "Critical Commentary," 55–59.

30 See the excellent discussion of these works and related issues in James Webster, *Haydn's "Farewell" Symphony and the Idea of Classical Style* (Cambridge, 1991).

31 Tovey, *A Musician Talks,* vol II: *Musical Textures* (London, 1941), 64, quoted in Forbes, ed., *Beethoven, Symphony No. 5,* 198ff.

32 For a close comparison of the two finales see Burnham, *Beethoven Hero,* 55–60.

THE "PASTORAL" SYMPHONY

1 *Briefe* No. 439; Anderson No. 256, dated May 2, 1810, from Vienna to Wegeler in Koblenz.

2 *Briefe* No. 436, Anderson No. 253, in a letter to Gleichenstein evidently written in April 1810 Beethoven writes of "the wounds with which evil persons have torn apart my soul."

3 *Briefe* No. 65; Anderson No. 51; dated 29 June 1801. Though earlier editions had assigned this important letter to 1800, it is securely dated 1801 by Brandenburg, *Briefe,* I, p. 81, n. 1. For an eloquent account of Beethoven's lifelong mental image of a "peasant hut" as refuge from the city and from his personal demons, see Solomon, *Late Beethoven*, 62–63.

4 *Briefe*, No. 442, Anderson 258, dated "toward the end of May 1810."

5 "Erwachen heiterer Empfindungen bei der Ankunft auf dem Lande."

6 Solomon, *Late Beethoven,* 62 and 256 n. 67; see also TF, 501, for a more complete text. I am combining elements from both translations.

7 TF, 501, citing his remarks inscribed on a sketch leaf in Vienna, Gesellschaft der Musikfreunde.

8 Sturm (1740–86) had been a minister in Magdeburg and Hamburg, son of a royal commissioner in Augsburg, and possessed a background in science. His treatise was first published in 1722 and went through numerous editions. Besides Beethoven's annotations in his own copy, he also used Sturm's book for an entry in his *Tagebuch* (No. 171). See Solomon, *Beethoven's Tagebuch*, in his *Beethoven Essays*, 294–95. On Sturm and all the annotations see Charles C. Witcombe, "Beethoven's Private God; An Analysis of the Composer's Markings in Sturm's 'Betrachtungen,'" M.A. Thesis, San Jose State University, 1998.

9 Beethoven attached these words to the score of the "Dona nobis pacem" of the

Missa Solemnis: "Bitte um innern und äussern Frieden" ("Prayer for inner and outer peace")

10 Although a good deal of ink has been spilled on the potential importance of this numbering, it seems to me quite possible that Beethoven may well have preferred to open the concert with the "Pastoral" Symphony, a new work that would be more easily accessible to his listeners, and then follow later with the more difficult Fifth Symphony. Conceivably it may only have been known to those who prepared the announcement of the event that the two new symphonies would be his Fifth and Sixth—but that they did not really know which was which. This at least is one of many plausible hypotheses for the numbering of the two works. For a full listing and discussion of the concert program, see TF, 446–49 and David Wyn Jones, *Beethoven, Pastoral Symphony* (Cambridge, 1995), 1–3.

11 As Wyn Jones notes in *Beethoven, Pastoral Symphony*, 89, n. 2, no copy of the original handbill has survived; his and all other accounts derive from the notice in the *AMZ* 11 (1808–9), cols. 267–68. He also notes some discrepancies between the movement-headings in the handbill and those in the first edition.

12 *ESk*, 159. This brief musical idea appears to be in A major, 4/4 time, and does not have any thematic resemblance to the Pastoral Symphony (as do several other entries in this sketchbook). For this reason Brandenburg, editing the autograph of the "Pastoral" Symphony, ruled out any likely connection. But the important fact remains that in this short entry Beethoven was expressly thinking about a "joyous" symphony, clearly in contrast to the tragic C-minor "Sinfonia" ideas that he had just written out on the pages directly preceding this entry.

13 *ESk*, vol. 1, 64, st. 1.

14 As an example, the finale theme of the G-major Violin Sonata Op. 96 was originally written in A major and conceived for the cello sonata Op. 69; the slow movement of the Seventh Symphony originated in a sketch for a possible slow movement for the Quartet Op. 59, No. 3 (see N II, 86).

15 This connection was found by William Kinderman; see *ESk*, vol. 1, 61.

16 First published by Nottebohm in N II, 375, who adds an unusually extensive commentary; also in Wyn Jones, *Beethoven, Pastoral Symphony*, 25. The entry bears the time-signature of Alla breve but is written in repeated-note triplets, yielding 12/8.

17 In his critical notes, Del Mar points out that in his autograph and an early copyist's score Beethoven added "quasi Allegretto" but then deleted those words from the autograph; they appear, however, in another early score copy and in the manuscript orchestral parts that were used for the 22 December 1808 concert and perhaps for earlier run-throughs at the Lobkowitz palace. See Del Mar's edition, "Commentary," 35.

18 "Der Titel der Sinfonie in F ist Pastoral-Sinfonie oder Erinnerung an das Landleben, Mehr Ausdruck der Emfindung als Mahlerey"—see *Briefe*, No. 370, dated from Vienna 28 March 1809. The words "Mehr Ausdruck [. . . etc.]" also appeared after the title in the program announcement for the 22 December 1808 concert, as we know from its having been reproduced in the *AMZ*, 11 Jg. (1808/09), col. 297ff.

19 *Musical Articles from the Encyclopedia Britannica*, 168.

THE SEVENTH SYMPHONY

1 *Briefe* No. 553; Anderson, No. 349, with some newly translated passages. Baron Krufft was in the Austrian imperial service and was apparently a capable musician. Johann Nepomuk Zizius was a professor of statistics at the university in Vienna and a founder of the Gesellschaft der Musikfreunde, who held musical gatherings at his home. All this information is from *Briefe*, vol. 2, p. 245, notes 5 and 6.

2 On the annuity see especially Solomon, *Beethoven*, 181, 191, 193f. A thorough account is found in Martella Gutierrez Denhoff, "'O Unseeliges Dekret.' Beethovens Rente von Fürst Lobkowitz, Fürst Kinsky und Erzherzog Rudolph," in Brandenburg und Gutierrez-Denhoff, *Beethoven und Böhmen* (Bonn, 1988), 91–145.

3 On Rudolph see Kagan, op. cit., and, most recently, my "Beethoven as Sir Davison," *Bonner Beethoven-Studien* 11 (2014), 133–40.

4 *Konversationshefte,* vol. 2, Heft 22 (January 20, 1823 to February 6, 1823): 365–67.

5 For the full text of the original letter, which has been published several times in facsimile, see *Briefe*, vol. 2, No. 582, and the endnotes by Brandenburg, 272. For a complete English translation see Solomon, *Beethoven*, 2nd ed., 209–11 and his extensive discussion on 211–46; also 502 for a review of the relevant literature up to 1998. A number of writers have brought forward claims for other individuals in the seemingly unending quest to identify the intended recipient of this letter—especially Countess Josephine Deym-Stackelberg, née Brunsvik. I continue to be persuaded by the arguments advanced by Maynard Solomon, which show that the most likely candidate is Antonie Brentano.

6 See my remarks in chapter 2 apropos the Heiligenstadt Testament and the Second Symphony.

7 Dahlhaus, *Beethoven: Approaches to his Music*, translated by Mary Whittall (Oxford, 1997), 3. See also my review in *19th-Century Music*, 16/2 (Summer, 1992): 80–85; and on the general subject of Beethoven biography, my "Reappraising Beethoven Biography," in the *Yearbook of Comparative and General Literature* 53 (2007): 83–100.

8 *Beethoven: Ein Skizzenbuch aus dem Jahre 1809 (Landsberg 5)*, ed. Clemens Brenneis (Bonn, 1992), vol. 1, 55, 87; also 50, st. 5–8, in F minor and Brenneis's comment in vol. 2, 35; and 59, st. 1–4, an Allegro in F major with a Largo "introduction" (*Eingang*) in F minor (thus marked by Beethoven), and which Brenneis thinks might be either a symphony or an overture (his comment in vol. 2, p. 36).

9 Solomon, "The Seventh Symphony and the Rhythms of Antiquity," in *Late Beethoven*, 102–34. For a critique of these claims see David Levy's review in *BF*, 12/2 (2005): 208f.

10 N II, 163.

11 Cf. the few other works by him that begin not simply with a slow introduction but with what amounts to a full slow movement—they include the so-called "Moonlight" Sonata, Op. 27 No. 2, and the Quartet Op. 131—coincidentally both in the key of C-sharp minor, which he uses nowhere else.

12 See Robert Gauldin, "Beethoven's Interrupted Tetrachord and the Seventh Symphony" *Integral* V (1991): 77–100. Gauldin proposes that the first ten bars of the introduction furnish the basic material for the tonal plans of all four movements.

13 As in, to pick from numerous examples, Haydn's D-major Cello Concerto, and the finales of several of Mozart's Piano Concertos, all four of his horn concertos, and his clarinet concerto.

14 Beethoven wrote a first movement in 6/8 in the piano sonata Op. 7 but then not until Op 101. In other genres we find it in his String Trio Op. 9, No. 3, the violin sonatas Op. 12, No. 2; Op. 23; and Op. 30, No. 3; also in the Andante opening of his cello sonata Op. 102, No. 1.

15 The anecdote, from Hiller's memoirs of Mendelssohn, was picked up by Grove, *Beethoven and His Nine Symphonies,* 238. The "smaller blanks" in the autograph MS were confirmed by Benito Rivera in a brilliant study, in which he showed that Beethoven's alteration of a number of phrases in the first movement enabled him to achieve stronger phrase-patterns that lead to several local climaxes; see his "Rhythmic Organization in Beethoven's Seventh Symphony: A Study of Canceled Measures in the Autograph," *19th-Century Music,* 6/3 (Spring 1983): 241–51.

16 See above for Beckett's letter on silences in the Seventh.

17 See Alessandra Comini, *The Changing Image of Beethoven,* 94f, and John Warrack, *Carl Maria von Weber,* 89–95.

18 *AMZ* (1816), reprinted in S. Kunze, ed., *Ludwig van Beethoven: Die Werke im Spiegel seiner Zeit* (Laaber, 1987), 295.

19 Grove, op. cit., 240. Also, Thomas Day, unpublished paper, 1981, 1.

20 John Knowles, "The Sketches for the First Movement of Beethoven's Seventh Symphony" (Ph.D. diss., Brandeis University, 1984), 64–68.

21 Berlioz, op. cit., 185.

22 See Barry Cooper, *Beethoven's Folksong Settings: Chronology, Sources, and Style* (Oxford, 1994), and Petra Weber-Bockholdt, *Beethovens Bearbeitungen britischer Lieder* (Munich, 1994). Also Nicole Biamonte, "Modality in Beethoven's Folksong Settings," in *BF,* 13/1 (2006): 28–63.

23 Biamonte, op. cit., 31.

24 Kunze, op. cit., 297.

THE EIGHTH SYMPHONY

1 *Briefe* No. 809 of 1 June 1815, letter to J. P. Salomon of 1815, in which Beethoven offers some new works for publication in England, including the Seventh Symphony ("one of my very best") and says that the Eighth is a "smaller symphony in F."

2 Czerny, *Anekdoten . . .* in *Über den richtigen Vortrag der Sämtlichen Beethoven'schen Klavierwerke* (Vienna, 1963), 16.

3 Tovey, *Essays in Musical Analysis,* vol. 1, 62.

4 The autograph of the Seventh Symphony is in Kraków (Berlin MS ms. Aut. Beethoven Mendelssohn 9). The autograph of the Eighth Symphony is divided as follows: the first, second and fourth movements are in Berlin, Staatsbibliothek; the third movement is in Kraków. The Petter Sketchbook is in Bonn, Beethoven-Haus, MS Mh 59; see JTW 207–19 and Brandenburg in *Zu Beethoven,* 117–48.

5 For the first movement, N II, 111–18 (as usual, selected and incomplete but pathbreaking for their time); and Brandenburg, "Ein Skizzenbuch Beethovens aus dem Jahre 1812 . . ." op. cit, 135–39. On the sketches for the second movement see Kathryn John, "Das Allegretto-Thema in op. 93, auf seine Skizzen befragt,"

in *Zu Beethoven* 2 (Berlin, 1984), 172–84. The full sketch material for the Eighth Symphony remains to be transcribed, published, and evaluated.

6 This discovery was made by Brandenburg, "Ein Skizzenbuch Beethovens aus dem Jahre 1812," *Zu Beethoven*, ed. H. Goldschmidt (Berlin, 1979), 117–48.

7 Petter Sketchbook, fol. 42r: "Concert in g" with an "adagio in Es"; also on this page "Concert in g oder E moll;" and a special idea for a slow movement (fol. 42r): "adagio in E dur Hörner sordino Echo etc." ["Adagio in E major with muted horns as an echo, etc."]. For all these entries see Brandenburg, "Ein Skizzenbuch . . ." 139.

8 See my study, "Beethoven's Unfinished Piano Concerto of 1815: Sources and Problems" in *The Musical Quarterly* LVI/4 (1970), 624–46.

9 On the movement-plan for a D-minor symphony in 1812, see Buurman, "Beethoven's Compositional Approach," 163–66, and Peter Cahn, "Beethovens Entwürfe einer d-Moll-Symphonie von 1812," *Musiktheorie*, 20/5 (2005): 123–29.

10 Buurman, op. cit., 167f.

11 Buurman, op. cit., 169–71.

12 Measures 1–12.

13 Measures 12–37.

14 Measures 38–51.

15 Measures 52–69.

16 Measures 70–90.

17 Measures 104–81.

18 Measures 190–301.

19 See Broyles, "Beethoven: Symphony No. 8," *19th-Century Music* 4/2 (1982): 39–46, for a summary of the problems of this passage and for changes suggested by such conductors as Felix Weingartner and Georg Szell.

20 For this view of the recapitulation—that it does not really take place at m. 190 but rather at m. 198—and with all the reasons here adduced amply described, see Broyles, "Beethoven, Symphony No. 8," op. cit.

21 For an amplification of the present remarks see chapter 9 of my *Beethoven: Studies in the Creative Process* (Cambridge, MA, 1992), 198–208, "Process vs. Limits: A view of the Quartet in F Major, Opus 59, No. 1." Also Lewis Lockwood and the Juilliard String Quartet, *Inside Beethoven's Quartets* (Cambridge, MA, 2008), 95–182, on Opus 59, No. 1, especially 112–15 on the recapitulation of the first movement.

22 For an overview see Kerman, "Notes on Beethoven's Codas,' in *BS* 3: 141–59.

23 Beethoven had tried out at least four other ways of concluding the movement, all of them after he had written out the full autograph manuscript. The first had been the shortest, a mere five measures of cadential material following the long fermata on the dominant. This was soon replaced by a longer ending in which he introduced the two sets of three chopped chords in the full orchestra, each followed by a bar of rest for all instruments except the timpani, then the final close (this last phrase was now ten bars long). This second version gave way to the third, in which the timpani entrances after the two sets of chords were now crossed out, so that these bars were left as complete silences. Finally Beethoven arrived at the fourth and last version, the one in the final score, which is now extended to much greater length than any of the preceding ones and made up of more than forty bars that end the coda with its highly contrasting thematic units.

24 *Beethoven by Berlioz*, 39. Quoted earlier by George Grove, *Beethoven and His Nine Symphonies*, 294.

25 Other quasi-slow movements marked "scherzoso" or "scherzando" are those of the quartet Op. 18, No. 4 and, at the end of his life, Op. 130, 3rd movement. Such movements always have staccato figures in long repetitions as a basic means of motion.

26 The long-held belief that this movement derived, or was in some other way related to, a canon on the name "Maelzel" ("Ta-ta-ta-ta"), WoO 162, has been shown to be another of Schindler's fabrications. See Standley Howell, "Beethoven's Maelzel Canon," *The Musical Times* 120 (1979): 987–90.

27 On the use of "solo cello" markings in Haydn symphonies see Andreas Friesenhagen, "Haydn's Symphonies: Problems of Instrumentation and Performance Tradition," *Early Music* 39 (2010): 256–58.

28 The first quotation is from the anonymous review in the *AMZ* (1918), col. 161–67, quoted in Kunze, op. cit., 316f.; the second, conjectured by Kunze to have been written by Anton Diabelli, is from the *Allgemeine Musikalische Zeitung mit besonderer Rücksicht auf dem österreichischen Kaiserstaat* Jg. 2 (1818), cols. 17–23; reprinted in Kunze, 318–23; this comment is from 321.

29 Mm 374–380. The change of key signature at m. 380 is curious. Since the musical content is unmistakably in F-sharp minor (mm. 30–91) the proper signature for this key would be that of three sharps; but Beethoven writes only two sharps and has to write in the third every time he needs it.

30 Broyles, *Beethoven: The Emergence and Evolution of Beethoven's Heroic Style*, 221.

31 Broyles, op. cit., 221.

32 Solomon, "Beethoven's *Tagebuch* of 1812–1818," *BS* 3, 193–288; this is part of Entry No. 1 (1812), 212.

33 Beethoven told the Archduke Rudolph that, in composing, he should work at the keyboard and keep a small table beside it, to write down his ideas. He himself undoubtedly maintained this practice much of the time, but could also compose away from the piano, as we know from his numerous pocket sketchbooks.

THE NINTH SYMPHONY

1 *AMZ* 28 (1826): 310. See *BML*, 460.

2 Igor Stravinsky and Robert Craft, *Dialogues and a Diary* (Garden City, 1963), 24.

3 Theodore Adorno, *Beethoven: The Philosophy of Music* (Stanford, 1993), 97, 136.

4 *Briefe* No. 1438; Anderson No. 1248. The date given by Anderson, 1823, is corrected in the *Briefe.*

5 *Briefe* No. 585; Anderson No. 376.

6 *Briefe* No. 1318 of July 29, 1819. The translation in Anderson, *Letters*, No. 955, is inadequate, and a better one is in J. S. Shedlock, ed., *Beethoven's Letters* (London, 1926), No. 314.

7 *Tagebuch,* No. 43.

8 *Tagebuch* No. 119 (1817).

9 See *Briefe*, No. 1129 and Albrecht, *Letters to Beethoven*, vol. 2, No. 239.

10 Beethoven to Ries, 9 July 1817; Briefe, No. 1140; Anderson No. 786 and 787.

11 For a thorough study of the Diabelli Variations see William Kinderman, *Beethoven's Diabelli Variations* (Oxford, 1987).

12 This theme in D minor is one that he was also considering for the finale of his projected symphony in C minor (which ultimately grew to be the Fifth Symphony). See William Meredith, "Forming the New from the Old: Beethoven's Use of Variation in the Fifth Symphony," in W. Kinderman, ed., *Beethoven's Compositional Process* (Lincoln, NE, 1991), 109. For the sketch in D minor marked "Sinfonia" see *ESk*, 177, and Commentary, 82.

13 Princeton, Scheide Sketchbook, 51. For a discussion and facsimile see Brandenburg, "Die Skizzen zur Neunten Symphonie," op. cit., 91 and Abb. 5.

14 Original text: "Sinfonie/erster anfang/in bloss 4 stimmen/ 2 Vi[oli]n Viol[e] Basso/ dazwischen forte mit andern stimmen und wenn möglich jedes/andre Instrument nach und nach eintreten lassen."

15 The final version of the first movement starts with the famous mysterious open fifths in the strings and horns, then the other instruments join in, as he says, "one after the other"—in order, solo clarinet (m. 5), second flute (m. 11), first flute (m. 13), then bassoons, low horns, trumpets—all in a slowly developing crescendo and with thematic fragments eventually coalescing into the colossal main theme at m. 17ff.

16 On the dating of sources for these years that relate to the Ninth as well as other works see Brandenburg, "Die Skizzen zur Neunten Symphonie" *Zu Beethoven 2* (Berlin, 1984), 95–103. For a valuable study of the first movement sketches, based on all material available up through 1987, see Jenny Kallick, "A Study of the Advanced Sketches and Full Score Autograph for the First Movement of Beethoven's Ninth Symphony, Opus 125" (Ph.D. diss., Yale University, 1987).

17 Bonn, Beethoven-Haus, MS BSk 8/56; see Brandenburg, "Die Skizzen . . ." 103. Brandenburg suggests a date of March/April 1818 for this leaf. The verbal entry for a "Pious song . . ." etc. was first published by Nottebohm in N II, 163.

18 See N II, 163; Brandenburg, "Die Skizzen . . ." 103; Cook, 13–17, where doubts are raised about the claim that Beethoven was actually thinking about a second symphony; Levy, *Beethoven: The Ninth Symphony*, 23–30, assembles the known sketch material from these years and accepts the idea that at least for a time Beethoven had two symphonies in mind.

19 Despite the original request from London for two symphonies, and some references by contemporaries (including the notoriously unreliable Schindler) to a "second" late symphony as a true project, there is no reason to disagree with Robert Winter that the sketch evidence for the last years "leaves little possibility that Beethoven did more than think on an occasion or two about a new symphonic work" (see Winter in *Beethoven Jahrbuch* 9 (1977): 550. And despite Barry Cooper's attempt to reconstruct, perform, and record the first movement of a "Tenth Symphony" (MCA Classics, MCAD-6269), the known evidence compels me to believe, with Robert Winter, that the resulting "work" was a speculative and quixotic project.

20 For a full discussion of all this material, with music examples, see Nicholas Marston, "Beethoven's 'Anti-Organicism'? The Origins of the Slow Movement of the Ninth Symphony," in *Studies in the History of Music*, vol. 3, *The Creative Process* (New York, 1992), 169–200.

21 Marston, op. cit., 181, 184 and sources cited there.

22 Marston, op. cit., 186.

23 On this point see Robert Winter, "The Sketches for the Ode to Joy," op. cit., 198f., and Nicholas Cook, op. cit., 17f. It appears that the third of Nottebohm's entries for the instrumental theme (which eventually went into Op. 132) is found, as Winter says (p. 198) "after the last finale sketches and keeps company with the first of the Op. 126 Bagatelles, to which Beethoven turned his attention—no doubt with some relief—after the symphony had been scored up."

24 These three versions of the theme later used for Op. 132 finale, here in D minor, were first published by Nottebohm, N II, 180f., and the sources for the first two have gone missing since Nottebohm saw them; see Winter, op. cit., 198. As Winter writes, "there is no reason to assume that they were entered when the chorale finale was especially advanced" (loc. cit.).

25 For this suppressed final verse see Gail K. Hart, "Schiller's 'An die Freude' and the Question of Freedom," *German Studies Review*, 32/3 (2009): 487f.

26 For an incisive and persuasive discussion of Schiller's transformation of his ideas of political freedom and revolt into the aesthetic ideals, see Klaus L. Berghahn, "*Gedankenfreiheit*: From Political Reform to Aesthetic Revolution in Schiller's Works," in Ehrhard Bahr and Thomas P Saine, eds., *The Internalized Revolution: German Reactions to the French Revolution, 1789–1989* (New York, 1992), 99–118.

27 See Solomon, "Beethoven and Schiller," in his *Beethoven Essays,* 205 and n. 3.

28 TF, 120f.

29 Robert Winter, "The Sketches for the 'Ode to Joy'," *Beethoven, Performers and Critics: International Beethoven Congress Detroit 1977*, ed. Robert Winter and Bruce Carr (Detroit, 1989), 177.

30 *Briefe* No. 1292 of 3 March 1819; Anderson No. 948 dates the letter "early June 1819" but this is too late; see *Briefe* 4, 247, n. 1 on the dating.

31 *Briefe* No. 1318; Anderson No. 955, July 29, 1819.

32 "Alte und Neue Kirchenmusik," first published in the *AMZ* of 1814.

33 Shown by Warren Kirkendale, "New Roads to Old Ideas in Beethoven's *Missa Solemnis*," *The Musical Quarterly*, 56 (1970): 665–701.

34 William Kinderman, "Beethoven's Symbol for the Deity in the *Missa solemnis* and the Ninth Symphony," *19th-Century Music*, IX (1985–86): 102–18.

35 *Briefe* No. 1875; Anderson No 1307 (16 September 1824).

36 *Beethoven*, 2nd ed., 401.

37 Measure 638. For astute comments on this passage see Leo Treitler, "'To Worship That Celestial Sound': Motives for Analysis," in his *Music and the Historical Imagination* (Cambridge, MA, 1989), 57 and 63.

38 This passage was one of the key points in William Kinderman's discussion of the connections between symbolism in the *Missa Solemnis* and in the Ninth Symphony (see n. 34); also David Levy, op. cit., 112f.

39 An example is Esteban Buch's book entitled *Beethoven's Ninth: A Political History* (Chicago, 2003), originally published in French as *La Neuvième de Beethoven* (Paris, 1999). Buch's book is a useful survey of the many political uses of the Ode melody. So far as I can tell on a close reading, nowhere in Buch's book is there any discussion of the earlier movements. Although he acknowledges (p. 4) that "it is true that the Ninth is, above all, a work of 'pure' music, an integral part of the classical repertoire," his position clearly is that there is no such thing as

"pure music," that "the most systematic refusal to make social or historical considerations a part of technical musical analysis still implies taking a position with regard to the social role of the work of art."

40 For sensitive discussions of the opening, rife in the literature, see Tovey, *Essays* II, 6; Schenker, Beethoven: Neunte Sinfonie, 2nd ed. (Vienna, 1969), 3; Treitler, "History, Criticism and Beethoven's Ninth Symphony," in his *Music and the Historical Imagination,* 19–22. My own earlier comments on the opening are in my "The Four 'Introductions' in the Ninth Symphony," in *Probleme der Symphonischen Tradition im 19. Jahrhundert,* ed. by Siegfried Kross unter Mitarbeit von Marie Luise Maintz (Tutzing, 1900), 97–113, especially 98–102.

41 Tovey, *Essays* II, 6. Tovey for once has it both ways.

42 See Jenny L. Kallick, "A Study of the Advanced Sketches." I refer to the earliest continuity drafts in the MSS Paris 96, the Engelmann Sketchbook, and other related sources, all listed by Kallick. Her discussion of the Exposition sketches is found on 33–50, her transcriptions of them are on 75–102.

43 For an eloquent discussion of key-relationships in the symphony see Treitler, *Music and the Historical Imagination,* 56ff.

44 There is no sign of a double bar in the autograph of the symphony, which has been published in facsimile several times, most recently by Bärenreiter (Kassel, 2010). See also Kallick, op. cit., 202.

45 This strategy—of having no repeat of the sonata-form exposition (which Beethoven would have called the "prima parte")—reminds us of his practice in the sonata-form first movement of the quartet in F major, Opus 59 No. 1, in which he had taken the historic step of eliminating the Exposition repeat. There too, as here in the Ninth, he opened the development section with an apparent return to the main theme that then moves on in new and surprising ways. On the formal plan of Opus 59, No. 1, see my *Beethoven: Studies in the Creative Process,* chapter 9, "Process vs. Limits: A View of the Quartet in F Major, Opus 59, No. 1," 198–208; and also my book co-authored with the Juilliard Quartet, *Inside Beethoven's Quartets* (Cambridge, MA, 2008), 95–146 (on Opus 59 No. 1) and the score of the first movement as annotated by the Juilliard Quartet, 147–79.

46 Marx, *Ludwig van Beethoven* (Leipzig, originally 1859) I cite the revised ed. of 1902, vol. II, 231; Tovey, *Essays* II, 18.

47 Susan McClary, in a much-discussed passage in her book *Feminine Endings: Gender, Music, and Sexuality* (Minneapolis: University of Minnesota Press, 1991), pp. 128-9, interprets the recapitulation as "one of the most horrifyingly violent episodes in the history of music" and sees the Ninth Symphony as "probably our most compelling articulation in music of the contradictory impulses that have organized patriarchal culture since the Enlightenment."

48 Treitler, *Music and the Historical Imagination,* 23; Levy, *Beethoven: The Ninth Symphony,* 62.

49 On this technique see Christopher Reynolds, *Wagner, Schumann, and the Lessons of Beethoven's Ninth* (Berkeley, 2015).

50 *Tagebuch* Entry No. 72, from perhaps around 1816.

51 Solomon, *Beethoven,* 2nd ed., 209. The original German is "Ach—Es gibt Momente, wo ich finde dass die sprache noch gar nichts ist"; *Briefe* No. 582.

52 The Largo as preface to the finale in Op. 106, and the Adagio that precedes the Arioso dolente in Op. 110, are among the most poignant and deeply expressive sections in all Beethoven's late works

53 The three-part Scherzi in the symphonies are those of the First, Second, Third, and Eighth (Tempo di Menuetto); the five-part Scherzi are those of the Fourth, Sixth, and Seventh.

54 This is well observed by Levy, op. cit., 73.

55 For a brief listing of the principal fugal movements in late Beethoven, see *BML*, 369f.

56 Unprecedented, that is, among the openings of Beethoven's Menuetti and Scherzi; he had used similar ways of opening fast movements with abrupt short phrases separated by rests from early on (e.g., the piano sonata Op. 10, No. 3, finale; Op. 22, first movement; and others). A good example for comparison with the opening of this Scherzo is that of his piano sonata Op. 28, which begins with descending octaves on F♯ over four bars and then four abrupt figures; but it is in no way as dramatic as the Ninth Symphony Scherzo opening.

57 On his use of this term in a variety of works from early to late see Günther Massenkeil, "Cantabile bei Beethoven," in *Beethoven-Kolloquium 1977*, ed. Rudolf Klein, (Kassel, 1978), 154–59; Peter Gülke, "Kantabile und Thematische Abhandlung," *Beiträge zur Musikwissenschaft*, 12 (1970): 252–73; and Carl Dahlhaus, "Cantabile und Thematischer Prozess," *Archiv für Musikwissenschaft*, 37 (1980): 81–98.

58 *Briefe* No. 2002, letter to Galitzin of c. 6 July 1825.

59 Schenker, *Beethoven's Ninth Symphony*, translated and edited by John Rothgeb (New Haven, 1992), 184; Tovey, *Essays*, I, 74–77 (but see also his extended remarks in *Essays*, II, 28–35; Levy, op. cit., 77–87; Cook, op. cit., 32–34.

60 Levy, op. cit., 84.

61 Berlioz, *A Critical Study of Beethoven's Nine Symphonies*, trans. Edwin Evans, Introduction by D. Kern Holoman (Urbana, IL, 2000), 123.

62 The primary sketchbook for the finale is Berlin, MS Landsberg 8/2, a "homemade sketch bundle" that he used between May 1823 and June 1824 (after the premiere of the Ninth). For its contents see JTW, 292–98; Winter, "The Sketches for the Ode to Joy," op. cit.; Brandenburg, "Die Skizzen . . ." 122–27. Important excerpts were already given by Nottebohm in N II, 157–92.

63 N II, 190f. Nottebohm's source was Berlin, MS Landsberg 8/2, Bundle VII, fols. 69 and 75 (see JTW, 298). Also reprinted from Nottebohm by Levy, 38.

64 N II, 189.

65 Winter, "The Sketches for the 'Ode to Joy'," op. cit., 184.

66 On the Scottish and Irish folksongs see my discussion of the Seventh Symphony finale and the song "Nora Creina," above, but also the collections WoO 157 (twelve folksongs, including one Sicilian and one Venetian alongside English, Scottish, and Irish) and WoO 158 (songs of various peoples, including songs from Denmark, Germany, the Tyrol, Poland, Portugal, Russia, Sweden, Spain, Italy, and Hungary).

67 For a brief summary, see Jean Mongredien, *French Music from the Enlightenment to Romanticism, 1789–1830*, translated by Sylvain Fremaux (Portland, OR, 1996), 38–48.

68 On the origins and uses of the melody see Grove, "National Anthems" and on

national anthems of this time, *BML*, 152–55. The Beethoven variations are WoO 78, and its companion piece, variations on "Rule Britannia," WoO 79. See, most recently, the commentary in *ESk*, vol. 1, 27f.

69 On this and much other music by Beethoven that is related to the political events of the period of the Congress of Vienna, and much before and after, see Nicholas Mathew, *Political Beethoven* (Cambridge, 2013).

70 Sketchbook MS Berlin Landsberg 5, ed. by Clemens Brenneis as *Beethoven: Ein Skizzenbuch aus dem Jahre 1809* (Bonn, 1992), 19.

EPILOGUE

1 For a recent appraisal of Beethoven's influence on later symphonic composers see Mark Evan Bonds, *After Beethoven* (Cambridge, MA, 1996).

2 Of many writings on Wagner's indebtedness to Beethoven, I can single out Klaus Kropfinger, *Wagner and Beethoven*, translated by Peter Palmer (Cambridge, 1991).

3 Alessandra Comini, *The Changing Image of Beethoven: A Study in Mythmaking* (New York, 1987), 14.

4 For one of many accounts of this famous performance see Klaus Geitel, "Exulting Freedom in Music," http://www.leonardbernstein.com/hc_berlin.htm.

5 Richard Rorty, "The Inspirational Value of Great Works of Literature," *Raritan* 16 (1996): 8–17, reprinted in his *Achieving Our Country* (Cambridge, MA, 1998), 125–40.

6 The statue, made by Thomas Crawford in the 1850s, is now in the New England Conservatory in Boston. In 1857, pianist, composer and Beethoven enthusiast Ignaz Moscheles commented on it favorably. See the new biography of Moscheles by Mark Kroll, *Ignaz Moscheles and the Changing World of Musical Europe* (Rochester, NY, 2014), 127.

7 The literature on the American Transcendentalist movement is voluminous, but in particular for its musical aspects and on John Sullivan Dwight, see Ora Frishberg Saloman, *Beethoven's Symphonies and J. S. Dwight* (Boston, 1995).

8 *Dwight's Journal*, the most important American music periodical of the century, ran for almost forty years, from 1852 to 1891.

9 Ora Frishberg Salomon, op. cit., 3. The strength of the Beethoven cult fostered the work of the first great Beethoven biographer, Alexander Wheelock Thayer, who moved in these circles and who published many of his early essays in Dwight's Journal. See Michael Ochs, "A. W. Thayer, the Diarist, and the Late Mr. Brown: A Bibliography of Writings in *Dwight's Journal of Music*," in Lewis Lockwood and Phyllis Benjamin, eds., *Beethoven Essays: Studies in Honor of Elliot Forbes* (Cambridge, MA, 1984), 78–95.

10 On this letter and Fuller's passionate devotion to Beethoven and his music see Charles Capper, *Margaret Fuller: An American Romantic Life*, 2 vols. (Oxford, 1992, 2007); the text of the letter was recently published on the internet by Greg Mitchell; see gregmitchellwriter.blogspot.com/2014/04 [dated 27 April 2014]. Also Ora Frishberg Saloman, "Margaret Fuller and Beethoven in America," *Journal of Musicology*, 10/1 (1992): 89–105.

11 In what follows I am borrowing from an earlier essay of mine, published in Dutch with the title, "Beethoven's moreel besef toen en nu" in *Europees human-*

isme in fragmenten, edited by Rob Riemen (Tilburg, 2008), 84–93.

12 The history of the Łódź ghetto was originally told by a number of chroniclers who lived through these appalling times and left their memoirs. A number of them have been published, and of these the most relevant for my narrative is that of Oskar Rosenfeld, whose notebooks were published first in German and later translated as *In the Beginning Was the Ghetto: 890 Days in Lodz,* edited and with an introduction by Hanno Loewy, translated by Brigitte M. Goldstein (Evanston: Northwestern University Press, 2002). The best modern account of the entire history of the ghetto is Gordon J. Horwitz, *Ghettostadt: Lodz and the Making of a Nazi City* (Cambridge, MA, 2008). I am grateful to Professor Horwitz for his help in locating the typescript of Rosenfeld's descriptions of the ghetto orchestra in the YIVO Institute for Jewish Research in New York. I am also especially indebted to Michael Ochs for his editorial help on this section.

13 The population figure given by Horwitz, op. cit., 335, n. 1, is estimated to have been 163,777 persons, based on a census made in June 1940. For a description of Rumkowski see Horwitz, op. cit., 14–17. The epithet "King of the Jews" comes from Leslie Epstein's novel of that name (1979).

14 Horwitz, op. cit., 127f. and 346, n. 44, citing the Lodz ghetto diary of Shlomo Frank, *Togbukh,* entry for 8 July 1941, p. 133.

15 A good summary on Rosenfeld appears in Saul Friedländer, *Nazi Germany and the Jews: The Years of Extermination* (New York, 2007), 310f., 314f. 446f. 493, 527, 630–32, 662. Rosenfeld is also quoted and discussed extensively in Horwitz, op. cit., passim; and on Rosenfeld's account of musical performances, 188–91.

16 This passage is taken from the excerpt from Rosenfeld's diary published in *Łódź Ghetto: Inside a Community Under Siege,* ed. by Alan Adelman and Robert Lapides (New York, 1989), 294f.

17 From Rosenfeld, *In the Beginning;* also partially quoted by Horwitz, 189f., and see his p. 357 n. 90 citing YIVO RG 241/858, O[skar] R[osenfeld], Kulturhaus-Konzerte.

18 Rosenfeld, *In the Beginning,* 79ff.; valuable excerpts are found in Horwitz, 189f.

19 Rosenfeld, *In the Beginning,* 80.

20 Beethoven, *Konversationshefte,* vol. I., Heft & (Leipzig, 1972), 235.

BIBLIOGRAPHY

ABBREVIATIONS

AMZ — *Allgemeine musikalische Zeitung.* Leipzig, 1798–1848.

Anderson — Beethoven, Ludwig van. *The Letters of Beethoven.* Translated and edited by Emily Anderson. 3 vols. London, 1961.

BF — *Beethoven Forum.* Lincoln, NE, and Urbana-Champaign, IL, 1992–2007.

BML — Lockwood, Lewis. *Beethoven: The Music and the Life.* New York, 2003.

Briefe — Beethoven, Ludwig van. *Briefwechsel: Gesamtausgabe.* Edited by Sieghard Brandenburg. 7 vols. Munich, 1996–98.

BS — Tyson, Alan, ed. *Beethoven Studies.* 3 vols. New York, etc., 1973–1982.

ESk — Lockwood, Lewis and Alan Gosman, eds. *Beethoven's "Eroica" Sketchbook: A Critical Edition.* 2 vols. Urbana, IL, 2013.

JTW — Johnson, Douglas, Alan Tyson, and Robert Winter. *The Beethoven Sketchbooks: History, Reconstruction, Inventory.* Berkeley, 1985.

Kinsky-Halm — Kinsky, Georg, and Hans Halm. *Das Werk Beethovens: Thematisch-bibliographisches Verzeichnis seiner sämtlichen vollendeten Kompositionen.* Munich, 1955.

N I — Nottebohm, Gustav. *Beethoveniana: Aufsätze und Mittheilungen.* Leipzig, 1872.

N II — Nottebohm, Gustav. *Zweite Beethoveniana: Nachgelassene Aufsätze.* Leipzig, 1887.

TF — Thayer, Alexander Wheelock. *Thayer's Life of Beethoven.* Revised and edited by Elliot Forbes. Princeton, NJ, 1964.

WORKS CITED

Adorno, T. W. *Beethoven: The Philosophy of Music*. Stanford, CA, 1993.

Albrecht, Theodor, ed. *Letters to Beethoven and Other Correspondence*. 3 vols. Lincoln, NE, 1996.

Beckett, Samuel. *The Letters of Samuel Beckett*, vol. 1, *1929–1940*. Cambridge, 2009.

Becking, Gustav. *Studien zu Beethovens Personalstil*. Leipzig, 1921.

Beethoven, Ludwig van. *Autograph Miscellany from Circa 1786 to 1799: British Museum Additional Manuscript 29801, ff. 39–162 (The "Kafka" Sketchbook)*. Edited by Joseph Kerman. 2 vols. London, 1970.

————. *Briefwechsel: Gesamtausgabe*. Edited by Sieghard Brandenburg. 7 vols. Munich, 1996–98.

————. *Konversationshefte*. Edited by Karl-Heinz Köhler, Grita Herre, Dagmar Beck, and Günter Brosche. 11 vols. Leipzig, 1968–2001.

————. *The Letters of Beethoven*. Translated and edited by Emily Anderson. 3 vols. London, 1961.

Berger, Karol. "The Ends of Music History, or: The Masters in the Supermarket of Culture." *Journal of Musicology* 31/2 (Spring 2014): 186–98.

Berghahn, Klaus L. "Gedankenfreiheit: From Political Reform to Aesthetic Revolution in Schiller's Works." In *The Internalized Revolution: German Reactions to the French Revolution*. Ed. by Ehrhard Bahr and Thomas P. Saine, 99–118. New York, 1992.

Biamonte, Nicole. "Modality in Beethoven's Folksong Settings." *BF* 13/1 (2006): 28–63.

Bonds, Mark Evan. *After Beethoven*. Cambridge, MA, 1996.

Brandenburg, Sieghard. "Ein Skizzenbuch Beethovens aus dem Jahre 1812." In *Zu Beethoven*, edited by Harry Goldschmidt, 117–48. Berlin, 1979.

————. "Die Skizzen zur Neunten Symphonie." In *Zu Beethoven 2*, edited by Harry Goldschmidt, 88–129. Berlin, 1984.

————. ed. *Kesslersches Skizzenbuch*. Bonn, 1978.

Brenneis, Clemens, ed. *Beethoven: Ein Skizzenbuch aus dem Jahre 1809*. Bonn, 1992.

Brinkman, Reinhold. "In the Time of the Eroica." In *Beethoven and His World*, edited by Scott Burnham and Michael Steinberg, 1–26. New York, 2000.

Broyles, Michael. *Beethoven: The Emergence and Evolution of Beethoven's Heroic Style*. New York, 1987.

————. "Beethoven: Symphonie No. 8." *19th-Century Music*, 4/2 (1982): 39–46.

Buch, Esteban. *Beethoven's Ninth: A Political History*. Chicago, 2003.

Burnham, Scott. *Beethoven Hero*. Princeton, NJ, 1995.

Busoni, Feruccio. *Von der Einheit der Musik, Verstreute Aufzeichnungen*. Berlin, 1922.

Buurman, Erica. "Beethoven's Compositional Approach to Multi-Movement Structure in his Instrumental Works." Ph.D. Dissertation, University of Manchester, 2013.

Cahn. Peter. "Beethovens Entwürfe einer d-Moll-Symphonie von 1812." *Musiktheorie,* 20/5 (2005): 123–29.

Czerny, Carl. "Anekdoten . . ." In *Über den richtigen Vortrag der sämtlichen Beethoven'schen Klavierwerke,* edited by Paul Badura-Skoda. Vienna, 1963.

Churgin, Bathia, ed. *Beethoven Werke, Symphonien II.* Munich, 2013.

Clive, Peter. *Beethoven and His World.* Oxford, 2001.

Claasen, P. A. *The Fate-Question in the Dramas and Dramatical Concepts of Schiller in Contrast to the Real So-called Fate-Dramas.* Leipzig, 1910.

Comini, Alessandra. *The Changing Image of Beethoven: A Study in Mythmaking.* New York, 1987.

Cook, Nicholas. *Beethoven: Symphony No. 9.* Cambridge, 1993.

Cooper, Barry. *Beethoven and the Creative Process.* Oxford, 1990.

———. *Beethoven's Folksong Settings: Chronology, Sources, and Style.* Oxford, 1994.

———. "Beethoven's Tenth Symphony." In *Journal of the Royal Musical Association,* 117 (1992): 324–29.

———. "Newly Identified Sketches for Beethoven's Tenth Symphony." *Music and Letters* 66 (1985): 9–18.

Coren, Daniel. "Structural Relations Between Op. 28 and Op. 36." In *Beethoven Studies 2,* edited by Alan Tyson, 66–83. Oxford, 1977.

Dahlhaus, Carl. *Beethoven: Approaches to His Music.* Translated by Mary Whittall. Oxford, 1991.

———. "Cantabile und Thematischer Prozess." *Archiv für Musikwissenschaft* 37 (1980): 81–98.

Daverio, John. *Robert Schumann: Herald of a "New Poetic Age."* New York, 1997.

Del Mar, Jonathan. "Beethoven's Five-Part Scherzos: Appearance and Reality." *Early Music,* 11/2 (2012): 297–305.

Denhoff, Martella Gutierrez. "'O Unseeliges Dekret.' Beethovens Rente von Fürst Lobkowitz, Fürst Kinsky und Erzherzog Rudolph." In *Beethoven und Böhmen,* ed. Sieghard Brandenburg and Martella Gutierrez Denhoff, 91–145. Bonn, 1988.

De Sola, Ralph, compiler and translator. *Beethoven by Berlioz: A Critical Appreciation of Beethoven's Nine Symphonies.* Boston, 1975.

Dusella, Reinhold. "Symphonisches in den Skizzenbüchern Schumanns." In *Probleme der Symphonische Tradition im 19. Jahrhundert,* edited by S. Kross, 203-24. Tutzing, 1990.

Einstein, Albert. "The Military Element in Beethoven." *Monthly Musical Record* 69 (November 1939): 270–74.

Ellman, Richard. *Golden Codgers: Biographical Speculations.* New York, 1973.

Epstein, David. *Beyond Orpheus.* Cambridge, MA, 1979.

Fétis, François-Joseph. *Biographie Universelle des Musiciens.* Paris, 1866.

Fishman, Nathan. *Kniga eskizov Beethovena za 1802–1803.* 3 vols. Moscow, 1962.

Floros, Constantin. *Beethovens Eroica und Prometheus-Musik.* Wilhelmshaven, 1978.

Forbes, Elliot, ed. *Beethoven: Fifth Symphony.* New York, 1960.

Friedländer, Saul. *Nazi Germany and the Jews: The Years of Extermination.* New York, 2007.

Friesenhagen, Andreas. "Haydn's Symphonies: Problems of Instrumentation and Performance Tradition." *Early Music* 39 (2010): 256–58.

Gauldin, Robert. "Beethoven's Interrupted Tetrachord and the Seventh Symphony." *Integral* 5 (1991): 77–100.

Geck, Martin. "V Symphonie in C moll, Op. 67." In *Die Neun Symphonien Beethovens,* edited by Renate Ulm, Kassel, 1994.

Goldschmidt, Harry. "Beethoven in neuen Brunsvik-Briefen." *Beethoven Jahrbuch* 9 (1973–77): 97–146.

Grigat, Friederike. *Die Sammlung Wegeler im Beethoven-Haus Bonn: Kritischer Katalog.* Bonner Beethoven-Studien 7 (2008).

Grove, George. *Beethoven and His Nine Symphonies.* London, 1896; reprinted New York, 2012.

Guerrieri, Matthew. *The First Four Notes: Beethoven's Fifth and the Human Imagination.* New York, 2012.

Gülke, Peter. "Kantabile und Thematische Abhandlung." *Beiträge zur Musikwissenschaft* 12 (1970): 252–73.

Haberl, Dieter. "Beethovens Erste Reise nach Wien: Die Datierung seiner Schülerreise zu W. A. Mozart." *Neues Musikwissenschaftliches Jahrbuch,* 14 (2006): 215–55.

Horwitz, Gordon J. *Ghettostadt: Łódź and the Making of a Nazi City.* Cambridge, MA, 2008.

John, Kathryn. "Das Allegretto-Thema in op. 93 auf seine Skizzen befragt." In *Zu Beethoven, 2: Aufsätze und Dokumente,* edited by Harry Goldschmidt, 172–84. Berlin, 1984.

Johnson, Douglas. "1794–1795: Decisive Years in Beethoven's Early Development." In *Beethoven Studies* 3, edited by Alan Tyson, 1–28. Cambridge, 1982.

———. *Beethoven's Early Sketches in the "Fischhof" Miscellany, Berlin Autograph 28.* 2 vols. Ann Arbor, 1980.

Johnson, Douglas, Alan Tyson, and Robert Winter. *The Beethoven Sketchbooks: History, Reconstruction, Inventory.* Berkeley, 1985.

Kagan, Susan. *Archduke Rudolph: Beethoven's Patron, Pupil, and Friend.* New York, 1988.

Kallick, Jenny. "A Study of the Advanced Sketches and Full Score Autograph for the First Movement of Beethoven's Ninth Symphony, Opus 125." Ph.D. diss., Yale University, 1987.

Kamien, Roger. "The Slow Introduction of Mozart's Symphony No. 38 in D, K. 405 ("Prague"): A Possible Model for the Slow Introduction of Beethoven's Symphony No. 2 in D, Op. 36." *Israel Studies in Musicology* 5 (1990): 113–30.

Kerman, Joseph. "Notes on Beethoven's Codas." *BS* 3 (1982): 141–59.

Kinderman, William. *Beethoven's Diabelli Variations.* Oxford, 1987.

———. "Beethoven's Symbol for the Deity in the *Missa Solemnis* and the Ninth Symphony." *19th-Century Music* 9/2 (1985–86): 102–118.

Kinderman, William and Joseph E. Jones, eds. *Genetic Criticism and the Creative Process.* Rochester, NY, 2009.

Kinsky, Georg and Hans Halm. *Das Werk Beethovens: Thematisch-bibliographisches Verzeichnis seiner sämtlichen vollendeten Kompositionen.* Munich, 1955.

Kirkendale, Warren. "New Roads to Old Ideas in Beethoven's *Missa Solemnis.*" *The Musical Quarterly* 56 (1970): 665–701.

Knowles, John. "The Sketches for the First Movement of Beethoven's Seventh Symphony." Ph.D. diss., Brandeis University, 1984.

Kroll, Mark. *Ignaz Moscheles and the Changing World of Musical Europe.* Rochester, NY, 2014

Kropfinger, Klaus. *Wagner and Beethoven.* Cambridge, 1991.

Kunze, Stefan, ed. *Ludwig van Beethoven: Die Werke im Spiegel seiner Zeit.* Laaber, 1987.

Küthen, Hans-Werner. "Beethovens 'wirklich ganz neue Manier'—Eine Persiflage." In *Beiträge zu Beethovens Kammermusik, Symposion Bonn 1984,* edited by Sieghard Brandenburg and Helmut Loos, 216–24. Munich, 1987.

Landon, H. C. Robbins. *Haydn: Chronicle and Works.* 5 vols. London, 1976–80.

Lenz, Wilhelm von. *Beethoven: Eine Kunststudie.* 4 vols. Hamburg, 1855–60.

Levy, David. *Beethoven: The Ninth Symphony.* Rev. ed. New Haven, CT, 2003.

Lockwood, Lewis. "Beethoven and His Royal Disciple." *Bulletin of the American Academy of Arts and Sciences* 57/3 (Spring 2004): 2–7.

———. "Beethoven as Sir Davison." *Bonner Beethoven-Studien* 11 (Bonn, 2004): 133–40.

———. "Beethoven before 1800: The Mozart Legacy." *BF* 3 (1994): 39–52.

———. "Beethoven, Florestan, and the Varieties of Heroism." In *Beethoven and His World,* edited by Scott Burnham and Michael P. Steinberg, 27–47. Princeton, NJ, 2000.

———. *Beethoven: Studies in the Creative Process.* Cambridge, MA, 1992.

———. *Beethoven: The Music and the Life.* New York, 2003.

————. "Beethoven's First Symphony: A Farewell to the Eighteenth Century?" In *Essays in Musicology: A Tribute to Alvin Johnson,* edited by Lewis Lockwood and Edward Roesner, 235–46. Philadelphia, 1990.

————. "Beethoven's Unfinished Piano Concerto of 1815: Sources and Problems." *The Musical Quarterly* 56/4 (1970): 624–46.

————. "Eroica Perspectives: Strategy and Design in the First Movement." In *Beethoven Studies,* edited by Alan Tyson, 85–106. New York, 1973.

————. "The Four 'Introductions' in the Ninth Symphony." In *Probleme der Symphonischen Tradition im 19. Jahrhundert,* edited by Siegfried Kross, with Marie Luise Maintz, 97–113. Tutzing, 1990.

————. "Reappraising Beethoven Biography." *Yearbook of Comparative and General Literature* 53 (2007): 83–99.

————. "Reshaping the Genre: Beethoven's Piano Sonatas from Op. 22 to Op. 28 (1799–1801)." *Israel Studies in Musicology* 6 (1996): 1–16.

Lockwood, Lewis and Alan Gosman, eds. *Beethoven's "Eroica" Sketchbook: A Critical Edition.* Urbana, IL, 2013.

Lockwood, Lewis and the Juilliard String Quartet, eds. *Inside Beethoven's Quartets.* Cambridge, MA, 2008.

Mann, Friedrich, and Alexander Mann, eds. *Musikalisches Taschenbuch auf das Jahr 1803.* Penig, 1803.

Marston, Nicholas. "Beethoven's 'Anti-Organicism'? The Origins of the Slow Movement of the Ninth Symphony." In *Studies in the History of Music, 3: The Creative Process,* edited by Ronald Broude, 169–200. New York, 1992.

Marx, A. B. *Ludwig van Beethoven.* Leipzig, 1859.

Massenkeil, Günter. "Cantabile bei Beethoven." In *Beethoven-Kolloquium 1977,* edited by Rudolf Klein, 154–59. Kassel, 1978.

Matthew, Nicholas. *Political Beethoven.* Cambridge, 2013.

Mayr, Karl Josef. *Wien im Zeitalter Napoleons.* Vienna, 1940.

Meredith, William. "Forming the New From the Old: Beethoven's Use of Variation in the Fifth Symphony." In *Beethoven's Compositional Process,* edited by William Kinderman, 102–21. Lincoln, NE, 1991.

Mies, Paul. "Quasi una fantasia." In *Colloquium Amicorum: Joseph Schmidt-Görg zum 70. Geburtstag,* edited by S. Kross and H. Schmidt, 239–49. Bonn, 1967.

Mongredien, Jean. *French Music from the Enlightenment to Romanticism, 1789–1830.* Translated by Sylvain Fremaux. Portland, OR, 1996.

Morrow, Mary Sue. *Concert Life in Vienna, 1780–1810.* Stuyvesant, NY, 1989.

Morrow, Mary Sue, and Bathia Churgin, eds. *The Eighteenth-Century Symphony.* Bloomington, 2012.

Murray, Sterling. "The Symphony in South Germany." In *The Eighteenth-Century Symphony,* edited by Mary Sue Morrow and Bathia Churgin, chapter 16. Bloomington, 2012.

Meyers, Jeffrey, ed. *The Craft of Literary Biography*. New York, 1985.

Misch, Ludwig. *Neue Beethoven-Studien und andere Themen*. Bonn, 1957.

Neubauer, John. *The Emancipation of Music from Language: Departure from Mimesis in Eighteenth-Century Aesthetics*. New Haven, CT, 1986.

Newman, Ernest. *The Unconscious Beethoven*. New York, 1927.

Nottebohm, Gustav. *Beethoveniana: Aufsätze und Mittheilungen*. Leipzig, 1872.

————. *Beethovens Studien*. Leipzig, 1873.

————. *Zweite Beethoveniana*, Leipzig, 1887.

Ochs, Michael. "A. W. Thayer, the Diarist, and the Late Mr. Brown: A Bibliography of Writings in *Dwight's Journal of Music*." In *Beethoven Essays: Studies in Honor of Elliot Forbes*, edited by Lewis Lockwood and Phyllis Benjamin, 78–95. Cambridge, MA, 1984.

Palisca, Claude. "French Revolutionary Models for Beethoven's *Eroica* Funeral March." In *Music and Context: Essays for John Ward*, edited by Anne Dhu Shapiro, 198–209. Cambridge, MA, 1985.

Riezler, Walter. *Beethoven*. 8th ed. Zurich, 1951. English translation, New York, 1972.

Ringer, Alexander. "A French Symphonist at the Time of Beethoven: Etienne Nicolas Méhul." *The Musical Quarterly* 37 (1951): 543–65.

Rivera, Benito. "Rhythmic Organization in Beethoven's Seventh Symphony: A Study of Cancelled Measures in the Autograph." *19th-Century Music* 6/3 (Spring 1983): 241–51.

Roeder, Erich. *Felix Draeseke: Der Lebens- und Leidensweg eines deutschen Meisters*, vol. 1. Dresden, 1932.

Ronge, Julia. *Beethovens Lehrzeit*. Bonn, 2011.

Rorty, Richard, "The Inspirational Value of Great Works of Literature," *Raritan* 16 (1996): 8–16, and in Rorty, *Achieving Our Country: Leftist Thought in Twentieth-Century America*, 125–40. Cambridge MA, 1998.

Rosenfeld, Oskar. *In the Beginning Was the Ghetto: 890 Days in Łódź*. Evanston, IL, 2008.

Saloman, Ora Frishberg, *Beethoven's Symphonies and J. S. Dwight: The Birth of American Music Criticism*. Boston, 1995.

Schachter, Carl. "Mozart's Last and Beethoven's First: Echoes of K. 551 in the First Movement of Opus 21." In *Mozart Studies*, edited by Cliff Eisen, 227–52. Oxford, 1991.

Schenker, Heinrich. *Beethoven's Ninth Symphony*. Translated and edited by John Rothgeb. New Haven, CT, 1992.

Schiedermair, Ludwig. *Der Junge Beethoven*. Leipzig, 1925.

Schindler, Anton Felix. *Beethoven as I Knew Him: A Biography*. Edited by Donald W. MacArdle, translated by Constance S. Jolly. Chapel Hill, 1966.

Schmidt, Hans. "Verzeichnis der Skizzen Beethovens." *Beethoven Jahrbuch* 6 (1965/68): 7–128.

Schmidt-Görg, Joseph. "Ein Schiller-Zitat Beethovens in neuer Sicht." In *Musik, Edition, Interpretation: Gedenkschrift Günter Henle,* edited by Martin Bente, 423–26. Munich, 1980.

Schmitz, Arnold. *Das Romantische Beethovenbild.* Berlin, 1927.

Schopenhauer, Arthur. *The World as Will and Representation.* 2 vols. Translated by E. F. J. Payne. New York, 1966.

Schumann, Robert. *Gesammelte Schriften über Musik und Musiker.* Leipzig, 1889.

Schumann, Robert. *On Music and Musicians.* Edited by Konrad Wolff, translated by Paul Rosenfeld. New York, 1946.

Schwartz, Boris. "Beethoven and the French Violin School." *The Musical Quarterly* 44 (1958): 431–47.

———. "French Instrumental Music between the Revolutions, 1789–1830." Ph.D. diss., Columbia University, 1950.

Senner, Wayne M., ed. *The Critical Reception of Beethoven's Compositions by His German Contemporaries,* vol. 1. Lincoln, NE, 1999.

Sessions, Roger. *The Musical Experience of Composer, Performer, Listener.* Princeton, NJ, 1949.

Sharpe, Leslie. *Friedrich Schiller: Drama, Thought and Politics.* Cambridge, 1991.

Shedlock, J. S. ed. *Beethoven's Letters.* London, 1926.

Sisman, Elaine. *Haydn and the Classical Variation.* Cambridge, MA, 1993.

Solomon, Maynard. *Beethoven.* 2nd ed. New York, 1998.

———. "Beethoven and Schiller." In *Beethoven, Performers, and Critics: The International Beethoven Congress Detroit 1977,* ed. by Robert Winter and Bruce Carr, 162-75. Detroit, 1977.

———. "Beethoven's 'Magazin der Kunst.'" *19th-Century Music* 7 (1984): 199–208.

———. "Beethoven's Tagebuch of 1812–1818." *BS 3,* edited by Alan Tyson, 193–288. Cambridge, 1982.

———. *Late Beethoven: Music, Thought, Imagination.* Berkeley, 2004.

Spitzer, John, and Neal Zaslaw. *The Birth of the Orchestra: History of an Institution, 1650–1815.* New York, 2004.

Stravinsky, Igor and Robert Craft. *Dialogues and a Diary.* Garden City, NY, 1963.

Sullivan, J. W. N. *Beethoven: His Spiritual Development.* New York, 1927.

Thayer, Alexander Wheelock. *Thayer's Life of Beethoven.* Revised and edited by Elliot Forbes. Princeton, NJ, 1964.

Tovey, Donald. *Companion to Beethoven's Pianoforte Sonatas.* London, 1931.

———. *Essays in Musical Analysis,* vol. 1, *Symphonies.* London, 1935.

———. *A Musician Talks,* vol. 2, *Musical Textures.* London, 1941.

Treitler, Leo. "To Worship That Celestial Sound: Motives for Analysis." In his *Music and the Historical Imagination,* 46–66. Cambridge, MA, 1989.

Tusa, Michael. "Beethoven's 'C-Minor Mood': Some Thoughts on the Structural Implications of Key Choice." *BF* 2 (1993): 1–27.

Tyson, Alan, ed. *Beethoven Studies.* 3 vols. New York, etc., 1973–82.

———. "The 'Razumovsky' Quartets: Some Aspects of the Sources." *BS* 3 (1973): 107–40.

Wagner, Cosima. *Cosima Wagner's Diaries,* vol. 2: 1878–1883. Edited by Martin Gregor-Dellin and Dietrich Mack; translated by Geoffrey Skelton. London, 1980.

Wallace, Robin. "Beethoven's Critics: An Appreciation." In *The Critical Reception of Beethoven's Compositions by His Germanic Contemporaries,* edited by Wayne M. Senner, vol. 2, 1–13.

Warrack, John. *Carl Maria von Weber.* Cambridge, 1968.

Weber-Bockholdt, Petra. *Beethovens Bearbeitungen britischer Lieder.* Munich, 1994.

Webster, James. *Haydn's "Farewell" Symphony and the Idea of Classical Style.* Cambridge, 1991.

Wegeler, Franz Gerhard, and Ferdinand Ries. *Biographische Notizen über Ludwig van Beethoven.* Koblenz, 1838; reprinted Hildesheim, 1972.

Wendt, Amadeus. "Über den Zustand der Musik in Deutschland." In *Allgemeine Musikalische Zeitung, mit besonderer Rucksicht auf den Österreichischen Kaiserstaat,* 6 (1822): col. 761–62.

Will, Richard. *The Characteristic Symphony in the Age of Haydn and Beethoven.* Cambridge, 2002.

Winter, Robert. "Noch einmal: Wo sind Beethovens Skizzen zur Zehnten Symphonie?" *Beethoven Jahrbuch* 9 (1973/77), 531–52.

———. "Of Realizations, Completions, Restorations, and Reconstructions: From Bach's *The Art of Fugue* to Beethoven's 'Tenth Symphony.'" *Journal of the Royal Musical Association* 116 (1999): 96–126.

———. [Response to Barry Cooper,] "Beethoven's Tenth Symphony." *Journal of the Royal Musical Association* 117 (1992): 329–30.

———. "The Sketches for the 'Ode to Joy'." In *Beethoven, Performers, and Critics: The International Beethoven Congress Detroit 1977,* edited by Robert Winter and Bruce Carr, 176–214. Detroit, 1977.

Witcombe, Charles C. *Beethoven's Private God: An Analysis of the Composer's Markings in Sturms "Betrachtungen."* M.A. Thesis, San Jose State University, 1998. UMI, 1998, No. 1389692.

Woodfield, Ian. "Christian Gottlob Neefe and the Bonn National Theatre, with New Light on the Beethoven Family." *Music and Letters* 93/3 (2012): 289–315.

Wyn Jones, David. *Beethoven, Pastoral Symphony.* Cambridge, 1995.

———. *The Symphony in Beethoven's Vienna.* Cambridge, 2006.

INDEX OF WORKS

Page numbers in *italics* refer to illustrations and music examples.

GENERAL INDEX

Page numbers in *italics* refer to illustrations.